EXPERIENCING COMICS

An Introduction to Reading, Discussing, and Creating Comics

Experiencing Comics is a visionary introduction to an emerging field—the study and creation of comics—that has been waiting for a treatment like this. Accessible, engaging, provocative, and inspiring, *Experiencing Comics* assembles some of the most potent and fascinating authorities in comicsdom, including creators, researchers, historians, and teachers. It presents a portrait of comics as the diverse, wide-ranging, and culture-shaping medium that it is today, the vibrant birthplace of blockbuster imaginations and underground possibilities. Rachelle Cruz is just the right teacher to wisely select resonant voices from the cutting edge of comics study, and present them in an engaging way to students, whether fresh to comics or familiar with only some sliver of the craft. The text will sharpen critical lenses while opening eyes to comics' variety. The questions will reinforce understanding and deepen analysis. The activities will unleash the creative language of comics for students themselves. I can't wait to use this book in my classroom.

—Paul Lai, Comics Educator and Host of *Comics Syllabus*,
a Multiversity Podcast

EXPERIENCING COMICS

An Introduction to Reading, Discussing, and Creating Comics

Written and edited by

Rachelle Cruz

Bassim Hamadeh, CEO and Publisher
Mieka Portier, Acquisitions Editor
Sean Adams, Project Editor
Emely Villavicencio, Senior Graphic Designer
Alisa Munoz, Licensing Coordinator
Natalie Piccotti, Director of Marketing
Kassie Graves, Vice President of Editorial
Jamie Giganti, Director of Academic Publishing

Printed in the United States of America.

ISBN: 978-1-5165-1698-8 (pbk) / 978-1-5165-1699-5 (br)

BRIEF CONTENTS

Introduction ix

List of Contributors xi

CHAPTER 1 Reading Comics 1

CHAPTER 2 Discussing Comics 35

CHAPTER 3 History and Background 67

CHAPTER 4 Creating Comics 119

Works Cited 161

About the Author and Editor 163

DETAILED CONTENTS

INTRODUCTION XI

LIST OF CONTRIBUTORS XIII

CHAPTER 1 Reading Comics 1

1.1 Defining Comics 2
1.2 Introduction to Comics Terms 6
1.3 Cartoonists on Comics They Love 11
1.4 Spotlight on Ashanti Fortson, Cartoonist 17
1.5 Getting Oriented 18
1.6 The Basics: How Do You Read a Comic? 18
1.7 Sample Visual on How to Read a Comic—*American Born Chinese* 19
1.8 Notice and Focus—*Student Example* 23
1.9 Spotlight on John Jennings, Cartoonist 26
1.10 Spotlight on *INK BRICK*, A Journal of Comics Poetry 30
1.11 A List of Further Reading 33

CHAPTER 2 Discussing Comics 35

2.1 Reading: "Panthers and Vixens: Black Superheroines, Sexuality, and Stereotypes in Contemporary Comic Books" by Jeffrey A. Brown 36
2.2 Discussion Questions 46
2.3 Reading: Excerpt from *The New Mutants: Superheroes and the Radical Imagination of American Comics* by Ramzi Fawaz 46
2.4 Discussion Questions 59
2.5 Reading: "The Difference a Mutant Makes"—*Los Angeles Review of Books Article* by Ramzi Fawaz 60
2.6 Discussion Questions 64
2.7 A List of Further Reading 65

CHAPTER 3 History and Background 67

3.1 An Introduction 67

3.2 Interview with Betsy Gomez, Editorial Director of the Comic Book Legal Defense Fund (CBLDF) 69

3.3 Spotlight on MariNaomi, Cartoonist and Founder of the Cartoonists of Color Database and the Queer Cartoonists Database 74

3.4 Activity: Students as Historians—Creator Profile 75

3.5 Reading: "Making Comics Respectable: How *Maus* Helped Redefine a Medium" by Ian Gordon 76

3.6 Discussion Questions 84

3.7 Interview with Keith Sicat, Director of *Komikero Chronicles* 85

3.8 Interview with Fred Van Lente, Author of *The Comic Book History of Comics* 91

3.9 Interview with Dr. Frederick Aldama, Author of *Your Brain on Latino Comics, Multicultural Comics, and Graphic Borders* 93

3.10 Interview with Dr. Deborah E. Whaley, Author of *Black Women in Sequence: Re-inking Comics, Graphic Novels, and Anime* 100

3.11 Cartoonists on Comics History 103

3.12 Interview with Jeff Yang and Keith Chow, Editors of *Secret Identities: The Asian American Superhero Anthology* and *Shattered* 108

3.13 Interview with Ryan North, Creator of the webcomic, *Dinosaur Comics* 113

3.14 A List of Further Reading 117

CHAPTER 4 Creating Comics 119

4.1 Introduction 119
4.2 Exercise 1: Self-Portrait as Icon 121
4.3 Exercise 2: A Monster's Exquisite Corpse 122
4.4 Cartoonists on Generating Ideas 124
4.5 Exercise 3: Character and Dialogue 129
4.6 Spotlight on Gene Luen Yang, Cartoonist 131
4.7 Exercise 4: Making Friends with Inner Demons 132
4.8 Spotlight on Andi Santagata, Cartoonist 135
4.9 Cartoonists on Perseverance in the Comics-Making Process 140
4.10 Exercise 5: Reverse Engineer a Movie Scene 145
4.11 Student Examples of Comics Final Projects 146
4.12 Cartoonists on Advice for Students of Comics 152
4.13 Cartoonists on Pitching 157
4.14 A List of Further Reading 158

Works Cited 163

Introduction

The idea for this textbook arrived in the second week or so of an introductory course to the graphic novel when one of my students sheepishly asked, "Wait, but *how* do you actually read comics?" Her initial question led others to chime in: "Do I read the words or the pictures first?" "How do I analyze comics?" The class contained students with a range of backgrounds in reading and writing about comics but a majority struggled with *how* to read comics. Several of them hadn't ever read a single comic book; others read them frequently but were so used to "binge reading" for enjoyment that they didn't often take notice of craft and storytelling elements. The first chapter of *Experiencing Comics,* "Reading Comics," is dedicated to the critical reading, thinking and writing processes and adapts David Rosenwasser and Jill Stephen's technique, "Notice and Focus," for slowing down the reading process in order to allow students to first make observations of what they're seeing and reading, then propose inferences based on their initial considerations. The "Notice and Focus" process helps guide thoughtful analysis, often deepening initial reads and observations and turning casual comics readers into scholars of the medium.

Although my syllabus includes foundational and oft-assigned texts, including Scott McCloud's *Understanding Comics*, Art Spigelman's *Maus*, Marjane Satrapi's *Persepolis,* I wanted to prioritize and include the sheer variety of voices, aesthetics, and backgrounds that aren't typically studied (and are frankly often historically excluded) in an introductory class. My syllabus foregrounds webcomics, independently published works (beyond Marvel and DC), and manga, and some of these titles include: Yumi Sakugawa's *Your Illustrated Guide to the Universe;* MariNaomi's *Dragon's Breath and Other True Stories;* Allie Brosh's *Hyperbole and a Half;* Kabi Nagata's *My Lesbian Experience with Loneliness;* excerpts from the political cartooning website, *The Nib,* among several others that deserve their own entire course of study. In addition to teaching comics, I've attended several conventions both as a presenter and a fan throughout the years, including the notable San Diego Comic Con, Geek Girl Con, and Wonder Con, and regional zine fests (L.A. Zine Fest and I.E. Zine Fest, both based in Southern California), where comics creators, writers, artists, letterers, and other industry folks engage in rich conversations about process, storytelling, collaboration, and publishing. I sought to capture the vitality of these conversations through the interviews with cartoonist sections throughout *Experiencing Comics,* which range in topics from each cartoonist's own writing background and process, to advice for beginning cartoonists. There are also spotlight features on comics creators such as John Jennings and Andi Santagata that give a more in-depth look at their processes and projects.

The second chapter of *Experiencing Comics*, "Discussing Comics," includes comics scholarship work by Jeffrey A. Brown, who wrote "Panthers and Vixens: Black Superheroines, Sexuality and Stereotypes," and an excerpt from Ramzi Fawaz's book, *The New Mutants: Superheroes and the Radical Imagination of American Comics*, in addition to an interview with Fawaz from the *Los Angeles Review of Books*. This chapter will encourage students to access literary theory and sociopolitical terms, such as intersectionality, hegemony, and liberal democracy; in order to broaden and deepen their comics conversations within a larger cultural context.

Chapter Three of *Experiencing Comics* is an introduction to varying movements and moments in comics history in the United States, and I must emphasize that this chapter is strictly an introduction, an entry point to the complexities and nuances of comics history. I interviewed Betsy Gomez, the editorial director at Comic Book Legal Defense Fund, about comics censorship and its legacies; Keith Sicat, director of *Komikero Chronicles*, a documentary on the history of Filipino comics (or *komiks*); Jeff Yang and Keith Chow about their historically significant anthology, *Secret Identities: The Asian American Superhero Anthology;* Fred Van Lente about his rendition of comics history told through the comics medium; Frederick Aldama on Latinx comics; cartoonist Ryan North on his long running webcomic, *Dinosaur Comics;* and Dr. Deborah Whaley on her interdisciplinary research and work in comics. I'm especially excited to include a Spotlight on the Cartoonists of Color Database and Queer Cartoonists Database, both founded by cartoonist MariNaomi, which showcase the tremendous number of people of color and queer cartoonists working in the industry today. Ian Gordon's essay, "Making Comics Respectable: How *Maus* Redefined a Medium," showcases the rise of the graphic novel's "respectablility" through the academic reception and acceptance of Art Spiegelman's *Maus*.

The fourth chapter is arguably the most interactive and perhaps the most fun. It provides comics-making exercises that can be done in class or at home and will give students a chance to practice craft and storytelling elements that cartoonists discuss throughout the textbook. Student examples from my own class are provided, in addition to excerpts of their final fifteen page comics projects, to show the range of style, aesthetics, and approach to craft.

My hope is that *Experiencing Comics* is accessible and inclusive of a wide variety of aesthetics and experiences and just the first step in investigating the enormous world of comics.

Special thanks to all of the incredible creators, cartoonists, writers, and scholars who so generously lent their time for this text; my amazing Creative Writing 155: Introduction to the Graphic Novel students; Paul Lai, friend and podcaster extraordinaire of *The Comics Syllabus*; Victoria Patterson, whose class on the graphic novel sparked inspiration for my further research into comics; Andrew Winer, Nalo Hopkinson, John Jennings, and the entire creative writing department at the University of California, Riverside; Mieka Portier, Sean Adams, and Alisa Muñoz at Cognella Publishing; Iris Law, for her careful eye on this book; all of my comics-loving cousins and family, especially Rico Reyes, Shaun Morris, Jason Morris, Christine Odena, Cheryl Dulce, Kevin Dulce; Maddy Dulce, Chloe Dulce, and Matteo Dulce; my sister, Julienne Cruz-Medina; my brother-in-law, Rhod Medina; Mary and Gulliermo; Sue and Keith; GW and DOTR; Laura; Julia; Tracy; of course, Anita and Romeo Cruz; Tess and Jess Alban; and my husband, Thomas Alban.

List of Contributors

Frederick Luis Aldama is Arts and Humanities Distinguished Professor of English and University Distinguished Scholar at The Ohio State University. In the departments of English as well as Spanish & Portuguese he teaches courses on and Latino & Latin American cultural phenomena, including literature, film, TV, music, sports, video games, and comic books. He is also an affiliate faculty of the Center for Cognitive and Behavioral Brain Imaging. He is the author, co-author, and editor of thirty books, including recently *Latinx Comic Book Storytelling*, *Latinx Superheroes in Mainstream Comics*, and his first book of flash-graphic fiction, *Long Stories Cut Short*. He is editor and coeditor of 7 different academic press book series, including the World Comics and Graphic Nonfiction series (University of Texas Press) and the trade-book graphic novel and nonfiction series, *Latinographix* (Ohio State University Press). He is founder and director of the White House Hispanic Bright Spot awarded LASER/Latino and Latin American Space for Enrichment Research. In 2016, Aldama received the Ohio Education Summit Award for Founding & Directing LASER. He is founder and co-director of Humanities & Cognitive Sciences High School Summer Institute at The Ohio State University. He has been honored with the 2016 American Association of Hispanics in Higher Education's Outstanding Latino/a Faculty in Higher Education Award. In 2017, Aldama was awarded Alumni Award for Distinguished Teaching and inducted into the Academy of Teaching. This same year he was also inducted into the Society of Cartoon Arts.

Rina Ayuyang is an Eisner- and Ignatz-nominated cartoonist based in Oakland, California. Stories from her self-published mini-comic series "Namby Pamby" were collected in the book *Whirlwind Wonderland,* co-published by Sparkplug Comic Books and Tugboat Press. Her online comic, *Beginning's End,* was nominated for an Eisner Award for Best Short Story. Her *A Cartoonist's Diary* contribution on TCJ.com was chosen as a silver medalist by the Society of Illustrators in the 2016 Comic and Cartoon Art Annual. Rina has self-published comics such as *Pet Project* and *Doodle DAZE* and contributed to various anthologies like *Unicorn Mountain #3, Stripburger,* and *Runner Runner.* She has exhibited at the Arlington Art Center and the Cartoon Art Museum and has been a cartoonist in residence at the Charles Schulz Museum. She also runs the comics imprint Yam Books and plays the "nice" co-host on the comics podcast *The Comix Claptrap.*

Keith Chow is co-editor of the Asian American comics anthologies *Secret Identities* and *Shattered* and the founder of TheNerdsofColor.org. His writing has also appeared in the *New York Times,* the Center for Asian American Media, and NBC News. Follow him on Twitter at @the_real_chow and @TheNerdsofColor.

Leela Corman is an illustrator, cartoonist, and Middle Eastern dancer. She is the author of *Unterzakhn* (Schocken/Pantheon, 2012) and *We All Wish For Deadly Force* (Retrofit, 2016). She is also an adjunct professor at the University of Florida's College of Fine Arts and a founding instructor at the Sequential Artists Workshop.

Ramzi Fawaz is assistant professor of English at the University of Wisconsin, Madison, where he teaches in the fields of queer theory, American cultural studies, and contemporary literature. He received his PhD in American studies at George Washington University. His first book, *The New Mutants: Superheroes and the Radical Imagination of American Comics* (NYU Press, 2016), received the Center for Lesbian and Gay Studies Fellowship Award for Best First Book Manuscript in LGBT Studies. His writing has been published in numerous academic journals, including *American Literature*, *Callaloo*, *GLQ*, and *ASAP/Journal*. He is currently coediting a special issue of *American Literature* with Darieck Scott titled, "Queer About Comics," which will be the first issue the journal has ever dedicated to the comics medium since its inception in 1929.

Ashanti Fortson is an illustrator and cartoonist with a deep love for kind stories and fantastical settings. They make a queer space fantasy webcomic called *Galanthus*, and they hope to one day see the Milky Way. *(Image credit: Ashanti Fortson)*

Sophie Goldstein is a cartoonist, illustrator and comics instructor based in the great city of Pittsburgh, PA. Her book *The Oven*, published by AdHouse Books, won two Ignatz awards and was nominated for the Cartoonist Studio Prize. Her latest book, *House of Women*, is a collection that comprises the eponymous Ignatz award-winning, self-published mini-comic series, was published by Fantagraphics in 2017. Goldstein first comics endeavor was *Darwin Carmichael is Going to Hell*, a webcomic cowritten with Jenn Jordan and that was self-published with funding from Kickstarter in 2013. Sophie has also illustrated a children's book, *Poopy Claws*, written by Gene Ambaum. In 2013 she graduated from the Center for Cartoon Studies and has been living la vida loca ever since. Her work has appeared in various publications, including *Best American Comics 2013*, *Fable Comics*, the *Pitchfork Review*, *Cricket Magazine*, *Sleep of Reason*, and *Symbolia Magazine*, among others.

Betsy Gomez is the editorial director for the Comic Book Legal Defense Fund, a nonprofit organization dedicated to defending the First Amendment rights of the comics community. Gomez manages the editorial content for CBLDF.org and CBLDF's print publications, including CBLDF's quarterly news magazine, *CBLDF Defender.* Gomez is the editor of CBLDF's book about the women who changed free expression in comics, *She Changed Comics.* With an extensive background in educational publishing, Gomez has worked as a content developer and editor for several companies, including Houghton Mifflin Harcourt and Pearson Education, among others. She began volunteering for CBLDF in 1998 and joined the CBLDF staff in 2011. Gomez was introduced to comics in college and has since been an advocate for the medium. Her work with CBLDF combines her love of the medium with her passion for the right to read. (*Photo credit: Katelyn Lucas*)

John Jennings is professor of media and cultural studies at the University of California, Riverside (UCR). Professor Jennings received his MA in art education in 1995 and the MFA in studio with a focus on graphic design in 1997 from the University of Illinois at Urbana–Champaign. He is an interdisciplinary scholar who examines the visual culture of race in various media forms, including film, illustrated fiction, and comics and graphic novels. Jennings is also a curator, graphic novelist, editor, and design theorist whose research interests include the visual culture of hip hop, afrofuturism and politics, visual literacy, horror and the ethnogothic, and speculative design and its applications to visual rhetoric. Jennings is co-editor of the Eisner Award–winning collection, *The Blacker the Ink: Constructions of Black Identity in Comics and Sequential Art* (Rutgers) and co-founder/organizer of the Schomburg Center's Black Comic Book Festival in Harlem. He is cofounder and organizer of the MLK NorCal's Black Comix Arts Festival in San Francisco and also SOL-CON: The Brown and Black Comix Expo at the Ohio State University. Jennings's current projects include the graphic novel adaptation of Octavia Butler's *Kindred* (with Damian Duffy), Tony Medina's police brutality–themed ghost story, *I Am Alphonso Jones* (with Stacey Robinson), and his hoodoo noir graphic novella, *Blue Hand Mojo* (Rosarium Publishing). Jennings is also a Nasir Jones Hip Hop Studies Fellow at the Hutchins Center at Harvard University. (*Photo credit: Rob Mach*)

Lucy Knisley is a critically acclaimed and award-winning comic creator. She lives in Chicago. She specializes in personal, confessional graphic novels and travelogues. Her last name is confusing and has a silent K. It's pronounced kind-of like "nigh-slee."

Jade F. Lee is a cartoonist whose works often use food and fantasy elements to explore narrative themes of identity, connection, and growth. She often draws inspiration from personal experience and stories from her family's food culture that is intimately rooted in their immigrant experiences. She is the creator of Half Moon Heroes, a martial fantasy adventure comic, and Coral, an upcoming middle grade novel about mermaids, the Dragon Boat Festival, and a Chinese-American girl learning to reconcile the challenges of growing up with self-acceptance. Her work can be found online at http://www.dumplingheart.com.

Sonny Liew's *The Art of Charlie Chan Hock Chye* was a *New York Times* and Amazon bestseller and the first graphic novel to win the Singapore Literature Prize. Other works include *The Shadow Hero* (with Gene Luen Yang), *Doctor Fate* (with Paul Levitz), and *Malinky Robot,* as well as titles for Marvel Comics, DC Comics, DC Vertigo, First Second Books, Boom Studios, Disney Press, and Image Comics. He has been nominated for multiple Eisner Awards for his writing and art (including six for *The Art of Charlie Chan Hock Chye*) and for spearheading *Liquid City,* a multivolume comics anthology featuring creators from Southeast Asia. *(Photo credit: Tom White)*

Jenny Lin is a multidisciplinary visual artist based in Montreal. Her practice centers around experimental narrative, including autobiography, fiction, and autobiographical fiction. She has created several alternative readings of mainstream narratives, particularly, reframing the ambiguous and fragmented tropes in storytelling as sites for transgressive actions and identities. Using digitally-rendered and hand-drawn imagery, she uses print media, video, or web-based platforms to explore formats, including 2-D print, artist books and zines, single and multi-channel video, installation, and interactive web projects. Some of her book projects were created in collaboration with Eloisa Aquino as B&D Press. Lin completed a BFA degree at the University of Calgary (1994–98) and an MFA at Concordia University (1998–2001). She currently teaches at Concordia University as a sessional instructor in the print media program area.

Nilah Magruder is a writer of children's books and comics. From her beginnings in the woods of Maryland, she developed an eternal love for three things: nature, books, and animation. She is the author of *How to Find a Fox* and *M.F.K.* She has also drawn for Disney and DreamWorks, and written for Marvel. When she is not drawing or writing, Nilah is reading fantasy novels, watching movies, rollerskating, and fighting her cat for control of her desk chair.

MariNaomi is the award-winning author and illustrator of *Kiss & Tell: A Romantic Resume, Ages 0 to 22* (Harper Perennial, 2011), *Dragon's Breath and Other True Stories* (2dcloud/Uncivilized Books, 2014), *Turning Japanese* (2dcloud, 2016), *I Thought YOU Hated ME* (Retrofit Comics, 2016), and the upcoming *Life on Earth* trilogy (Graphic Universe, 2018–2020). Her work has appeared in over sixty print publications and has been featured on numerous websites, such as The Rumpus, *the Los Angeles Review of Books,* Midnight Breakfast and BuzzFeed. MariNaomi's comics and paintings have been featured by such institutions as the Smithsonian, the De Young Museum, the Cartoon Art Museum, the Asian Art Museum, and the Japanese American Museum. In 2011 and in 2018, Mari toured with the literary roadshow Sister Spit. She is the creator and administrator of the Cartoonists of Color Database and the Queer Cartoonists Database. She has taught classes for the California College of the Arts Comics MFA program and was a guest editor for PEN Illustrated. She is the cohost of the comedy advice podcast *Ask Bi Grlz* with Myriam Gurba.

Ryan North is the (*New York Times* bestselling, Eisner award-winning) creator of *Dinosaur Comics*, the coeditor of the Machine of Death series, and the author of *To Be or Not To Be*, the choose-your-own-path version of *Hamlet*! He has written the *Adventure Time* comic and writes *The Unbeatable Squirrel Girl* for Marvel Comics, which you might know from their movies about an iron man. He also once reviewed the novelization of *Back to the Future*, page by page, which was crazy, which you can buy on Qwantz.com. He lives in Toronto, Canada, with his wife, Jenn, and his dog, Noam Chompsky.

Danica Novgorodoff is an artist, writer, graphic designer, and horse wrangler from Louisville, Kentucky, currently living in Brooklyn, New York. Her books include *A Late Freeze; Slow Storm; Refresh, Refresh* (included in *Best American Comics 2011*); and *The Undertaking of Lily Chen*. Her art and writing has been published in *Best American Comics, Artforum, Esquire, VQR, Slate, Orion, Seneca Review, Ecotone Journal*, and many other periodicals. She was awarded a 2015 New York Foundation for the Arts fellowship in literature, and was named Sarabande Books' 2016 writer in residence. She has been a fellow at the MacDowell Colony, Blue Mountain Center, VCCA, Brush Creek, and Willapa Bay AiR.

Glynnes Pruett is the owner of the Comic Book Hideout in Fullerton, California, where she is also a comics educator.

Born in Puerto Rico and based in Columbus, Ohio, **Rafael Rosado** is a seasoned writer, director, and storyboard artist for the animation industry. He began his career at Character Builders in Columbus, Ohio, as an assistant animator. He quickly worked his way up to become a character designer, storyboard artist, and commercial director. During his tenure there he worked on such shows as Fox's Emmy Award–winning *Life With Louie*, HBO's *Happily Ever After* and Fox's *Where in The World Is Carmen San Diego?* After leaving Character Builders in 1994, Rafael went to work for Warner Brothers Animation, storyboarding on *Pinky and The Brain* and Emmy-nominated *Animaniacs*, for which he also wrote two episodes. He was the recruited by the newly founded Sony Television Animation division, where he worked on eleven shows, including directing episodes of CBS's *Project GeeKeR* and NBC's *Sammy*. He was promoted to supervising director on *Extreme Ghostbusters* and producer on *Men In Black: The Animated Series*. After five years honing his skills in Los Angeles, Rafael moved back to Ohio to raise his family. He is now one of the most highly sought-after storyboard artists, working for major studios such as Warner Brothers, the Walt Disney Company, Sony, Universal, and the Cartoon Network. Highly diverse, he has storyboarded on action, comedy, and preschool shows, shows as diverse as *Boondocks, Teenage Mutant Ninja Turtles, The Batman, The Venture Brothers*, and *Curious George*. Rafael's first graphic novel, *Giants Beware!*, was published by First Second Books in early 2012. His short film *The Tortured Clown* was acquired by and featured on the Sundance Channel. *(Photo credit: Gil Whitney)*

Alexander Rothman is a cartoonist and poet based in Philadelphia. He's the publisher and editor in chief of Ink Brink, a small press dedicated to comics poetry, and he spreads knowledge of the form through presentations, workshops, and critical writing. You can learn more about the press at inkbrick.com and see some of his work at versequential.com.

Yumi Sakugawa is an Ignatz Award–nominated comic book artist and the author of *I Think I Am In Friend-Love With You, Your Illustrated Guide to Becoming One with the Universe, There Is No Right Way to Meditate,* and *The Little Book of Life Hacks.* Her comics have also appeared in *The Believer, Bitch, the Best American NonRequired Reading 2014, The Rumpus, Folio, Fjords Review,* and other publications. She has also exhibited multimedia installations at the Japanese American National Museum and the Smithsonian Arts and Industries Building. A graduate of the fine arts program of the University of California, Los Angeles, she lives in Los Angeles.

Andi Santagata is a cartoonist and illustrator living in White River Junction, Vermont. They're probably most known for their autobio comic *Trans Man Walking*, receiving a 2017 DINK Fellowship, and/or drawing on the bathroom walls at the Center for Cartoon Studies. *(Photo credit: Whiteley Foster)*

Keith Sicat is an independent filmmaker and comic book creator who has screened his films in local and international film festivals. He was heavily involved with painting and photography before falling in love with cinema. Under the Kino Arts banner, he has a total of twelve features under his belt as a director, writer, or producer, including award winners *Rigodon, ka Oryang, The Guerrilla is a Poet,* and *Woman of the Ruins,* their subjects ranging from social-realist documentaries to gothic fiction. A number of the films screened in museum spaces such as the Ayala Museum, the Lopez Museum, the Smithsonian Institute (Washington, DC), and the Museum of Modern Art (MoMA, New York). He served as head of concepts for animation firms in the Philippines, culminating in the first Philippine-Japanese anime coproduction, *Barangay 143,*

with TV Asahi, which is due for release next year. He is constantly developing new documentaries and fictional feature films.

Taneka Stotts is a queer, little tumbleweed that stopped rolling somewhere in Portland, Oregon. After spending quite a few years as a spoken-word artist, Taneka's focus shifted to comics, a medium full of collaboration and imagination. Taneka writes the webcomics *Full Circle* and *Love Circuits,* as well as the Eisner-nominated webcomic *Deja Brew.* Taneka has edited a few comics anthologies, including, most recently, the award-winning *Beyond: The Queer Sci-Fi and Fantasy Comic Anthology* and Ignatz winner for outstanding anthology and Eisner Best Anthology Winner, *Elements: Fire—an Anthology by Creators of Color* (Beyond Press). Taneka is currently working on *Kingmaker!* with Mildred Louis and *Last Bell* with Ria Martinez.

Fred Van Lente is the number-one *New York Times* bestselling, award-winning writer of comics like *Archer & Armstrong* (Harvey Award nominee, Best Series), *Action Philosophers!* (American Library Association Best Graphic Novel for Teens), and *Cowboys & Aliens* (with Andrew Foley), the basis for the feature film. In 2017, Van Lente branched into the world of prose with his debut novel, the stand-up murder mystery *Ten Dead Comedians.* His follow-up novel, *The Con Artist*, set in the comic book industry, will be out in 2018. His many other comics and graphic novels include *Weird Detective, The Comic Book History of Comics, The Incredible Hercules* (with Greg Pak), *Taskmaster, Marvel Zombies,* and *The Amazing Spider-Man.* He lives in Brooklyn with his wife, the playwright Crystal Skillman, and some mostly ungrateful cats.

Deborah Elizabeth Whaley is senior scholar for Digital Arts and Humanities Research Digital Scholarship and Publishing Studio. She is professor of American and African American studies at the University of Iowa. *(Photo credit: Crystal Skillman)*

Ronald Wimberly is an artist who works primarily in design and narrative. He is also an accomplished cartoonist, having designed several graphic novels, as well as shorter works for DC/Vertigo, Nike, Marvel, Hill and Wang, and Dark Horse. His most recent works of note were the critically-acclaimed *Prince of Cats* and the cartoon essay "Lighten Up" for *The Nib* on Medium.

Born in Taiwan, **Belle Yang** spent part of her childhood in Japan. At age seven she immigrated to the United States with her family. She attended Stirling University in Scotland and graduated from the University of California, Santa Cruz, in biology but went on to study art at Pasadena Art Center College of Design and the Beijing Institute of Traditional Chinese Painting. She worked and traveled in China for three years and returned to the United States late in 1989 after the Tiananmen Massacre. She returned with gratitude in her heart for the freedom of expression given her in America, certain she would firmly grasp this gift with both hands.

Jeff Yang writes frequently for CNN. He is a columnist for *The Wall Street Journal* Online and can be heard on radio as a contributor to shows such as PRI's *The Takeaway* and WNYC's *The Brian Lehrer Show.* He is the author of *I Am Jackie Chan: My Life in Action* and editor of the graphic novel anthologies *Secret Identities* and *Shattered.*

Gene Luen Yang is a cartoonist and author of *American Born Chinese,* which won the American Library Association's Michael L. Printz Award and an Eisner Award. It was also the first graphic novel to be nominated for a National Book Award. Gene is the author of *Boxers and Saints, The Shadow Hero* (along with Sonny Liew), and the *Secret Coders* series (with Mike Holmes). He served as the Library of Congress' fifth National Ambassador for Young People's Literature.

Student Contributors

Lili Berni studies creative writing at UCR. She can be found working on projects at her library, binging Netflix on her beloved couch, or at a hospital where she moonlights as a respiratory therapist known for her high quality chest compressions. She loves a hamster named Helena and a boy named Evan.

Justin M. Jones received his BA in Creative Writing from the University of California, Riverside. In 2017, he was inducted into the Phi Beta Kappa academic honor society.

Susana Martinez is a creative writing major at UCR. When she isn't writing she's crocheting things she doesn't need or creating D&D campaigns from her shelved story ideas.

Jacquelyn Nille will be a creative writing graduate of the University of California Riverside's 2019 class. She is always eager for any chance to combine both her poetic and artistic abilities.

A UVA YWW and CSSSA alumna, **Kini Sosa** is currently a UCR undergraduate who spends her days napping and writing love letters to the ocean. (She has yet to receive one in return.)

Cloud Whorl (they/them) is a queer/trans/disabled writer. Their work includes poetry, fiction, and scripts. Cloud loves to read comic books, play video games, and plan their next tattoos.

Reading Comics

1

Introduction

As you begin your foray into comics, you may have several questions and concerns, such as:

> "I'm used to reading prose and poetry, NOT comics. How do you read and analyze comics?"
>
> "What's the difference between comics and graphic novels?"
>
> "I've read comics since childhood, but I read them like I'm eating chips. How do you slow down in order to notice details?"
>
> "Are comics just about superheroes?"
>
> "What are comics, anyway? How do you define them?"

This chapter seeks to approach answers to these questions and, in doing so, serves as the launch pad for your exploration into comics. It provides some definitions for the term "comics" as defined by cartoonists and scholars; basic terms and vocabulary, which will allow you to identify these craft elements at play in your own reading; interviews with cartoonists about comics that proved influential to their careers; and it will give you a set of strategies to, first, get oriented with reading comics and, second, to allow you to think and read critically in order to deepen your understanding of comics.

Whether you're new to comics or not, this chapter serves as a toolbox for students to read, analyze, write, and discuss comics in an effective and constructive way.

Learning Objectives

- Explore and discuss various definitions of the term "comics."
- Identify and describe key terms and craft elements related to the comics-making process and the form/structure of comics, such as panels, the splash page, and word balloons.
- Engage in various critical reading strategies that will allow students to get oriented with reading comics and to slow down their reading in order to examine craft elements.

Learning Outcomes

- Gain an introduction to professional and renowned cartoonists who are successful in making thought-provoking comics and read about the comics that were influential to their reading and writing lives.
- Apply critical thinking and reading techniques, such as "Notice and Focus."
- Analyze singular comics panels and develop connections to larger craft and story concerns.

Key Terms

- **Comics**
- **Comic book**
- **Floppy**
- **Graphic novel**
- Icon
- Medium
- Universality

1.1 Defining Comics

There are plenty of comics textbooks and scholarly articles that delve into the debate of what comics is and what it isn't and the issues with trying to define comics in the first place. Rather than diving into these debates, this section is meant for you to get an introductory understanding of how comics is defined by practitioners and scholars and to see what these definitions include and what they do not. We'll look at the differences between the term comics, the comic book, and the graphic novel.

Comics

In Will Eisner's *Comics and Sequential Art*, the cartoonist and theorist argues, **"Comics communicate in a 'language' that relies on a visual experience common to both creator and audience"** (7; emphasis added). Comics creator and scholar Scott McCloud, in his foundational text on comics theory, *Understanding Comics*, similarly emphasizes that comics is a language, or a medium, in which a variety of stories can be told. He writes: **"the artform—the medium—known as comics is a vessel which can hold any number of ideas and images."** inside the same panel, there is an image of a glass pitcher (which is a metaphorical stand-in for "comics") and the list of words "writers, artists, trends, genres, styles, subject matter, and themes" on the inside of the pitcher to signal the liquid inside (6; emphasis above added). No matter what genre a cartoonist wants to convey—horror, mystery, humor, action, comedy, etc.—or topic/theme—politics, love, identity, migration, etc., the glass pitcher remains the same though the beverage it contains may change, depending on the storyteller.

McCloud defines **comics** as **"n. plural in form, used with a singular verb. 1. Juxtaposed pictorial and other images in deliberate sequence, intended to convey information and/or to produce an aesthetic response in the viewer** (9; emphasis added):

Jessica Abel and Matt Madden's fantastic guide to making comics, *Drawing Words, Making Pictures*, provides a definition by scholar David Kunzle, who wrote *History of the Comic Strip*. Abel and Madden write:

> In order to distinguish between comics and comics-like art, such as the Bayeux tapestry and Mayan codices, [Kunzle] invented a definition that was more narrowly construed than Eisner's or McCloud's definition. To elaborate, **he proposed four prerequisites to make a comic a comic:**
>
> 1. There must be a sequence of separate images.
> 2. There must be preponderance of image over texts.

3. The medium in which the strip appears and for which it is originally intended must be reproductive; that is, in printed form, a mass medium.
4. The sequence must tell a story that is both moral and topical (5).

In *The Power of Comics*, scholars Randy Duncan and Matthew J. Smith discuss the term "comics" as a catch-all term for a plethora of stories of various subject matter: ". . . most of the early American comic books started out as collections of repasted newspaper comic strips. By the time that innovation took hold, the label of 'comics' had already been semantically stuck to that art form, even though adventure and science fiction stories not told for laughs had become popular features among them. For more than eight decades the label has endured, although it does seem to be a sizeable misnomer, given the fact that comic books address many more types of stories than just humorous ones (4)."

In Charles Hatfield's essay "Defining Comics in the Classroom; or, The Pros and Cons of Unfixability," he points to "a newly self-conscious field" that has been "particularly notable for [. . .] anxious throat-clearing about how to define its object." He argues that this preoccupation with definition-making not only deals with the analytical but with the tactical, as well. Hatfield references McCloud's definition of comics, which was "influenced by a desire to liberate the form from suffocating presumptions about content and market. Note, for example, how this definition serves to bring woodcut novels and picture books into the comics fold (19)."

Hatfield discusses his strategy in bringing different definitions for comics into his classroom: "This approach means putting competing definitions of comics on the table, discussing the tactical nature of definitions in general, and helping students see why the question of comics' definition has been so aggravated. An advantage to this approach is that it avoids a too exclusive, naively presentist, or historically inauthentic definition of comics. But it has disadvantages, or at least awkwardness. [. . .] Comics shouldn't be easy to define, as they are an interdisciplinary, indeed, antidisciplinary, phenomenon, nudging us usefully out of accustomed habits of thought and into productive gray areas where various disciplines—such as literature, art, semiotics, and mass communications—overlap and inform one another (see Hatfield). That's why I've never been satisfied with newfangled phrases that are designed to do the same work as the word *comics* yet with greater respectability, phrases like *sequential art* or *graphic narrative*, which always seem to err on the side of narrowness and exclusion. The more particular the term, the less expansive; hence less useful."

Discussion Questions on Comics Definitions

1. What does each definition by Eisner, McCloud, and Kunzle prioritize in terms of evaluating comics?
2. What are the similarities and differences between the definitions of comics by McCloud, Eisner, and Kunzle? Do they prioritize different elements?
3. After looking at the similarities and differences between these definitions, discuss: Which are more inclusive or exclusive in terms evaluating comics?
4. Discuss Hatfield's position on comics definitions and the process of defining comics in the classroom.
5. Is a series of panels without words a comic?
6. Does a comic need pictorial images to be considered a comic? Why or why not?

Try it!

1. **Close Reading**: Rewrite one of the above definitions and define each word using the dictionary. What new insights have you gained from looking closely at this definition? What do you notice now that you hadn't prior to this close reading of the definition? Discuss your findings with a partner.
2. **Write your own definition of comics.** What would you include? Exclude? Why? Describe your reasoning after writing your definition.

The Comic Book

The Comic Book as "Floppy"

When you visit your local comic book shop, you'll notice rows of staple-bound, short comic books, also known by many comic book sellers and readers as "floppys." These floppys often contain a single issue from a five-to-eight-story arc in an ongoing comic series though, some floppys are self contained and are considered "single shots." Floppys are often protected with plastic sleeves and thin sheets of cardboard, which are called "bags and boards."

A shelf of "floppy" comics

Duncan and Smith define the term "comic book: "As an art form, a comic book is a volume in which all aspects of the narrative are represented by pictorial and linguistic images encapsulated in a sequence of juxtaposed panels and pages. . . . By volume, we mean a collection of sheets of paper bound together."

The Graphic Novel

As an attempt to elevate comic books, many scholars, creators, and publishers have embraced the term "graphic novel" in order to escape the connotations that comic books carried with them, such as being a lower form of entertainment, "just for kids," and crude or cheap. However, graphic novels maintain similar, if not the same, qualities as defined above—narrative, image, and text juxtaposed in sequence.

In this book, we will make no effort to differentiate between the two, except, perhaps, in size since they encapsulate the same aesthetic and linguistic considerations.

A shelf of graphic novels

Try it!

1. Visit your local comic shop. You can find yours here: www.comicshoplocator.com. Check out the floppys that they have on display in addition to the graphic novels. Pick one floppy and one graphic novel that stand out to you. What do you notice about them in terms of aesthetic? In terms of production? What do they have in common? Where do they differ? Record your findings.
2. At the local comic shop, make a list of different topics, genres, and subject matters you find among the various comics you observe. Which topics, genres, and subject matters seem to dominate? Which are lesser represented? Why do you think this is? Take notes on your observations.
3. At your local comic shop, ask the staff for recommendations based on your own interests. Which titles piqued your interest? Why?

1.2 Introduction to Comics Terms

A Note on Comics as a Collaborative Process

(From ReadWriteThink.org: "Roles in Comic Book Production")

- **Writer:** the person who writes the script from which the story will emerge.
- **Artist**: the person who draws the script, using a variety of media from pencil to watercolor.
- **Inker:** the person who goes over the artist's pencil lines with ink to make them stand out.
- **Colorist:** the person who colors the inker's and artists' work, sometimes by hand and sometimes using software.
- **Letterer:** the person who puts the words in the right places and makes them clearly legible. The letterer might also put in the sound effects.

Parts of a Comic Book

- **Script**: provides written descriptions of settings, characters, action, dialogue and plot for an artist to use for collaboration.
- **Panels**: square or rectangular blocks that contain the action and dialogue of a comic. However, panel shapes and sizes may vary.
- **Sound Effect**: a word or phrase that communicates sound (and uses onomatopoeia).
- **Word balloons**: depicts dialogue between characters.
- **Thought balloons**: shows characters' thoughts and are often shaped like bubbled clouds.
- **Narratory blocks**: panels that indicate the narrator's exposition or storytelling.
- **Open panels**: panels that don't have lines or borders to contain them.

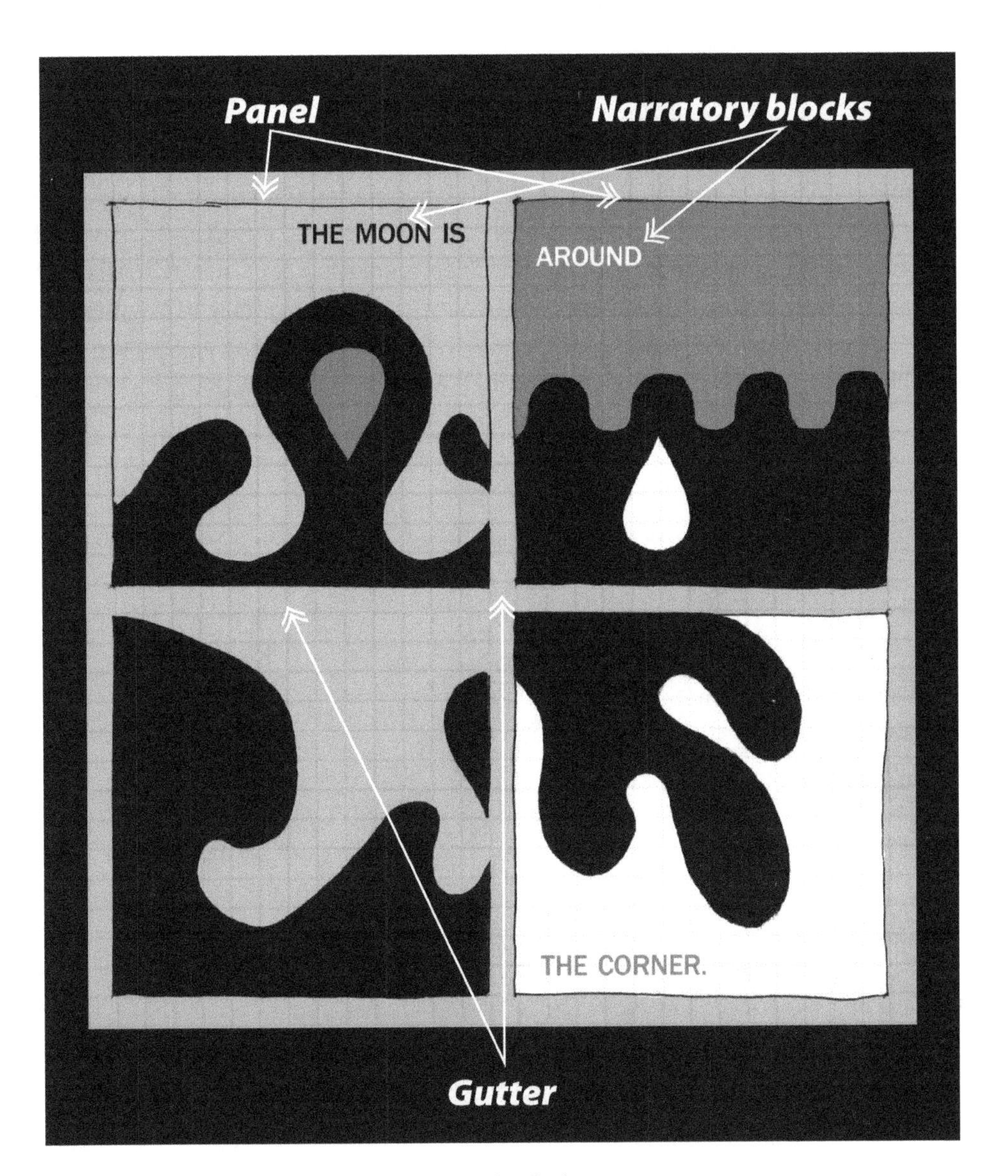

"The Moon is Around the Corner" by Alexander Rothman

- **Splash pages**: panels that are typically the size of an entire page. They are used to zoom in on significant moments within a story, introduce a main character, or to give the reader a wider view of an important event.
- **Credits**: give information about writers, editors, pencillers, inkers, color artists, letterers, cover artists, graphic designers, and the publishing company.
- **Gutter**: the space between panels.

- **Closure**: Scott McCloud, author of Understanding Comics, argues that that the gutter is essential in the reader's barely perceptible process of completing a story or sequence of images based on past experience and incomplete information (63-68) . This is illustrated in McCloud's example of a woman playing a game of Peek-A-Boo; one panel shows her face and a word balloon that states her dialogue, "Peek-A-Boo!" then the next image shows the woman covering her face with a blanket (67). The latter image is a more explicit visual representation of closure that fills in the blanks between panels. Even without this image of the woman covering her face in between the two Peek-A-Boo panels, we can still intuit that there is something happening in between panels. The same applies for the following strip of the walking figure."

From *Understanding Comics* by Scott McCloud (67).

On Inconography

An icon is "an image used to represent a person, place, thing or idea," as McCloud broadly defines the term. In *Understanding Comics*, McCloud discusses "amplification" of particular details, i.e. certain facial features, "through simplification" and states that "when we abstract an image through cartooning, we're not so much eliminating details as we are focusing on specific details. By stripping down an image to its essential 'meaning' an artist can amplify that meaning in a way that realistic art can't" (30).

McCloud argues for the "universality" of simplified cartoon imagery, which readers are able to immediately identify with and become immersed in the storytelling experience. In fact, McCloud writes that through "simplification through amplification," "we don't just observe the cartoon, we become it!" (36; see above).

From *Understanding Comics* by Scott McCloud (36-37).

From *Understanding Comics* by Scott McCloud (36-37).

Discussion Questions

1. Referring to McCloud's panel above (31), do you agree or disagree that "the more cartoony a face is [...] the more people it could be said to describe"? Why or why not?
2. Define and analyze the term "universal." What are the connotations behind this term? What is a "universal" experience? Whose is a "universal" experience?
3. What are some of the challenges and concerns behind McCloud's concept of "amplification through simplification"?
4. How can icons be useful for comics creators? Comics readers?
5. How can icons be limiting for comics creators? Comics readers?
6. When would a more realistic art style more useful and even preferable for comics creators?

1.3 Cartoonists on Comics They Love

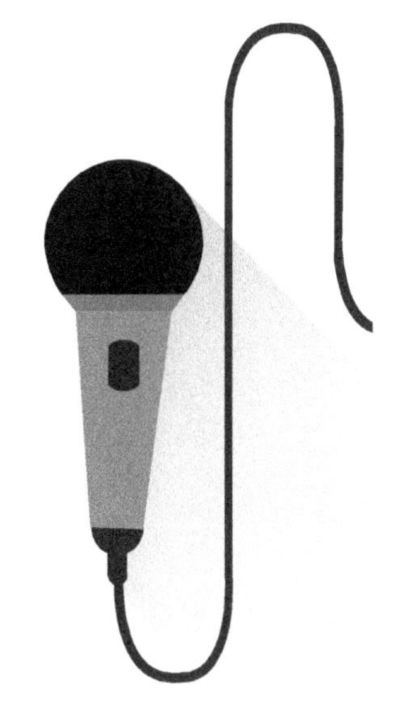

Question

Which comics did you fall in love with when you first started reading comics? Which ones were crucial in your development as a cartoonist? How?

Gene Luen Yang: The first comic I bought was *DC Comics Presents* #57 starring Superman. It was set in a nuclear wasteland. Superman teamed up with these guys called the Atomic Knights. That book blew my mind. I read a ton of superhero comics as a kid, mostly because that was what was available. I also read a bunch of Disney comics. I loved Carl Barks's and Don Rosa's work on the Disney Duck books. Those guys are geniuses. In college, I was heavily influenced by Lynda Barry's *One Hundred Demons* and Jeff Smith's *Bone.* Osamu Tezuka's *Adolf* made me into a manga fan.

Yumi Sakugawa: I feel very fortunate that I had exposure to both North American and Japanese comics during the formative years of my youth. For American comics, my first exposure was newspaper comics (particularly *For Better or For Worse, Luann*), which, when I think about it now, feels like the perfect training for thinking of storytelling and character development in very economical terms within a limited space. As for manga, I grew up reading *Chibi Maruko-chan*, *Dragon Ball Z*, *Sailor Moon*, and *CLAMP* comics. I am especially grateful to my manga upbringing because I was exposed to a culture where comics by women for women and girls was already the established norm, and that certainly was not the case for American comic culture when I was growing up.

Ryan North: I really loved the autobiographical comics of Eddie Campbell, and then I found Chris Onstad's *Achewood* comics online, and I thought (and still do!) that they were spectacular. His were the only online comics I knew of, so I thought when I started *Dinosaur Comics* that I'd be the second comic. Turns out, I wasn't close to second, and there were literally thousands of webcomics out there, but it's probably best I didn't know that because then I may never have started my strip!

Sonny Liew: Growing up, there was everything from the *Beano* to Disney comics, *Tintin* to *Lao Fu Zi* and *Richie Rich*. I don't think I was very discriminate at that age. The more conscious influences came a bit later—Bill Watterson's *Calvin and Hobbes* was probably the main one when I started drawing comics of my own.

"I am especially grateful to my manga upbringing because I was exposed to a culture where comics by women for women and girls was already the established norm, and that certainly was not the case for American comic culture when I was growing up." - Yumi Sakugawa

Taneka Stotts: When I was younger, I started out with what was available: *MAD Magazine*, *Creepshow*, *Casper*, and *Wendy*. A little later, I had access to more mainstream titles but found myself reading indie comics before diving headfirst into manga and manhwa. I would say the most crucial to my development as a writer was *Sailor Moon* by Naoko Takeuchi. It was the first series that told me that women creators were very valid and had amazing stories to tell.

Lucy Knisley: I was big into *Archie* comics as a kid. When my parents divorced, especially, I would beg them for the subscriptions by mail and drag my dad to the comic shop every week when I'd get to see him. My father, being a writing professor, disapproved of the literary merits of *Archie* comics. My mother, being an artist and feminist, disapproved of their content and quality. I had to convince them to buy them for me by looking at comics critically from a young age—picking out words I'd learned by reading them to convince my father or relating stories that shed a positive light on the women in the comic in order to convince my mother. I also read a lot of *Calvin and Hobbes*, *For Better or for Worse*, and *FoxTrot*, as well as Lynda Barry's Marlys comics. I didn't really come upon graphic novels until I was in high school.

Leela Corman: If we're going all the way back, *Archie*, *Tintin*, and those strips that ran all the way through *Cricket Magazine*. Oh, and of course, *Peanuts*. I used to wake up extra early when I was little just to read *Peanuts* in my bed, but I'd laugh so hard that I'd wake the household. I think I stopped reading comics around age ten or so and then rediscovered them when I was fifteen, thanks to a friend who had a copy of "Are We Having Fun Yet?", a *Zippy the Pinhead* collection. I immediately fell in love with it. I found a place that sold *Zippy* and other Last Gasp comics, and then around that same time, I discovered *RAW Comics* and *Love and Rockets*. Those were completely formative for me. I could feel the ground shifting beneath me when I read them for the first time, like my first kiss, like hearing the Stooges for the first time, like the first time I saw modern art. A path opened up, though I didn't know it at the time. I thought I was going to be a painter and that comics were too hard. But I was wrong about the latter and partially wrong about the former.

Fred Van Lente: My dad had a copy of this book the cartoonist Jules Feiffer did, *The Great Comic Book Heroes* (which we talk about in the *Comic Book History of Comics*, come to think of it), that had this essay Feiffer wrote for *The New Yorker* along with a bunch of Golden Age superhero stories: Batman, Superman, Captain America, the Spirit, like a dozen in all. I just loved it. I was like three, four. I begged my mother to read it to me and read it to me until she got sick of it and insisted I start reading some other books. So I just stared at the pictures and the words until I associated the one with the other, so I could read a lot earlier than the other kids when I entered kindergarten. She was impressed by that!

I didn't set foot into a comic book store until I was old enough to drive. But that was the time of the black-and-white boom, and it was the first time I discovered more literary comics, like Will Eisner's graphic novels. The one that made the biggest impression on me was *Kings in Disguise*, which Kitchen Sink came out with as a comic, and I see Norton has just brought back as a trade edition. That was a story about homeless people in the Depression—"hobos" to you and me—that had no fantastical elements and was very clearly drawn. It made me realize that comics could be about literally anything and opened a lot of exciting doors in my mind that later influenced me as a writer.

> “I first read comics around the time I was starting to go extra girl crazy. I would look at the lurid, saturated pages of my buddy’s X-Men comics mostly for Psylocke, Storm, and Rogue.” - Ronald Wimberly

Nilah Magruder: I started reading manga as a teenager, back in the late 90’s. Some of my faves were *Naruto, Paradise Kiss, Mars, One Piece, Peach Girl, Shaman King, Bleach, 20th Century Boys.* I LOOOOVED *Beck* (a.k.a. Mongolian Chop Squad). I also fell hard for webcomics: *Strings of Fate* by Jen Wang, *Same Difference* by Derek Kirk Kim, *Fallen* by Yuko Ota, and a lot of others that have been lost to time.

MariNaomi: As a kid, I used to clip *Bloom County* out of the newspaper so I could binge-read it all in one sitting. I had a huge crush on Opus the penguin.

When I was in my early twenties, I came across alternative comics, specifically Scott Russo’s *Jizz,* which was essentially a personal zine put out by a fancy publisher (Fantagraphics). I’d never seen anything like it. Within its pages were autobio comics about going to Catholic school, Xeroxed letters he had sent to politicians, form letters he had gotten back (and hilarious “translations” of what they really meant), crude jokes, and the occasional rant. It was angry, funny, sometimes shocking stuff, and I ate it up.

It wasn’t until a few years later, when I read the comics anthology *Twisted Sisters*, that my brain made the switch. It was Mary Fleener’s comic “The Jelly” that made me think, “Hey, I have stories, and I like to draw! Maybe I should make comics too!”

My biggest influences were true-life comics from that time period. After reading *Twisted Sisters,* I sought out other all-women anthologies, like *Tits and Clits, Real Girl*, stuff like that. I was also into Dennis Eichhorn’s anthology, *Real Stuff.* They were his stories, drawn by other people. I basically loved all real-life stories about sex, drugs, and heartache, which was an abundant genre at the time.

Ronald Wimberly: I first read comics around the time I was starting to go extra girl crazy. I would look at the lurid, saturated pages of my buddy’s X-Men comics mostly for Psylocke, Storm, and Rogue. But I didn’t fall in love with those any more than I fell in love with the Benny Hill show; in fact, I preferred the collector cards with the stats on the back. I suppose I fell in love with *Appleseed, Batman vs. Grendel, Akira*, and “Slow Jams” in Non.

Appleseed was something I picked up because I had already been introduced to anime by then. Darkhorse was putting out slim, floppy albums. I loved the notes in the gutters and the world-building portions in the back of the book.

Batman vs. Grendel stood out to me because of the design of the work, the character development, and the storytelling. Grendel was far more interesting to me than Batman. Looking back, it’s almost as if, to me, Wagner presented Grendel as a counterpoint to superhero comics and the ideas therein at large.

I found “Slow Jams” in Non when I was in high school. I had mostly stopped reading American comics altogether; there was little I found interesting there. The way the writer’s voice blended with the drawing and collage immediately hooked me. It would be the only reason I walked into a comic shop for the next few years . . . waiting for the next installment.

Rafael Rosado: I was born and raised in Puerto Rico, so most of the comics I read as a kid were translations of American comics or comics in Spanish from Mexico or Central and South America. As a very young kid, I read Disney comics, *Little Lulu, Sugar and Spice,* and *Henry,* among others. I moved on to Spanish language comics like *Condorito, Mafalda, Kaliman*, and wrestling comics/fumetti like *El Santo* and *Blue Demon*. Later on, I discovered Marvel and DC Comics and the work of Jack Kirby. That changed everything for me. His drawings had incredible energy, great staging, and were full of virtuoso drawing. I'm influenced by his work to this day.

Sophie Goldstein: The earliest comics I remember reading are *Archie* comics. I had stacks of the digest-size collections as well as the single issues. I also remember reading a lot of *Sonic the Hedgehog* comics even though I wasn't allowed to play video games. My dad would let me pick out a comic when we would go to the drugstore, so I was limited to whatever was in the spinner rack.

I also read the funny pages in the newspaper every day. When I went to summer camp or, later, to college, my dad would cut comics he liked out of the paper and mail them to me. He still had *Calvin and Hobbes* strips taped to his fridge years after the comic ended—up until he got a new fridge.

Belle Yang: My parents took me from authoritarian Taiwan to Japan in 1967, so I began reading manga avidly at age five. We were too poor to subscribe to the monthly issues of girls' manga, so I read my neighbor's, but, occasionally, my mother would buy me an issue with its melodramatic storylines and cliffhangers. I began drawing the saucer-eyed girls in kindergarten and elementary school. I also remember the scary manga set in the Samurai era. One that sticks in my mind was about a ruler who hated cats so much he tried to behead them all. When his first child was born, the baby had the eyes of a cat and would grow up to take revenge on him. Atom, or here, known as Astro boy, was a comic book I was quite familiar with.

Danica Novgorodoff: I came to reading comics late—it wasn't until my last year of college that I really started seeking them out. The first graphic novel I ever bought was Chris Ware's *Jimmy Corrigan*. It was so beautiful and depressing, and I loved it! In my midtwenties, I worked as a designer for First Second Books, and I was exposed to a lot of European authors, like Joann Sfar, Emmanuel Guibert, Marjane Satrapi, Gipi, David Beauchard, Clement Oubrerie, and Marguerite Abouet. When I was a kid, my favorite was *Calvin and Hobbes.*

Jenny Lin: The first comics I read were my brother's superhero comics, especially *Batman*. He had a huge collection, and I loved the visuals and the way that the same basic formulae of stories

“When I went to summer camp or, later, to college, my dad would cut comics he liked out of the paper and mail them to me. He still had *Calvin and Hobbes* strips taped to his fridge years after the comic ended—up until he got a new fridge.” - Sophie Goldstein were repeated over and over but with variations. I also had or have a soft spot for really old Wonder Woman comics.

When I started reading comics again as an adult, R. Crumb's comics really blew my mind and really influenced me. I felt encouraged to work with weird, subversive, and uncomfortable subject matter and just to go with my imagination really intuitively. I learned about Julie Doucet's work after I moved to Montreal and found her work so quirky and playful, but also, she's so totally astute in her character depiction, of capturing a particular mix of strangeness, banality, and also of intimacy in her stories and of creating an empathetic, engrossing read even with the most "despicable" characters in her comics.

Andi Santagata: I grew up in Hong Kong, which was in the process of assimilating back into China post-Communism, so comics were pretty hard to come by. I grew up reading newspaper comics like *Calvin and Hobbes* and *Adam At Home*, but it wasn't until my aunt dropped off a box full of *Archie* comics digests she'd collected from her teenhood in Hawaii (circa 1960!) that things started to really "click." Classic *Archie* is full of cheesy jokes, clean lines, swooping shapes, and an underlying sense of companionship—I believe it was Dan Parent who said, "Riverdale is where people already understand you"—that meant a lot to someone growing up in a rough time. *However*—and it's a big one—it wasn't until I discovered underground comics in middle school, particularly Jhonen Vasquez (*Johnny the Homicidal Maniac, Squee*) and Julie Doucet (*My New York Diary*, autobio works) that I realized I was supposed to be making comics (loud, angry, *loud* comics). Vasquez, Doucet, and their predecessors—R. Crumb, Derf, and even Harvey Kurtzman's weirder Playboy comics—did super honest, extremely hard-hitting, dense, gory, personal, and aesthetically wild stuff that was doing on paper what my brain was doing in my head. Funnily enough, lots of cartoonists are inspired by both classic Archie and the polar opposite, underground comics—Jaime Hernandez of *Love and Rockets*, for one!

Rina Ayuyang: I fell in love with comics at an early age and would read serialized comic strips in the newspaper, especially the Sunday funnies. I loved *Peanuts, Nancy, Blondie, For Better or for Worse, The Far Side, and The Family Circus*. I loved the humor and the richness of the characters in these strips. I also admired the drawing skills of the cartoonists who made them. I always wanted to be a newspaper cartoonist but always thought that only a handful of iconic artists like Charles Schulz could get a strip in the newspaper. So I abandoned the idea of being a cartoonist but still focused on artmaking. During college, I was in the art program and focused on painting, conceptual art, and new media art. It was only when I read Chester Brown's *I Never Liked You*, Adrian Tomine's *Optic Nerve*, and John Porcellino's *King Cat* that I discovered I could self-publish my own mini-comics and write the stories I wanted and really cared about. So I got back into cartooning again. I've been a cartoonist now for seventeen years.

"It was only when I read Chester Brown's *I Never Liked You*, Adrian Tomine's *Optic Nerve*, and John Porcellino's *King Cat* that I discovered I could self-publish my own mini-comics and write the stories I wanted and really cared about. So I got back into cartooning again. I've been a cartoonist now for seventeen years." - Rina Ayuyang

Jade Lee: The first comics I really got into (that I remember) were Magical Girl manga from the 1990s–early 2000s, specifically, *Sailor Moon* and *Cardcaptor Sakura*, which I was obsessed with as a kid, and continues to inspire my work today. Although I will say I was watching more anime at this time in my childhood, and I aspired to be an animator more so than a cartoonist. In college, I studied to be a fine artist instead, but my perspective took a really hard shift to comics in my junior year when I attended the Small Press Expo on a whim and got introduced to the hidden-but-expansive world of independently published comics and webcomics. While my personal comics tastes have changed a lot since, webcomics such as *Rice Boy* by Evan Dahm, *Johnny Wander* by Yuko Ota and Ananth Hirsch, and *Strings of Fate* by Jen Wang had a profound impact on me at the time. It was the first time that I realized the comics form was limitless in the types of stories I could use it to tell.

1.4 Spotlight on Ashanti Fortson, Cartoonist

"My introduction to comics was Miyazaki's *Nausicaä of the Valley of the Wind* at around nine years old—not entirely age-appropriate, but it was and still is incredibly important to me. Its beautiful, meticulously hatched panels and its profoundly human story made me love comics. More than that, it helped me realize that I could become an artist and a storyteller if I wanted to. I did, so I did.

After reading *Nausicaä*, I read the entire manga section at my local library. In fact, I first started to draw by tracing panels from *Inuyasha*. When I became active online in my teens, I read lots of webcomics. *Gunnerkrigg Court* by Tom Siddell stood out to me because of the incredible growth visible in the author's art. I felt encouraged by this! Anyone could make a comic, and I mean that in the best way possible. Comics (especially webcomics) felt accessible.

Despite my long history of reading and loving comics, it took me until 2015—my first year of college—to draw my first comic. Since then, the work of other contemporary cartoonists and webcomickers has been essential in helping me grow as a creator and a person. So much incredible work is being made right now, and I want to keep learning from it and doing my best."

An excerpt of "Spell It Out," a fairytale-inspired comic, by Ashanti Fortson.

1.5 Getting Oriented

Reading Text and Image

Will Eisner argues in *Comics and Sequential Art* that the act of reading of words is no different from the reading of images or the combination of image and text. Eisner cites Tom Wolf's research and writing on the act of reading published in the *Harvard Educational Review* in 1977:

> . . . research has shown that the reading of words is but a subset of a much more general human activity which includes *symbol decoding, information integration and organization* [. . .] The reading of words is one manifestation of this activity; but there are many others—*the reading of pictures, maps, circuit diagrams, music notes.*

This "reading of pictures, maps, circuit diagrams, music notes" can, of course, also be applied to reading comics. Eisner later writes:

> The format of the comic book presents a montage of both word and image, and the reader is thus required to exercise both visual and verbal interpretative skills. *The regimens of art (e.g., perspective, symmetry, brush stroke) and the regimens of literature (e.g., grammar, plot, syntax) become superimposed upon each other.* The reading of the comic book is an act of both aesthetic perception and intellectual pursuit. . . . Wolf's reconsideration of reading is an important reminder that the psychological processes involved in viewing a word and an image are analgous. The structures of illustration and of prose are similar (Eisner, 8; italics added).

1.6 The Basics: How Do You Read a Comic?

You may be overwhelmed, terrified, or quite familiar with the process of reading comics. No matter your level of experience with reading comics (or lack thereof) the below suggestions are:

- Take a breath and go slow. If you're reading comics for the very first time, it can take a while to adapt to reading words and images in combination.
- Resist the urge to skim quickly through the text without reading the images, as well, and vice versa.
- Look at the smaller details that may hide in the background.

Here Are Some Ways You Can Slow Your Reading Down and Engage with the Texts on Deeper Levels.

1. Read **the title and the cover art.** What do you notice? What predictions can you make before reading the comic? How does the comics creator (or cartoonist) set the tone for the work before the reader begins?
2. **Circle** words or lines you don't understand. Look these words up, and make a list of their definitions. Group the words that have similar meanings among the definitions you've looked up. What do you notice and observe about these groups of words? When you read these definitions, what story do they tell about the comic?

3. **Underline** words or sentences you feel are important to the reading. Look these words up even if familiar. What are the similarities and differences between these words? What are these words' qualities and characteristics? When you read these definitions, what story do they tell about the comic?
4. Choose two to three of the following **craft elements** to focus on, and choose a panel or a page to unpack these tools at work. What do you notice about the tools (or elements of craft) that the writer uses, such as:

- Word choice?
- Panel Size?
- Panel Shapes?
- Gutters?
- Sound effects?
- Tone?
- Repetition?
- Imagery?
- Use of color?
- Background?
- Line?
- Dialogue?
- Character design?
- Panel?
- Character?
- Metaphor and simile?
- Setting?
- Symbolism?
- Dialogue?
- Narratory blocks?

5. Write down **five to seven questions** you have about the text regarding craft elements such as word choice, color, etc. For example, "Why does the cartoonist repeat the word 'same' in every panel on the page?"? Try to answer your own questions using context clues from the text.
6. **Make Observations:** Write down **two to three observations** about the cartoonist's choices for this text. For example, "The voice in this story is told from a child's point of view" or "The creator spends a lot of time describing the poor conditions of New York City tenements."
7. **Make Inferences:** Based on your observations, what is the text trying to say? Write down **two to three inferences**. What are your final interpretations?

1.7 Sample Visual on How to Read a Comic—*American Born Chinese*

Notice and Focus

In their book, *Writing Analytically*, David Rosenwasser and Jill Stephen write about reframing a reader's habits of mind: "Not 'What do you think?' & not 'What do you like or dislike?' but 'What do you notice?'" They provide these questions to prompt the reader to guide his or her thinking: "What do you find most INTERESTING? What do you find most STRANGE? What do you find most REVEALING?"

Notice and Focus is a guide for close reading and drawing observations and inferences when reading comics. You can go through the entire process for an in-depth, thorough close reading, or you can select one or two questions from each reading to explore.

Instructions

Step 1: Cast a wide net by continuing to list details you notice. Go longer than you normally would before stopping—often the tenth or eleventh detail is the one that eventually leads to your best idea."
An example of Step 1 after reading a panel in Gene Luen Yang's *American Born Chinese*:

1. The colors in the background are light brown, grey, yellow.
2. Jin is wearing green and orange, which makes him blend into the background..
3. Wei Chen is wearing bright, vivid colors.
4. "Bump-da-da-bump" is written in bright yellow.
5. "Bump-da-da-bump" is an onomatopoeic word.
6. The purple car has bright green colors.
7. There's a Chinese symbol on the door.
8. It says "Xtreme" at the top of Wei Chen's windshield.
9. Both characters have black hair.
10. The car is purple.

Panel from Gene Luen Yang's *American Born Chinese* (228).

Step 2: Focus inside what you've noticed. Rank the various features of your subject you have noticed. Answer the question: "What details (specific features of the subject matter) are most interesting (or significant or revealing or strange)?" The purpose of relying on interesting or one of the other suggested words is that it will help deactivate the like/dislike switch of the judgement reflex and replace it with a more analytical perspective."

Example

Ranking of most interesting (1) to least interesting (10):

1. The car is purple, is **interesting** . . .
2. There's a Chinese symbol on the door that is **revealing** to me about Wei Chen . . .
3. It says "Xtreme" at the top of Wei Chen's windshield, which is **strange** . . .
4. "Bump-da-da-bump" is written in bright yellow and is **revealing** because . . .
5. "Bump-da-da-bump" is an onomatopoeic word.
6. The colors in the background are dull: light brown, grey, yellow.
7. Jin is wearing green and orange, which makes him blend into the background.
8. Wei Chen is wearing bright, vivid colors.
9. The purple car has bright green colors.
10. Both characters have black hair.

Step 3: Say why three things you selected struck you as the most interesting (or revealing or significant or strange). Saying why will trigger interpretive leaps to the possible meaning of whatever you find most interesting in your observations."

Example

1. I find it **interesting** that Wei Chen drives a deep purple car, which can symbolize his feelings of royalty and his desire to be different, to stand out.
2. The Chinese symbol on the side of Wei Chen's front door is **revealing** to me because it shows his pride in his cultural roots.
3. The "Xtreme" sign at the top of Wei Chen's windshield at first seemed quite **strange**, but it symbolizes him going from one extreme to another: from being an innocent, "fresh-off-the-boat" nerd to "rice rocket" gangster.
4. The bright yellow "bump-da-da-bump" hip-hop sounds coming from Wei Chen's car **reveal** his entering the foreground of the text and becoming his own individual instead of blending into the background as an outsider.

Note: After applying Notice and Focus, you may use your analysis from all three steps to include in your academic work on comics.

Example

In *American Born Chinese*, Wei Chen's wavering loyalty to his friend Jin made him decide to commit human vice and rebel against his father. After Jin encounters Wei Chen for the first time after getting punched in the face, Jin recognizes an enormous difference in Wei Chen's character. **In this panel, Wei Chen sits in his deep purple car with a sign that states "Xtreme" at the top of the windshield and a Chinese symbol that appears to symbolize his family name. Wei Chen uncharacteristically draws a lot of attention by bumping hip-hop music in the neighborhood, which takes Jin aback who is hesitant to approach his friend (228).** With the decision to purchase a flashy, purple car with his family last name engraved on the driver's side door, Wei Chen shows his pride for his cultural roots, his family name, and his father's status as Monkey King. It symbolizes his feelings of royalty and his desire to be different, to stand out. The "Xtreme" sign at the top of Wei Chen's windshield shows his journey from going from one extreme to another, from being an innocent, "fresh-off-the-boat nerd" to "rice rocket" gangster. The "bump-da-da-bump" hip-hop sounds coming from Wei Chen's car symbolize Wei Chen commanding the foreground of the text and becoming his own individual instead of blending into the background as an outsider. This shows how Wei Chen refuses to be Jin's sidekick after Jin punches him in the face. Wei Chen's assumptions about Jin being an unconditional best friend were false, and so he decides to embrace himself, become independent without Jin, and refuse to be influenced by his peers and father.

Try it!

Notice and Focus

Choose a panel from one of the comics you're currently reading. This can be a panel that confuses or surprises you or a splash page that demands your attention—your choice. It should be a panel that elicits your interest to dig deep into the craft elements and tools at work.

1. Go through all three steps of Notice and Focus.
2. Write 500 words that coalesce your findings in Notice and Focus.
3. Write on these questions: What did you notice as you slowed your reading process down? What did Notice and Focus allow you to see in the text?

1.8 Notice and Focus—*Student Example*

The Assignment: Choose a page from Black Panther: World of Wakanda *to analyze using Notice and Focus. Please use the comics terms and vocabulary we learned on the first day of class and in the first chapters of* Understanding Comics and Experiencing Comics, *as well.*

The page I am choosing from *Black Panther: World of Wakanda* is the page in which Ayo and Aneka first have physical contact outside of the fights. They are in a hallway, arguing, when Ayo pins Aneka against the wall and touches her face. The contact gets more intimate before the two are forced to spring apart because another group of initiates is coming into the hallway.

Panel from *Black Panther: World of Wakanda* written by Roxane Gay and Yona Harvey; art by Alitha E. Martinez and Afua Richardson.

Step 1

1. The colors of the background are mostly golden and warm.
2. There are four panels on the page, with blank space in the spaces that the panels do not take up.
3. The most intimate panel is the smallest.
4. Aneka and Ayo both are wearing similar clothing (small top, loose pants, gold jewelry), but Aneka's is purple, while Ayo (and the initiates that enter at the end of the page) are more of a grayish color.
5. Aneka runs down the stairs, whereas Ayo runs up.
6. There are not traditional gutters, but the panels are outlined ink thick black lines.
7. Aneka has tattoos/scarification on her face, but Ayo does not.
8. Both Aneka and Ayo are wearing earrings, but Aneka has dangly earrings, while Ayo has a gold ear cuff.
9. The speech bubble of the initiates when they first walk in is just abstract squiggly lines that is simply meant to convey talking that Aneka and Ayo can't fully hear.
10. When Aneka turns her head away from Ayo, the intimacy increases, but the size of the panel decreases.

Step 2

1. When Aneka turns her head away from Ayo, the intimacy increases, but the size of the panel decreases.
2. The most intimate panel is the smallest.
3. There are not traditional gutters, but the panels are outlined ink thick black lines.
4. Aneka and Ayo both are wearing similar clothing (small top, loose pants, gold jewelry), but Aneka's is purple, while Ayo (and the initiates that enter at the end of the page) are more of a grayish color.
5. Aneka runs down the stairs, whereas Ayo runs up.
6. Aneka has tattoos/scarification on her face, but Ayo does not.
7. There are four panels on the page, with blank space in the spaces that the panels do not take up.
8. Both Aneka and Ayo are wearing earrings, but Aneka has dangly earrings, while Ayo has a gold ear cuff.
9. The speech bubble of the initiates when they first walk in is just abstract squiggly lines that is simply meant to convey talking that Aneka and Ayo can't fully hear.
10. The colors of the background are mostly golden and warm.

Step 3

1. When Aneka turns her head away from Ayo, the intimacy increases, but the size of the panel decreases.
2. The most intimate panel is the smallest.

   I think these observations are interesting for very interconnected reasons. The artist chose to decrease the size of the panel in order to increase the intimacy because it literally brings the reader in with Aneko and Ayo, as they are moving closer together. The panel also zooms in, and no longer shows their whole faces, but just the bottom halves of their faces and their hands. The emphasis is also placed clearly on their lips in order to increase the sensuality of the moment, but the space has shrunk in order for it to feel more intimate even in size and reading experience.

3. There are not traditional gutters, but the panels are outlined in thick, black lines.

   I found this particularly interesting throughout reading the whole graphic novel because a lot of the panels were open panels or almost full splash panels. They didn't always have boundaries, or even when they did have boundaries sometimes, that black borders would blend into the coloring of the panels themselves because many of them (even on just this page for instance) have fairly dark coloring for their backgrounds. I think that using panels of literally varying sizes and placements on the page and then allowing for there to be actual blank space on the page adds a lot of simplicity and beauty to the piece itself. It doesn't feel as cluttered as sometimes graphic novels feel, and everything flows really cleanly.

4. Aneka and Ayo both are wearing similar clothing (small top, loose pants, gold jewelry), but Aneka's is purple, while Ayo (and the initiates that enter at the end of the page) are more of a grayish color

   This one is probably the most interesting to me personal (though I ranked it lower because I feel the importance of the aforementioned points contributes to this one). Slowing down my reading really made look at both Aneka and Ayo visually and stop and think and describe their outfits. And in all honesty, both are wearing fairly "skimpy" clothes. They both have very loose, low-hanging pants and very short, tight, cleavage-exposing, almost bra-like tops. In other scenes these elements are emphasized in incredibly sexy (and still tasteful, in my opinion) ways. However, in this particular scene, they are not. The two panels in which we see Aneka and Ayo getting closer and closer show from the very tops of their shoulders up. And even the bareness of their shoulders is deemphasized by jewelry, movement, and where the panel cuts off. Instead, all the sensuality is placed on their faces, their hands, their lips, their cheeks, their noses, their nails—all things that are very rarely ever showcased on women in comic books. Rather than showcasing large breasts, a big ass, a toned stomach, wide hips, or long/luscious hair, the artist chooses a very human, very realistic way of making a situation truly sexy and truly intimate. The tension in the scene is palpable because the sexuality is kept so simple and so genuine.

Cloud Whorl

1.9 Spotlight on John Jennings, Cartoonist

Which comics did you fall in love with when you first started reading comics?

The comics that got me started in the medium were *The Mighty Thor, Daredevil*, and the *Amazing Spider-Man*. I was a huge Marvel fan at first. My mother bought them for me, and I've been hooked ever since.

Which ones were crucial in your development as a writer and cartoonist?

Of the original batch, I'd say that Frank Miller's *Daredevil* had a huge effect on me. Loved his visual style, his writing, and the personality that he managed to inject into Matt Murdock. Later, I truly fell in love with DC's horror comics in the late 70s and into the early 80s. So, books like *Tales of the Unexpected, House of Secrets*, etc.

Which writing and drawing exercises were helpful for you as you worked on and developed your craft?

I think that Burne Hogarth's book *Dynamic Anatomy* was pivotal in my development as an artist. I think I may have had three copies of that book. I just drew from it continually. Another book that was very influential was *How to Draw the Marvel Way.*

This textbook examines the history of comics in the U.S. in the beginning chapters. Are there any influential and/or underrepresented moments, movements, or figures in comics history that have influenced you and your work in any way?

A lot of my work is influenced by the design and illustrations done during the Harlem Renaissance and also the Black Arts Movement. The independent black comics movement that began in the mid-90s was also a huge influence on my work. So books like *Brotherman, Ramses, Original Man* and others helped me find my way as a creator. *Brotherman*, in particular, was a massive inspiration for me.

John Jennings, Cartoonist

How do you get started on a project once you've explored the seed of an idea? And perhaps more importantly, how do you persevere after the initial excitement over an idea?

I usually take a lot of notes on a project. So, sometimes the project starts out as just an idea. I'll jot that down in my notes and start doing research on it. Then, as the idea grows, I start doing world building and character development. The story ideas sort of "self-select." As the stories began going form, the ones that are stronger ideas tend to remain in the forefront. The initial excitement is maintained by the force of seeing something start from being an idea into a real, totally functional visual narrative. Sometimes, it takes months. Sometimes it takes years. I am very obstinate when it comes to projects, and I will get them done regardless of the time frame or the method.

You're incredibly active in the comics community, particularly when it comes to fostering and supporting comics spaces and nerd spaces for Black folks and people of color. Can you talk about your work with the Black Comic Festival at the Schomburg Center in Harlem and other festivals/spaces that put cartoonists and fans of color at the forefront?

I became very interested in comics and representation while I was at UIUC. Since then, I've managed to make some really amazing alliances with institutions across the country who are dedicated to empowering underserved youth through the power of comics. I've also put together a number of art shows, published collections and books about identity politics in comics. Six years ago I cofounded the Schomburg Center's Black Comic Book Festival with Dr. Jonathan Gayles, Deirdre Hollman, and Jerry Craft. The event is held at the historic Schomburg Center for Research in Black Culture. The convention is totally free and has now grown to a two-day event that happens the Friday and Saturday before MLK Holiday in January. The event brings in around seven to eight thousand people and has some of the most talented African American comics creators in the country. That same weekend, I helped create the Black Comix Arts Festival. This festival is a part of the MLK celebration that is put on by the city of San Francisco and is in collaboration with the Northern California King Foundation. The festival is held at Yerba Buena Art Center's CityView Metreon and brings in about three thousand people. I am also the cofounder of SolCon, the Brown and Black Comix Expo along with Dr. Frederick Luis Aldama and Ricardo Padilla, the co-founder of the Latino Comics Expo. I have dedicated a great deal of time as a cultural activist putting on symposia, conferences, conventions, and exhibitions that are geared towards pushing back against symbolic annihilation of people of color and other designated minorities and underserved groups. Everyone deserves to see themselves represented in the society in which they participate.

> "I have dedicated a great deal of time as a cultural activist putting on symposia, conferences, conventions, and exhibitions that are geared towards pushing back against symbolic annihilation of people of color and other designated minorities and underserved groups. Everyone deserves to see themselves represented in the society in which they participate."

You also have a palpable presence in academia. You teach in the media and culture studies department at UC Riverside; you collaborate with other professors in the Creative Writing Department there, as well; and you're a Nasir Jones Hiphop Fellow at Harvard. Phew! How do these roles help you further understand your process and thinking about comics? How does teaching inform your comics creation practice, and vice versa?

I think that comics, by nature, is a hybridized storytelling medium. My interdisciplinary practice has always informed the way that I design and write. Hip hop and science fiction definitely inform my comics work in various ways. The sampling and remix aspects of hip hop culture inform the way that I think about making comics and also my research methods. I honestly think that being a hip hop scholar has informed almost every aspect of how I move through the academy. In a sense, every part of my practice is informed by principles of hip hop culture. In turn, the visual aspects of cultural studies, production and design also inform my pedagogy.

Can you discuss your work with Professor Frances Gateward in coediting *The Blacker the Ink: Constructions of Black Identity in Comics and Sequential Art?* What was your process in selecting the essays for this anthology, and how did the critical work you came across influence your thinking about comics?

We wanted to find a narrative beyond black superheroes. The idea was to look at the various modes of how blackness was being interpreted in the comics medium. So, we went after brilliant scholars who were doing groundbreaking analysis of black identity but also looking at work that really has been overlooked due to the overwhelming presence of superheroes in the public sphere.

I am not sure how much the work shifted how I was thinking about comics, but it was an amazing experience, and I am very proud of the five-year journey that we took to get to the end result.

Promotional flyer for The Schomburg Center's Annual Black Comic Book Festival, which was co-founded by John Jennings, Dr. Jonathan Gayles, Deirdre Hollman, and Jerry Craft. Art by John Jennings.

Kindred, a graphic novel adaptation of Octavia Butler's celebrated novel by Damian Duffy and John Jennings.

Can you talk about collaboration with Damian Duffy in adapting Octavia Butler's *Kindred*? What was especially challenging about this process? What was the most rewarding part about it?

The most challenging thing about *Kindred* was dealing with the overwhelming traumatic effect of visualizing the horrors of slavery. Nothing prepares you for finding the perfect way to illustrate pain. The most rewarding thing about the book was turning in the project and hearing that the Butler Estate had no changes. Nothing can beat the feeling. Except for maybe debuting at number one on the *New York Times* bestseller list!

Which comics are you reading now that you love?

I love horror so, comics I am really loving [Cullen Bunn's] *Harrow County;* Becky Cloonan's *Southern Cross* and *Black Cloud*. I am also a big fan of *Southern Bastards, Noble* and a lot of the Lion Forge's *Catalyst Prime* comics. I am also a huge fan of Gail Simone's *Clean Room.*

What would you tell students who are just getting into creating comics? Any words of encouragement for beginning students who feel like they suck at drawing or writing?

I always ask my students, "How do you get really good at throwing a punch?" The answer is: "Throw a lot of punches." I am a huge believer in "failing safely." Practice. Practice. Practice. Also, if want to be unhappy, compare yourself to others. Find your own voice and strengthen your voice. It will take a long time; just remember that there's no "app" for success and that hard work usually breeds success.

1.10 Spotlight on *INK BRICK*—A Journal of Comics Poetry

An Interview with Alexander Rothman, one of the founding editors of INK BRICK.

What is comics poetry? And how has your understandings of comics poetry changed in the past few years of editing *INK BRICK*?

I define comics poetry as work that uses the visual language of comics to compose poetry.

That's still pretty vague, so I usually give my working definitions of "poetry" and "comics" as well. Basically, I think of poetry as the form most directly concerned with language. To some extent, fiction requires plots, essays require arguments, and plays require characters. These things are available to poets, of course, but I'd argue that if she wants to, a poet can focus on the creative problem, "What else can language do?" (And of course other writers can tackle that question, too.)

And I approach comics as a form that uses images the way other forms use words. So put poetry and comics together, and you get a form that asks, "What else can comics do?"

I like that definition because I think it's fundamentally generative. If anything, it risks letting too much work in the door, but our mission is to move the form forward, to offer proofs of concept as to what's possible. And that's what I love most about editing *INK BRICK*. Our contributors constantly surprise me with new ways to think about juxtaposition, or reading paths, or the function of gutters, and on and on.

" I approach comics as a form that uses images the way other forms use words. So put poetry and comics together, and you get a form that asks, "What else can comics do?" "

How did *INK BRICK* get started?

In 2013, Paul and I were living in NYC, as were the cartoonist-poets Bianca Stone and Gary Sullivan. We met up a few times and discussed ways to pool our resources and collaborate. We ended up developing the press out of that. Alexey Sokolin joined the editorial board as of issue three, and Matthea Harvey just joined us as of issue nine.

Which writers and artists are the literary ancestors of comics poetry? Whose work has influenced your understanding of this form?

I always like to say that when I first started meeting other cartoonist-poets, we all thought we'd invented the form. But people have been intentionally combining comics and poetry since at least the 1960s, when Joe Brainard collaborated with the New York School poets. For me it was huge to discover work by John Hankiewicz, Warren Craghead, and Keren Katz. George Herriman is my patron saint. Really, there are too many inspiring creators working to count—folks like Alyssa Berg, Madeleine Witt, Deshan Tennekoon, Daryl Seitchik, Anthony Cudahy, Laurel Lynn Leake . . .

Recent issues of *INK BRICK*, A Journal of Comics Poetry.

Since you started *INK BRICK* back in 2014, have you noticed any shifts or trends in comics poetry?

Mostly just that there's been a total explosion of work. When we started this, I worried that we'd struggle to find enough work to fill issues. Instead we've practically doubled our page count and we're getting more than we know what to do with. I'm also gratified to see this work in mainstream publications like *Poetry*. It's truly an exciting time for the form.

What surprises have you encountered while editing *INK BRICK*? How have poet-cartoonists defied your expectations of poetry, comics, and/or comics poetry?

I touched on this earlier, but I'm constantly surprised by our contributors. There are just so many unique ways to mine the expressive potential of comics. Let's just consider the idea of juxtaposition, which I'd argue is the foundational unit of comics. Mostly we think about that in terms of panel sequences. But comics also juxtaposes words and images, and both of those elements with structural components like word balloons and captions, and also nonsequential panels with each other, and potentially pages within a spread, and also other image units, like the parts of a single composition—and all of that is just scratching the surface.

I love to see creators really exploring the difference between, say, putting text in a caption and running it under a panel, like in a *New Yorker* cartoon. My spouse just ordered some comics by Peony

Gent, and they came with postcards that featured empty word balloons with the text written beside them. I love things like that.

Can you speak on your own backgrounds and histories with comics, poetry, and comics poetry?

I grew up reading and making comics. My dad introduced me to Pogo Possum when I was young, and I went from being a huge Spider-Man fan to reading *Sandman*, and then things like *Maus* and *True Swamp*, and out from there. I also ended up studying poetry as an undergrad. I wrote a creative thesis under Jorie Graham's guidance that collected original poems and translations from Ukrainian.

By the time I graduated I knew that I wanted to combine the two forms, but I didn't really know where to start. I spent several years kind of flailing around, and then a major reason I wanted to start *INK BRICK* was to refine my own thinking about the form, find a community, and cultivate a forum for everyone's work.

Issue Five of *INK BRICK*, A Journal of Comics Poetry.

Have you made your own comics poetry? If so, can you describe this process?

I do. I consider myself a creator much more than an editor or publisher.

A lot of my process is trying to get out of my own way. After years of trying to compose images and language simultaneously, I've come to terms with the fact that I'm much more verbal than visual. I use a few simple grids of either four or six panels. (Frank Santoro's ideas about the grid have been hugely helpful to me.) The constraint frees me from the anxiety of coming up with wild layouts.

These days I draw mostly on an iPad Pro using Procreate. I'll iterate language, move it around, and I draw using a lot of reference.

What words of encouragement would you give to beginning writers and artists as they dive into this form?

Play. There are so many tools to facilitate creation and get your work out there. Don't think you can draw? Try working with procedurally generated images or collage photos in GIMP, or just mess around arranging typography in panels. The field is young, and there are endless places to go with it.

There's also no money whatsoever in this and very little prestige. And that's freeing, too. There are no excuses not to do whatever you want.

Do you have any reading recommendations in comics poetry, comics, or poetry in general?

I'll just mention one book here, since any kind of list is going to leave too many people out. Fantagraphics recently came out with an edition of John Hankiewicz's *Education,* and that's about as accomplished a book as comics poetry has produced yet.

"Love," a comic-poem by Alexander Rothman.

1.11 A List of Further Reading

Bennett, Tamryn. "Comics Poetry: Beyond 'Sequential Art.'" *Image and Narrative,* vol. 15, no. 2, 2014, www.imageandnarrative.be/index.php/imagenarrative/article/viewFile/544/397.

Betts, Tara. "When Comics and Poetry Intersect." The Ploughshares Blog, 16 July 2016, http://blog.pshares .org/index.php/when-poetry-and-comics-intersect/.

Eisner, Will. *Graphic Storytelling and Visual Narrative.* W. W. Norton, 2008.

Karasik, Paul, and Mark Newgarden. *How to Read Nancy: The Elements of Comics in Three Easy Panels.* Fantagraphics, 1994.

Lai, Paul. *Comics Syllabus* (podcast). Multiversity Comics, 2017–2018, http://www.multiversitycomics.com/tag/comics-syllabus/.

"Strip Panel Naked." YouTube, uploaded by HassanOE, https://www.youtube.com/channel/UCYJAToPH5GSGShP7Yoc3jsA.

Discussing Comics

2

Introduction

As you begin to learn about the history, terminology, and language of comics, it is also imperative to observe and learn how contemporary comics scholars in the field engage in the comics themselves. Scholars use different lenses to read and **engage** in discourse using literary criticism and theory, such as critical race theory, queer theory, gender studies, and more, in order to create and deepen critical conversations about comics, which, as discussed in chapter three on the history of comics, have been historically and easily dismissed as unworthy of study and discussion. As you read the critical discourse in this chapter, it is quite evident that the medium of comics "contains multitudes" (as the poet Whitman wrote) to discuss, unpack, and analyze, and these works are just a few of the fine examples of the excellent comics scholarship that continues to proliferate today.

Jeffrey A. Brown's essay "Panthers and Vixens: Black Superheroines, Sexuality, and Stereotypes in Contemporary Comic Books" effectively illustrates the damaging stereotypes of Black women in the media and the comics that challenge these stereotypes through characters, Marvel's Black Panther and DC's Vixen. Brown writes: "Both Black Panther and Vixen have costumed identities and powers associated with animals. This animalistic association is a clear remnant of colonial stereotypes that characterized African women as the embodiment of an abnormal, voracious, and almost bestial sexuality" (143). Brown argues that creator Reginald Hudlin's run of *Black Panther: Deadliest of Species* and G. Willow Wilson's run of *Vixen* are

Learning Objectives

- Read and analyze scholarly essays by Jeffrey A. Brown and Ramzi Fawaz.
- Define and discuss key concepts such as, hegemony, masculinity, Orientalism, fetishization, comic book cosmopolitics, fluxability, and more.
- Apply comics terminology from Chapter 1: Reading Comics to the scholarly essays.

Learning Outcomes

- Evaluate the intersectionality of race, class, nationality, gender, and sexuality in comics and graphic novels.
- Interpret the term "stereotype" in comics and sociopolitical contexts.
- Deconstruct the term "diversity" in comic books as posited by comics scholar Ramzi Fawaz.

specific, illuminating examples of comics that have resisted stereotypes in a medium that can so easily uphold them.

The New Mutants: Superheroes and the Radical Imagination of American Comics by Ramzi Fawaz is an incisive and accessible examination and analysis of superhero comics contextualized through the lens of post–World War II radical movements, such as the Black Power movement, women's liberation, and the LGBTQ movement. An excerpt from *The New Mutants* is provided here in order to show the ways in which Fawaz incorporates a series of overlapping and interconnected lenses to view superhero comics from history to queer theory and gender studies. Additionally, a personal essay by Fawaz entitled "The Difference a Mutant Makes," originally published by the *Los Angeles Review of Books,* details his connection to comics and his ambition to study and write about them today.

There are discussion questions provided after Brown's essay and Fawaz's excerpt in order to propel you into critical discussion about these works and to apply these concepts to your own study of comics. This chapter will also introduce you to, or deepen your understanding of, foundational concepts in feminism, queer theory, gender studies, critical race theory, and more in order to broaden your critical thinking and discussion about these works and other comics you read in any classroom community.

Key Terms

- Hegemony
- Masculinity
- Intersectionality
- Fetishization
- Stereotype
- Orientalism
- Feminism
- Queer theory
- Gender studies
- Comic Book Cosmopolitics

2.1 Reading: "Panthers and Vixens: Black Superheroines, Sexuality, and Stereotypes in Contemporary Comic Books"

by Jeffrey A. Brown

COMIC BOOK SUPERHEROES HAVE BEEN AN IMPORTANT PART OF AMERICAN popular culture ever since Superman first appeared in 1938. Though the medium of comic books and the genre of superheroes are typically derided as inconsequential and formulaic children's entertainment, the enduring presence of costumed super beings makes them a useful subject for tracking cultural changes. In fact, it is precisely because superheroes are considered innocuous fantasies that they warrant serious consideration. Everyone knows who Superman, Batman, Spider-Man, and Wonder Woman are. Even if we have never read a comic book, seen their movies, or watched their television series, we know their basic stories. We also know what they look like, know of their never-ending crusades for justice, and are at least familiar with their unique powers. As omnipresent characters in Western culture, superheroes help shape our ideologies. They reveal some of our most basic beliefs about morality and justice, our conceptions of gender and sexuality, and our attitudes towards ethnicity and nationality. The primary focus of this chapter is the depiction of black superheroines in contemporary comic books and how they are portrayed according to specific racial and sexual stereotypes. When looking specifically at recent stories focused on the black superheroines Black Panther and Vixen, it becomes apparent that while many of the superficial ingredients may reinforce racial and sexual stereotypes, they can also present tales that move beyond derogatory stereotypes to provide positive and heroic examples of black women in popular culture.

Background: Gender and Ethnicity In Comic Books

Despite many cultural advances over the last fifty years, black women in the media, especially within the superhero genre, are still constructed as exotic sexual spectacles, as erotic racial "Others." In contrast to the dominant model of male heroes, and in distinction to non-ethnically identified female characters in the comics, black superheroines are often presented as hypersexual and metaphorically bestial. Moreover, popular black superheroines—like Storm, Vixen, Pantha, and the Black Panther are explicitly associated with exoticized notions of Africa, nature, noble savagery, and a variety of Dark Continent themes, including voodoo, mysticism, and animal totemism. While heroic images of black women challenge the dominant model of superheroes and represent some very real, and very positive changes, the continued use of stereotypes reinforces some of our most rudimentary racial conceptions. In the cases of Black Panther and Vixen, there is a small step forward to representing black superheroines who are more than just a cluster of racial stereotypes.

> "As omnipresent characters in Western culture, superheroes help shape our ideologies. They reveal some of our most basic beliefs about morality and justice, our conceptions of gender and sexuality, and our attitudes towards ethnicity and nationality."

The colorful stories of comic book superheroes have always been concerned first and foremost with parables of justice and of basic cultural values about heroism, and of good triumphing over evil. But, as a great deal of research over the past two decades demonstrates, issues of gender and sexuality are also central implicit themes played out in superhero tales. Week after week, new issues hit the stands with depictions of perfectly muscled men, what Anthony Easthope (1988) refers to as "super-masculine ideals" (29), ready to defend America against any array of criminals, terrorists, or alien invaders. In addition to teaching lessons about right and wrong, superhero comic books have always provided a clear and rudimentary example of gender ideals. In comic books, women have historically been damsels in distress or—at best—plucky reporters. But men in superhero stories have always been paragons of masculinity. Male superheroes are depicted as incredibly powerful, smart, confident, and always in control. Moreover, the illustrations emphasize the muscles and the stature of the heroes as perfect male specimens. The Clark Kent and Peter Parker side of the characters may exist, but these wimpy secret identities only stress the exceptional nature of Superman and Spider-Man. Alan Klein argues that "comic book depictions of masculinity are so obviously exaggerated that they represent fiction twice over, as genre and as gender representation" (Klein 1993, 267). The conventional superhero is an adolescent fantasy of hegemonic masculinity, either literally or figuratively armored against possible threats. Scott Bukataman points out that in contemporary comics the superhero's body is "hyperbolized into pure, hypermasculine spectacle" (Bukataman 1994, 106). The masculine ideal embodied by heroes such as Superman, Batman, Iron-Man, and Captain America represent a reassuring fantasy about the eminence of patriarchal authority for the genre's mostly young and male readership.

The dominant male superheroes embody masculine ideals and serve as a point of identification for readers. Female superheroines, on the other hand, are primarily depicted as scantily clad and erotically posed fetish objects. Despite some major advancement for female characters, and an increasing presence of female writers and illustrators, women in the comics continue to be portrayed primarily as sexual spectacles.

In his analysis of comic book mutants and bodily trauma, Scott Bukataman argues that "the spectacle of the female body in these titles is so insistent, and the fetishism of breasts, thighs, and hair so complete, that the comics seem to dare you to say something about them that isn't just redundant. *Of course* the female form has absurdly exaggerated sexual characteristics; *of course* the costumes are skimpier than one could (or should) imagine; *of course* there's no visible way that these costumes could stay in place; *of course* these women represent simple adolescent masturbatory fantasies (with a healthy taste of the dominatrix)" (Bukataman 1994, 112). The unequal presentation of gender is certainly not unique to comics. In most forms of popular culture, men are depicted as strong and authoritative figures, while women are, to borrow Laura Mulvey's (1975) famous phrase, valued for their "to-be-looked-at-ness." That this gender dichotomy is taken to an extreme in comics, where men are crafted as hypermasculine heroic ideals and women as scantily clad and extremely curvaceous sexual objects, may not be surprising given the genre's target audience of young males, but it does perpetuate sexist beliefs and is indicative of the medium's reliance on stereotypes.

Just as superhero comics have always relied on gender stereotypes of the most extreme sort, ethnicity in the comics has predominantly been portrayed according to racial stereotypes. In his discussion of shifting forms of black identities within superhero stories, Marc Singer notes that "comic books, and particularly the dominant genre of superhero comic books, have proven fertile ground for stereotyped depictions of race" (Singer 2002, 123). It is this reliance on stereotypes that makes truly progressive depictions of black superhero characters difficult within mainstream comics from industry giants like Marvel and DC Comics. Black male superheroes have come a long way since Blaxploitation-influenced characters like Luke Cage, Black Panther, Black Lightning, and Black Goliath first appeared in the 1960s and 1970s (for a more detailed discussion of black male superheroes, see Brown 2001, Singer 2002, McWilliams 2010, or Cunningham 2010). In the 1960s and 1970s, Blaxploitation-inspired superheroes were mostly stereotypical "black male brutes" who focused on street crime in inner-city ghettos. Contemporary black superheroes have become far more powerful, diverse, and respected. For example, where originally Luke Cage was an ex-convict who fought pimps and drug dealers in Harlem while uttering his trademark expletive "Sweet Christmas!" the current version of Cage is a husband and father, a trusted and revered superhero who fights urban blight in inner cities as well as world-class supervillains and alien invasions; most significantly, he is also the newest leader of Marvel's legendary super-team, the Avengers. While Luke Cage may be the most remarkable example of a black superhero who has risen to prominence within the genre, he is joined by a growing number of other characters who represent a challenge to the traditionally white-dominated heroic landscape. Whether part of a team or headlining their own series, there are a substantial number of black superheroes currently populating the Marvel and DC universes, including such fan favorites as Cyborg, Steel, Blade, Icon, Static, Bishop, Mister Terrific, War Machine, and Deathlok.

While significant advancements have been made with black male superheroes, in both their sheer numbers and the manner in which they are portrayed, the development of black female superheroines has been slower. There are several notable examples of popular black superheroines in mainstream comics, including Marvel's new female version of the Black Panther and DC's Vixen, both of whom will be discussed in detail below, but they are often depicted in a manner that is more problematic than portrayals associated with either white superheroines or black superheroes. Elsewhere (Brown 2011), I contended that ethnically diverse superheroines continue to traffic in Orientalist conceptions of exotic fetishism because their portrayal is dictated by the twin burdens of racial and sexual stereotyping. In my earlier piece, I was concerned with ethnic superheroines as a general type. I argued "the power of exoticism is still a dominant trope played out on the body of the female Other, especially in visual mediums, in a manner that reduces her to a racially charged sex object and a readily consumable body" (Brown 2011, 170). Here, I want to address how the figure of the black superheroine reinforces and challenges specific racial markers. Nearly all comic book superheroines who are identified as ethnic minorities are treated as erotic spectacles, as hypersexual "Others." For example, Latina superheroines like Arana (aka Spider Girl), White Tiger, Fire, Feral, and Tarantula are routinely depicted as seductive and hot-tempered beauties, often referred to in the comics as "hot tamales." Likewise, Asian superheroines such as Lady Shiva, Katana, Hazmat, Psylocke, and Colleen Wing are portrayed as mysterious and alluring dragon ladies. By virtue of their ethnicity and their femininity, black superheroines are presented as exotic beauties in a manner similar to other female characters from different minority backgrounds. It is worth noting that, in addition to black characters, minority representation is restricted in mainstream comics almost exclusively to Asian and Latina (extraterrestrial superheroines may have different skin colors but they are physically depicted as Aryan). In addition to hypersexuality, black superheroines are also specifically aligned with Afro-centric stereotypes related to nature, mysticism, and totemism.

Volumes of research have explored the ways that black women have been constructed and reproduced in the popular imagination as supremely racialized and sexualized figures (see, for example, McClintock 1995, hooks 1992, Collins 2005, and Negra 2001). Based historically in a colonial logic that sought to contain and marginalize non-whites, and thus to valorize whiteness as a cultural category which was personified in the figure of chaste white womanhood, black women in particular became the locus for a specific set of intertwined racist assumptions. In her treatise on the colonial imagination, Anne McClintock notes the centuries-old tradition in Europe of conceptualizing Africans with unbridled sexuality: "popular lore had firmly established Africa as the quintessential zone of sexual aberration and anomaly" (McClintock 1995, 22). Patricia Hill Collins echoes the same sentiments when she argues that "through colonial eyes, the stigma of biological Blackness and the seeming primitiveness of African cultures marked the borders of extreme abnormality" (Collins 2005, 120). And most importantly, as McClintock clarifies, African "women figured as the epitome of sexual aberration and excess. Folklore saw them, even more than the men, as given to a lascivious venery so promiscuous as to border on the bestial" (Collins 2005, 22). Likewise, in his discussion of nineteenth-century depictions of black women, Sander Gilman noted that they were characterized as "more primitive, and therefore more sexually intensive" than white women and that their bodies and sexuality were described as "animal-like" (Gilman 1992, 177). This colonialist and imperialist worldview allowed white Europeans to accept a system of race-based hierarchy as natural. It also facilitated demeaning and dehumanizing practices whereby black bodies were seen as available commodities to be bought and sold in systems of slavery and where black female bodies, especially, could be presented for sexual entertainment or displayed as sexual curiosities.

Contemporary representations of black women are still haunted by the colonialist conception of African females as "animal-like" hypersexual creatures. bell hooks notes that "representations of black female bodies in contemporary popular culture rarely subvert or critique images of black female sexuality which were part of the cultural apparatus of nineteenth-century racism and which still shapes perceptions today" (hooks 1992, 114). These stereotypes still function, at least in part, as a means to sanctify white female sexuality by contrast. In their discussion of women in modern music videos, Railton and Watson argue that depictions of sexuality are intimately grounded in these long-standing conceptions about race and gender:

> These imperial discourses are only one branch of a long tradition of cultural representation which produces white and black womanhood as very different. Much of this difference turns upon a series of binary oppositions, oppositions which both disguise the complexities of lived experience and structure thinking in ways which tend to mask and shore up hierarchies of power. Simply stated, within this tradition of representation, white women are defined by asexuality in direct contrast to the presumed hypersexuality of black women. On the one hand, black women's "hypersexuality" is seen to derive from a series of apparently natural traits that link them to the animal, the primitive and the "dirty." In defining the black woman first and foremost through a series of physical characteristics, her body is not only made available to both white and black men but the buttocks of that body are figured as emblematic of black womanhood generally and the icon of black female sexuality more precisely. (Railton and Watson 2005, 56)

The colonial tradition which Railton and Watson, Collins, hooks, McClintock, and countless others have documented clearly still informs media representations of black women as hypersexual, "booty-licious," and wild. Recent popular performers continue to present the commodifiable images of the wild black woman, from Grammy-winning singers Beyonce and Nicki Minaj, to award-winning actresses like Halle Berry, to tennis champions Venus and Serena Williams, to reality television stars like New York. Likewise, the variations of this stereotype have been explored in dozens of recent academic studies, including such specific examples as music videos (Railton and Watson 2005), sports (McKay and Johnson 2008), and even video pornography (Miller-Young 2010).

The Modern Black Superheroíne

The depiction of black women as superheroines in comic books shares many of the same traits associated with black female representations in other media forms. But the very nature of superheroines facilitates a different type of representation than typically occurs when black women appear as singers, actresses, models, porn stars, and even as celebrity athletes. Despite the sexual spectacle that is an inherent aspect of contemporary superheroines, they are also undeniably strong and heroic characters. While the compounded hypersexuality of being both costumed superheroines *and* black women means that black superheroines run the risk of simply reinforcing racial and gendered stereotypes, they also have the potential to embody progressive and empowering concepts about black female strength and heroics. After all, the entire narrative purpose of any superhero is to right wrongs, to defend the weak, and to be a champion for justice. Black female characters in popular culture rarely have the potential to be as explicitly and unabashedly heroic as they do in superhero comic books.

Unfortunately, there are still relatively few black superheroines in mainstream comics. Characters like Marvel's Storm, Misty Knight, and Monica Rambeau (aka Captain Marvel), as well as DC's Thunder, Onyx, and Bumble Bee, may have a devoted following among serious comic book fans, but none of them are considered popular enough to headline their own monthly series. Most of these characters stay in circulation as minor to middling heroines on various super-teams like the Teen Titans, the Outsiders, or Heroes for Hire. Even Storm, who is arguably the most widely recognized black superheroine of all time thanks to the overwhelming popularity of the X-Men comics, cartoons, and movies, remains a character in super-team books with only an occasional one-shot or miniseries of her own. Thus, it was surprising that in 2009 both Marvel and DC chose to feature black superheroines as title characters. Marvel rebooted the *Black Panther* series with a female character taking over the role that had previously been held only by men. The first six issues of the series, in which the African princess Shuri assumes the heroic identity from her fallen brother, proved very popular and were reprinted in the trade paperback collection *Black Panther: The Deadliest of the Species* (Hudlin and Lashley 2009). At DC, the character of Vixen, who has bounced around the DC universe on various super-teams since the early 1980s, was given the opportunity to headline her own miniseries after positive fan reactions to her increased presence as a member of the newly revised Justice League of America. The title won the 2009 Glyph Fan Award (from the East Coast Black Age of Comics Con) for best comic and is available in the trade paperback collection *Vixen: Return of the Lion* (Wilson and Cafu 2009). These two books coincidentally have a lot more in common than just featuring black superheroines. Both characters are African citizens, and the stories take place in fictional African settings. Moreover, both of the adventures are about characters coming into their own as superpowered beings and accepting the truth about themselves and their responsibilities. The stories of both Black Panther and Vixen involve mysticism and nature as a central plot point, and both characters have powers closely associated with animals. Though these parallel tales mobilize a range of traditional stereotypes, they each manage to present black superheroines who are ultimately far more than just wild, bestial, or hypersexual spectacles.

Black Panther's and Vixen's Stories

The original Black Panther debuted within the pages of Marvel's *Fantastic Four* £52 in 1966, becoming the first black superhero to appear in mainstream American comic books. The Black Panther was part of the comic book industry's initial wave of Blaxploitation heroes but was popular enough to remain in circulation well after many of his imitators had perished. His biography, powers, and base of operations have been revised many times over the years, but at his core he is T'Challa, the wise ruler of the fictional and technologically advanced African nation of Wakanda. The Black Panther has a mystical connection with the Wakandan panther god that grants him superhuman senses and abilities, including increased strength, speed, agility, and stamina. By the mid-2000s, the T'Challa version of the Black Panther was firmly established as a top-tier hero, with his marriage to Ororo Monroe (aka Storm) treated as a company-wide event.

The events of *Black Panther: Deadliest of the Species* take place shortly after T'Challa's wedding. During a surprise attack by the villainous Dr. Doom, T'Challa is left comatose, and Wakanda is rendered vulnerable to an impending assault by the mystical Morlun—Devourer of Totems. Ororo assumes the role of Wakanda's ruler, traveling to the underworld with the help of an ancient witch doctor in order to return her husband's soul to his body. And because Wakanda must have a military leader to survive, T'Challa's sister, Shuri, undertakes a spiritual test to become the new Black Panther. After some physical trials that pose no real challenge to Shuri, she ingests a magical herb that allows her to commune directly with the panther god. When Shuri declares herself worthy to be the next Black Panther and demands the magical gifts that go with the position, the panther god scolds her hubris and rejects her pleas. Shuri is disheartened by her failure but refuses to give up on her people in their hour of need as Morlun destroys Wakanda's army and ravages the city. Despite having no superpowers, Shuri dons the mantle of the Black Panther and sets forth on an apparent suicide mission to battle Morlun. But in the midst of the struggle Shuri's bravery is rewarded and she becomes the one true Black Panther, and destroys Morlun. "The panther god is subtle and wise," explains the witch doctor Zawavari in the final pages. "You threw yourself into the fight . . . not for glory, but for your people. And in doing so, you *became* the Black Panther." *The Deadliest of the Species* is a typical superhero story about bravery and self-sacrifice that both utilizes and challenges centuries-old stereotypes about Africa and black women.

In the DC Comics universe, Vixen was one of the first black superheroines to turn up when she made her initial appearance in the pages of *Action Comics* £521 in 1981. Vixen is really Mari Jiwe McCabe, who was raised in a small village in the fictional African nation of Zambesi. After Mari's parents are killed, she moves to America and becomes a successful fashion model but eventually returns to Africa to take back the magical Tantu Totem that her uncle had murdered her father for. The Tantu Totem is a mystical icon that allows Mari to tap into the Earth's "morphogenetic field" and assume the characteristics of any animal she desires—she can fly like a hawk, run with the speed of a cheetah, fight with the strength of a bear, and so on. For two decades, Vixen bounced around the DC universe on various super-teams, such as Suicide Squad, Birds of Prey, and Checkmate, before finally ending up as a core member of the Justice League of America. During his run in the mid-2000s as the writer of the revamped JLA series, Dwayne McDuffie (one of the cofounders of Milestone Media and a leader in the development of ethnically diverse superheroes) raised Vixen's profile within the team and paved the way for her own spin-off miniseries, *Vixen: Return of the Lion*.

Written by G. Willow Wilson and illustrated by Cafu, *Vixen: Return of the Lion* features a heroine who is initially insecure about her place among such superpowered luminaries as Superman, Batman, and Black Canary. The solo adventure begins when Vixen decides to return on her own to Zambesi when new information about her mother's murder comes to light. She returns to her childhood village to visit friends but finds them living in fear. Vixen is soon wounded and left to die on the African plains after an initial fight with the seemingly superpowered villain, Aku Kwesi, who both murdered her mother and continues to terrorize the village. In her weakened state, Vixen's connection to her magical animal powers begins to fade, and she seems to be near death until a friendly lion finds her and delivers her to the care of Brother Tabo, a monk who helps her recover both her health and her connection to animal powers. Tabo teaches Vixen that she can have unlimited access to the spirit of the animals, even without the Tantu Totem, if she just frees her mind and soul to accept their mystical gifts. While Vixen was recovering with Brother Tabo, other members of the Justice League discovered that Kwesi was more than just a local warlord: he was helping to organize the super-villains known as "Intergang" so they could gain a foothold on the African continent. Several of the League's top guns travel to Africa but are ambushed by Intergang, who manage to poison Superman and Black Canary and turn them into mindless zombies who attack their own teammates. Vixen arrives with a newfound confidence and sense of purpose and first fights with and then cures Superman moments before he could kill all of the heroes. Vixen then returns to the village and defeats Kwesi on her own before returning to America a renewed superheroine.

Recurring Themes

That both *Black Panther: Deadliest of the Species and Vixen: Return of the Lion* are set in Africa is atypical for the superhero genre. Stories are usually set in either real or fictional American cities, thus allowing the heroes to explicitly defend "the American way." When Africa, or any other foreign locale, is utilized, the setting characteristically implies an atmosphere of unfamiliar danger. That both Black Panther and Vixen are African lends the setting more authenticity. Africa is not presented in either story as a mysterious or unknowable place for the heroines. They are familiar with the customs, the people, and the landscape. The overall effect, though, does conform to what Edward Said (1979) famously described as Western "Orientalist" notions of Africa as a treacherous Dark Continent. In the colonialist fantasy that Said outlines, the West perceives the East, and in fact all who can be categorized as "Others," as mysterious and exotic mythical places filled with primitive natives, bizarre customs, and dangerous environments. This collective fiction of the "Orient" has long provided a justification for the Western world's domination and subjugation of non-Western nations and people. As in conventional adventure stories, danger lurks around every corner in both Deadliest of the Species and Return of the Lion, and much of it is presented as specifically wild African dangers. For example, the Black Panther has to fight off real panthers and battle African sorcery, and Vixen is attacked by lions, as well as the warlords who target her village.

In addition to the omnipresence of dangerous wild panthers and lions, it is the presence of voodoo throughout both of the stories that most stereotypically aligns Africa and these black superheroines with ideas of Africa as a mysterious and primitive land. Shuri is granted her Black Panther superpowers by the mystical panther god and eventually defeats the black magic of Morlun with the aid of an ancient witch doctor. Vixen has to reconnect with the magic powers of her amulet totem and is renewed by the faith and teachings of an African monk. In both stories, the people of Africa are depicted as superstitious, resorting to mystical herbs and witch doctors to help save Wakanda, and repeatedly accusing Vixen of being a "voduun" witch for her powers. To their credit, the Black Panther stories also depict Wakanda as a technologically advanced society, complete with supercomputers, hi-tech medical equipment, and flying motorbikes. But since this is a genre in which people can fly, shoot laser beams out of their eyes, and ice from their fingers, voodoo is an accepted reality in superhero comics. The presence of voodoo is never questioned or treated as out of the ordinary in these stories. More specifically, voodoo is not treated as a uniquely African motif. Taken as singular examples, these stories might compound stereotypes of Africa as a dark, mysterious, and mystical place, but for regular readers of superhero comics, it is only part and parcel of the genre itself.

Both Black Panther and Vixen have costumed identities and powers associated with animals. This animalistic association is a clear remnant of colonial stereotypes that characterized African women as the embodiment of an abnormal, voracious, and almost beastial sexuality. The trade paperback covers for both *Black Panther: Deadliest of the Species and Vixen: Return of the Lion* depict strikingly similar images that clearly suggest a range of stereotypes about black women as exotic sexual fantasies. The cover illustration for *Deadliest of the Species* shows Shuri in the skintight black leather panther costume that covers her entire body, head, and face. With just a thin belt slung low around her hips and a long necklace hanging across her breasts, the costume seems to be, in typical comic book fashion, simply painted onto her body. Every curve is emphasized as this female Black Panther leans back against a jungle tree with one arm entwined with a branch and her head tilted in an inviting pose (It is difficult to imagine Marvel portraying T'Challa's male version of the character in a similar cheesecake pose). Under her other arm is a large, muscular, and snarling black panther. Similarly, the cover for *Return of the Lion* features Vixen splayed out in the tall grass of the African plains in her signature skintight, mustard-colored body costume complete with clawed gloves and a plunging neckline that shows off much of her chest. Vixen is lying back with one leg flirtatiously pulled up across the other, her head is tilted, and her expression is, like Black Panther's, both confidently challenging and seductive. Accompanying Vixen is a majestic male lion that she is leaning against, with one arm stretched out behind his mane and the other stretched across his torso.

These purely symbolic images (neither depicts a scene that actually occurs in the stories) are typical of the way that superheroines are portrayed as sexual objects on comic book covers. While male characters usually strike heroic action poses, superheroines are far more likely to be illustrated as pinups or centerfolds. Given both the ethnicity of these two specific superheroines and the nature of these adventures, the covers of both *Deadliest of the Species* and *Return of the Lion* symbolically also allude to a level of racial fetishization. The jungle and the plains settings suggest an aura of savage primitivism associated with Africa as the Dark Continent. The costumes, like those of all superheroines, clearly mark the characters as promising the possibility of erotic and/or fetishistic adventures or what Bukataman referred to in the earlier quotation as "simple adolescent masturbatory fantasies (with a healthy taste of the dominatrix)" (Bukataman 1994, 112). And the presence of the panther and the lion symbolizes the heroines' powers, but also their affinity with nature and these deadly beasts. That each heroine is posed seductively with an arm around these ferocious African cats further implies that the women's sexuality may be alluring, but it is animalistic and threatening as well.

That both Black Panther and Vixen are explicitly associated with big cats is especially noteworthy. Of course, Black Panther's powers are based in those of a real panther and are magically bestowed by a panther god, so her animal association makes sense narratively. But Vixen, whose magical totemic powers grant her access to the abilities of all animals, is repeatedly aligned with lions specifically—as the title, *Return of the Lion*, makes clear. At various points in her story, Vixen is ambushed by a lion, saved by one, and has to fight another that has gone mad and attacked a village. When Vixen slays this rogue beast, she repeats the mantra, "I *am* the lion. I *am* the lion." The strong association of these heroines with wild African cats is easy to interpret as both racial and sexual in nature. This symbolic alignment of superheroic identities with animals is a common convention in comic books and is not restricted to women or ethnically identified characters. The genre is ripe with this type of hero: Batman, Spider-Man, Hawkman, Animal-Man, the Blue Beetle,

Vixen cover, © DC Comics

Black Panther cover, © Marvel Comics

the Falcon, etc. But the overloaded sexual symbolism of cats and their specifically feminine connotations is hard to ignore. Male superheroes associated with cats do exist, such as the original Black Panther or the villain Cat-Man, but they are far fewer and much less sexually charged than female-costumed cat characters. The best known may be Catwoman (often described as "the original feline fatale"), but she is joined by the likes of Black Cat, Pantha, Tigra, Cheetah, Hellcat, Shadowcat, Alley Cat, and Feral.

The sexual inference of these various "catwomen" is clearer in some cases than others. Both Tigra and Cheetah, for example, are literally drawn as sexy cats and sometimes are even called "pussies" by other characters. They each have ideal female bodies but are covered in actual fur, stripes and all, and have tails. To stress the exoticism of their sexy feline/female bodies, Tigra and Cheetah wear only the skimpiest of bikinis as their costumes. As one adolescent superhero in training says of Tigra in *Avengers Academy* £8: "She walks around practically naked." It is worth noting that both Tigra and Cheetah are Latina characters, so their sexual depiction also serves to reinforce their ethnic stereotyping. Other feline-costumed characters, like the white women Catwoman and Black Cat, are only symbolically associated with cats through their roles as cat burglars and their cat-themed costumes. Yet Catwoman and Black Cat are both portrayed as eminently erotic—as sex kittens, who flirtatiously and shamelessly flaunt their figures in revealing outfits. All of these fictional catwomen in comics are a modern embodiment of the centuries-old conception of cats as feminine, sexual, and untrustworthy (see, for example, Darnton 1984). Black Panther and Vixen also fit into this catlike sexual iconography, but no more so than any of the other characters. In other words, their identities as black women who are depicted as catlike does have racist stereotype implications, but it is also a formulaic convention of the larger superhero genre. Yes, these feline heroines are eroticized, but their sexualization seems to have less to do with their ethnicity than it does with the genre itself. Black Panther and Vixen may be animal-like, but their totemic association is not explicitly linked to their sexuality (as it is with Tigra, Catwoman, and Black Cat); instead, it is tethered to their physical strength. At least in *Deadliest of the Species* and *Return of the Lion*, the heroines' animal natures are not explicitly about sex.

To say that the wild animal natures of both Black Panther and Vixen's superheroine identities are not explicitly linked to their sexuality in these stories is not to say that they are exempt from sexualized depictions. They are both illustrated as extremely attractive, fit women in skintight costumes. And, as the cover illustrations make clear, they are both positioned and sold as erotic spectacles. Yet neither story contains romantic subplots or erotic scenes, and no one comments on their attractiveness or even makes a sexist remark. Furthermore, despite the pinup quality of the covers, the interior artwork does not overtly stress their idealized bodies—certainly no more that any other comic book depiction of women (and far less than most). In these particular stories, Black Panther and Vixen are no more sexualized than white superheroines usually are. Given that the superhero genre routinely depicts women visually in a highly fetishistic manner, and that black women continue to be represented as hypersexual in the media, it would seem logical for these characters to be determined first and foremost by their sexuality. By not overemphasizing Black Panther's and Vixen's sexuality, according to centuries-old racial stereotypes, these stories do not contribute to the accumulative and persistent type of characterization that Railton and Watson argue occurs in other media forms like music videos.

Railton and Watson conclude that "through regular and explicit references to the natural and the animal, the black female body and black sexuality continue to be figured as primal, wild, and uncontrollable" (Railton and Watson 2005, 58). Black Panther and Vixen are clearly associated with animals but not in a manner that links their sexuality to being "primal, wild, and uncontrollable." The stories move the characters beyond such simple classifications. It is unfortunate that the covers still rely on this type of stereotype to promote the books because they do not do justice to the progressive representations of black superheroines that the books offer.

This over-reliance and easy association of black women with animalistic hypersexuality as a way to market black female characters is the persistent problem. Individual stories such as *Deadliest of the Species* and *Return of the Lion* can represent a progressive step away from rudimentary stereotypes, but the stories and the characters still exist within a larger stereotypical context. In other comics, Shuri's version of the Black Panther is lusted after and illustrated to show off her ideal figure to maximum effect. Likewise, Vixen—her very name implies a seductress—is often portrayed as sexually active, physically attractive (she is a supermodel, after all) and even a bit of a superheroine homewrecker. But in these two books the heroines' sexuality is downplayed in favor of their heroism. The most sexually evocative moment in either story involves the supporting character of Storm, who has to strip naked in order to travel to the underworld to rescue her husband T'Challa in *Deadliest of the Species*. Thus, a black superheroine is displayed as a sexual spectacle, but it is not one of the title characters. And even this minor instance of Storm's disrobing is a far cry from the blatantly erotic way she is normally depicted. It is also very different from the way other black superheroines are routinely hypersexualized, such as Big City Comics' Ant (aka Hannah Washington), who is always illustrated with her butt thrust out evocatively, or Marvel's Misty Knight, who at times seeks out rough-and-dirty recreational sex with other superheroes just to blow off some steam (for a more detailed discussion, see Brown 2011, 178). In contrast to the way most superheroines—black or otherwise—are depicted, these solo adventures of Black Panther and Vixen are remarkably chaste.

Drawing Conclusions

As the highest-profile books to feature Black Panther and Vixen, *Deadliest of the Species* and *Return of the Lion* demonstrate that comics featuring black superheroines can be successful without reducing the characters to the most sexist and racist stereotypes associated with black women. I would not go so far as to suggest that black superheroines in general are moving beyond the colonial-influenced jezebel stereotype; it is an unfortunate fact that the superhero genre of comic books continues to rely heavily on stereotypes of all kinds. It is not a medium or a genre that lends itself to mature and nuanced storytelling. But it is a form of mass-mediated popular culture where individual writers and artists can present radically different versions of characters. The fact that both *Deadliest of the Species* and *Return of the Lion* strive to represent black superheroines as fully three-dimensional characters can be attributed to the fact that the books were written and illustrated by creators who are explicitly concerned with the political ramifications of depicting race and gender.

Reginald Hudlin, the author of *Black Panther: Deadliest of the Species*, is an African American writer with a long history of creating progressive black characters. Similarly, G. Willow Wilson, the author of *Vixen: Return of the Lion*, is a woman whose work consistently addresses issues of gender, religion, and Middle Eastern cultures. In a medium where individual creators can have a direct impact on characterization (more so than in mediums like film or television), the increasing presence of writers and illustrators from a diversity of backgrounds bodes well for the future of diverse superheroes and superheroines.

Even within a genre that is typically derided as juvenile, and which traffics predominantly in stereotypical characterizations and extreme portrayals of gender and sexuality, there can be progressive representations of black women. The wild, animal-like hypersexual stereotype of black women that continues to dominate in film, television, music, and even sports exists in superhero comics as well, but as the specific examples of Black Panther and Vixen indicate, there is a very real possibility of challenging the one-dimensional racist and sexist logic. Although Black Panther and Vixen may initially appear to simply reinforce the colonialist stereotype of African women (literally "at first glance," given the deceiving erotic come-on of the covers), the stories reveal a message of heroism attributed to these black superheroines. Rarely are black women portrayed in any medium as independent, intelligent, and both physically and spiritually strong. Heroic black women who avoid racist and sexist stereotypes do appear on several police procedural shows on television, but such shows generally feature ensemble casts with white male leads. In headlining their own comic books, Black Panther and Vixen represent rare instances of black heroines taking center stage without resorting to any excessive fetishization of their bodies. While these characters may be costumed in the standard superheroine uniform of revealing, skintight outfits, their heroic actions far outweigh the spectacle of eroticism. In these specific cases, Black Panther and Vixen are heroes, first and foremost. They save their families, their villages, and their fictional African nations. They also save themselves from numerous physical and emotional dangers, and model new possibilities for the representation of black women in popular culture.

2.2 Discussion Questions

1. Brown writes about the conventional superhero as an "adolescent fantasy of hegemonic masculinity either literally or figuratively armored against possible threats." Define the term "hegemony." How this concept plays into expectations for a "masculine" superhero?
2. Define the term "fetishization." How does this particular phenomenon happen to Black women in comics and the media beyond?
3. What is the "male gaze"? How does this lens apply to the ways in which female characters are viewed in comics?
4. What is Edward Said's theory, "Orientalism?" How does it apply to the way Black female protagonists are rendered in comics?
5. Define the term "intersectionality." How does this theory apply to the reader's understanding of Vixen and Black Panther?
6. What is a "stereotype"? How are visual stereotypes used in comics in a **stylistic or craft** way?
7. How does the medium of comics specifically lend itself to the perpetuation of stereotypes?
8. Identify stereotypes of Black women as influenced by the legacy of slavery and colonialism. How do the writers of *Black Panther* (Reginald Hudlin) and *Vixen* (G. Willow Wilson) resist stereotypes of Black women in their comics?
9. Brown writes: "The unequal presentation of gender is certainly not unique to comics. In most forms of popular culture men are depicted as strong and authoritative figures while women are, to borrow Laura Mulvey's (1975) famous phrase, valued for their 'to-be-looked-at-ness.'" Cartoonist and creator Kelly Sue DeConnick coined the term "the sexy lamp test." She argues that if there is a female character in a comic or any other media form that can be replaced with a lamp, then the character isn't well developed, fleshed out; her presence is akin to a piece of furniture. Make a list of female characters in comics, film, or television who are "sexy lamps" and a list of female characters who aren't. Compare and contrast this list.

2.3 Reading: Excerpt from *The New Mutants: Superheroes and the Radical Imagination of American Comics*

by Ramzi Fawaz

Introduction: Superhumans in America

We might try to claim that we must first know the fundamentals of the human in order to preserve and promote human life as we know it. But what if the very categories of the human have excluded those who should be described and sheltered within its terms? What if those who ought to belong to the human do not operate within the modes of reasoning and justifying validity claims that have been proffered by western forms of rationalism? Have we ever yet known the human? And what might it take to approach that knowing?

—JUDITH BUTLER, *Undoing Gender* (2004)

We've changed! All of us! We're more than just human!
—*THE FANTASTIC FOUR* #1 (November 1961)

Starting in the late 1950s, this model of the American superhero as a local do-gooder and loyal patriot was radically transformed by a generation of comic book creators who reinvented the figure to speak to the interests and worldviews of postwar youth. Unlike their fictional forebears, whose powers were natural extensions of their bodies, postwar superheroes gained their abilities from radioactive exposure, technological enhancement, and genetic manipulation. Where once, superheroes were symbols of national strength and paragons of U.S. citizenship, now they were framed as cultural outsiders and biological freaks capable of upsetting the social order in much the same way that racial, gendered, and sexual minorities were seen to destabilize the image of the ideal U.S. citizen. Rather than condemn these figures, superhero comics visually celebrated bodies whose physical instability deviated from social and political norms. Consequently they produced a visual lexicon of alliances between a variety of "inhuman" yet valorized subjects as a cultural corollary to the cosmopolitan worldviews of movements for international human rights, civil rights, and women's and gay liberation.

The traditional view of the superhero as a nationalist icon has blinded scholars of cold war cultural history to the dynamic role the figure has played in offering alternative and often radical reinterpretations of the central political terms of liberal democracy in the post–World War II period. I complicate this view by exploring how superhero comics articulated the tropes of literary and cultural fantasy to a variety of left-wing projects for political freedom. In the chapters that follow I show how postwar superhero comics made fantasy a political resource for recognizing and taking pleasure in social identities and collective ways of life commonly denigrated as deviant or subversive within the political logics of cold war anticommunism and an emergent neoconservatism. In case studies of *The Justice League of America* (1960) and *The Fantastic Four* (1960), I show how these comic book series recast the vigilante superhero as a member of a democratic collective through the invention of the "superhero team." The egalitarian image of the superhero team as an intergalactic peacekeeping force provided readers with a popular fantasy for imagining alternative social and political responses to the cold war, including international cooperation and cross-cultural alliance, rather than unilateral military power. In later chapters I investigate the emergence of mutant, cyborg, and alien superheroes in comic books like *The Silver Surfer* (1968), *The X-Men* (1974), and *The New Mutants* (1981) as visual allegories for racial, gendered, and sexual minorities. Though socially outcast by a bigoted humankind for their monstrous biology and alien lineages, benevolent mutant superheroes like the X-Men and alien warriors like the Silver Surfer were celebrated in comic books as figures who sought alliances on the basis of shared ethical goals rather than national or ethnoracial identity. Tracking these and a variety of other fictive innovations in superhero storytelling, I argue that postwar comic books used fantasy to describe and validate previously unrecognizable forms of political community by popularizing figures of monstrous difference whose myriad representations constituted a repository of cultural tools for a renovated liberal imaginary. *The New Mutants* tells the story of these monsters and the world of possibilities they offered to readers who sought the pleasures of fantasy not to escape from the realities of cold war America but to imagine the nation and its future otherwise.

From American Marvels to the Mutant Generation: Reinventing the Superhero

The superhero was introduced to American culture in 1938, when Superman made his first appearance in *Action Comics* £1, a variety adventure serial produced by publisher Detective Comics (later known as DC Comics). The superhero's debut launched the comic book medium to national notoriety

"I argue that postwar comic books used fantasy to describe and validate previously unrecognizable forms of political community by popularizing figures of monstrous difference whose myriad representations constituted a repository of cultural tools for a renovated liberal imaginary."

while providing Americans with a fantasy of unlimited physical power and agency in an era when the promise of individualism and self-determination appeared all but impossible in light of an unremitting economic depression. Comic books emerged as a distinct cultural form in the early 1930s, originally sold as pamphlets containing reprinted newspaper comic strip materials; cheap, portable, visually sensational, and accessible for repeat readings, comic books embodied the populist ideals of folk culture but packaged in mass cultural form. As the medium gained public attention and sales figures expanded, publishers began developing original content in a variety of genres, including crime and suspense, romance, and war stories. It was the invention of the superhero, however, that would cement comics as one of the most influential forms of twentieth-century American popular culture, by linking the populist character of the comic book medium to a fantasy figure that embodied American ideals of democratic equality, justice, and the rule of law. DC Comics initially refused to publish Joe Shuster and Jerry Siegel's *Superman* comic in 1936, fearing that the character was too "unbelievable," but they soon discovered that if someone could draw the Man of Steel, readers would believe in him.

First introduced as the opening feature of *Action Comics* £#1, Superman immediately became a national sensation, soon starring in his own series and spawning countless imitations that would compose a growing pantheon of American superheroes. Between the late 1930s and the end of World War II, superhero comic books like *Superman* (1938), *Batman* (1939), and *Captain America* (1941) reached monthly circulation figures of nearly 900,000 issues, making superheroic fantasy a common fixture in American households and an anticipated monthly escape for GIs on the front lines of war.[5]

Gifted with abilities beyond the ken of normal humans, superheroes possessed an unprecedented capacity to extend their bodies into space and manipulate the material world with physical powers—among them extraordinary strength, speed, agility, and energy projection—that mimicked the capacities of modern industrial technologies. Both scholarly and fan literature often locate the American superhero at the tail end of a long tradition of mythic folk heroes, namely the frontier adventurers and cowboy vigilantes of nineteenth-century westerns. Though the superheroes of the late 1930s limned these figures through recourse to heroic masculinity and the embrace of vigilante justice, the superhero is historically distinguished from these previous icons by its mutually constitutive relationship to twentieth-century science and technology. Unlike the frontier hero escaping the constraints of civilization, the modern superhero is an embodiment of the *synthesis* between the seemingly "natural" biological self and the technologies of industrial society.

What distinguished the superhero from the merely superhuman, however, was its articulation of an extraordinary body to an ethical responsibility to use one's powers in service to a wider community. When attached to the prefix *super*, the word *hero* irrevocably transforms the concept of a body gifted with fantastic abilities by framing the bearer of such power as an agent of universal good. At once capable of refashioning the world in his image yet ethically committed to the well-being of a broader community beyond his own self-interest, the superhero has historically functioned as a visual meditation on the political contradiction between the values of individual liberty and collective good.

I conceive of the superhero's dual relationship to individual agency and public life as embodying the central tension of American liberal democracy, which articulates a belief in the unfettered autonomy of the individual with a form of governance dedicated to protecting political freedom for all citizens through collective political representation. Liberalism can be defined broadly as a worldview that values individual agency as the ultimate goal of organized politics and recognizes the rights of individuals on the basis of their universal humanity;[6] alternately, democracy is a collective solidarity between disparate individuals equally vested with political power, who seek to achieve a common good for a community above the pursuit of individual license. In the United States the uneasy alliance between liberalism and democracy has consistently been threatened by the historical exclusion of those deemed outside the boundaries of legitimate humanity, including the disabled, the stateless, and those believed to lack the capacity for reason on the basis of their race, gender, or class.[7] In its commitment to protecting the political interests of these alienated social groups the superhero had the potential to redefine the meaning of political freedom in America by recognizing the rights of those excluded from the national community. The lack of definition surrounding the superhero's ethical purview—whether her commitments ended at the borders of the nation or the broader sphere of humanity or included all life in the cosmos—and to whom the superhero was ultimately accountable in the use of her powers made the figure a generative site for imagining democracy in its most radical form, as a universally expansive ethical responsibility for the well-being of the world rather than an institutional structure upholding national citizenship.

During World War II this creative potential was mitigated by the superhero's affirmative relationship to the state. The comic books of this period depicted the superhero as an American patriot with definite national loyalties; often deploying his abilities in service to national security, the superhero's robust masculinity served as a metaphor for the strength of the American body politic against the twin evils of organized crime at home and fascism abroad. As Bradford Wright argues, the superheroes of this period embodied an idealized form of liberal citizenship as champions of individual freedom who supported outside intervention (whether in the form of the superheroic vigilante himself or the strong state) to protect and expand the political rights of individuals and maintain law and order.[8] This form of liberal citizenship embraced the use of science and technology in forwarding the goals of American democracy by imagining that mechanical or biological enhancement of the body would grant Americans an unprecedented ability to perform acts of civic duty beyond the physical capacity of ordinary humans.

The most famous cultural product of comics' articulation of science and liberal citizenship during World War II was Marvel Comics' Captain America (1941). Once a sickly army reject, Steve Rogers is transformed into the supersoldier Captain America, the nation's premier Nazi fighter, when the government backs the invention of a "super-serum" that alters his physiognomy, granting him unparalleled strength, speed, agility, and invulnerability.[9] With his exceptional physical powers and rigorous military training, Rogers is able to take on the Nazis with few physical or moral limits. Captain America manifested the belief that science was a vehicle for political freedom and that scientific and technological enhancement of the human body could produce more capable citizens. As Rogers's transformation from scrawny stripling to muscular powerhouse suggested, this particular image of ideal citizenship through scientific intervention was consistently coded as masculine and virile (not to mention white and heterosexual); with rare exceptions the defining characteristic of World War II superheroes was an invulnerable male body whose physical strength functioned as a literal bulwark against threats to the nation's borders and ideological values. No surprise, then, that this period of superhero storytelling is traditionally dubbed "the Golden Age" of comics, implying a nostalgic reverence for an era defined by the superhero's triumphant embodiment of American ideals.

Alternatively, postwar superheroes emerged as the monstrous progeny of the age of atomic and genetic science, no longer legitimate citizens of the state or identifiable members of the human race. Their mutated bodies and bizarre abilities—variously obtained from radiation exposure, genetic mutation, and alien science—suggested that the innovations of molecular engineering might destabilize the biological integrity of the human, producing political subjects whose abnormal physiologies rendered them unfit to engage in national civic life. What comic book historians call "the Silver Age" of comics was defined by an interest in exploring how various experiences of superhuman transformation might change what it means to be human and, consequently, what kind of community the superhero might affiliate with when the traditional markers of belonging—namely, proper humanity and national citizenship—no longer held true.

A variety of historical circumstances made this creative project viable for the comic book industry beginning in the late 1950s, including demographic shifts in reading audiences; changing social attitudes toward race, gender, and sexuality; new technologies of media production and circulation; and national interest in atomic and genetic science. A central motivating force, however, was the transformation of the relationship between the comic book industry and the U.S. government from one of mutual affirmation during World War II to one of clashing political and cultural interests in the postwar period. Following the war, crime and horror comics supplanted superhero stories as the highest selling genres among teenage readers. Narrating the violent exploits of criminals and social deviants, these comics joined other contemporary cultural genres such as film noir and dystopian science fiction that uncovered the seamy underside of postwar prosperity.[10] Responding to public criticism of the violent content of crime and horror comics by Catholic decency groups, psychologists, and school officials, in 1954 the House Un-American Activities Committee convened a special Senate session on juvenile delinquency, which threatened comic book publishers with regulatory action if they refused to develop content standards for their publications.[11] In the wake of government chastisement, mainstream comic book producers returned to the superhero as a fantasy figure traditionally understood to embody patriotic American values. Ironically this creative shift allowed writers and artists to explore bodies whose monstrous abnormality offered a rich site for critiquing the regulatory powers of the state and its inconsistently applied guarantee of national citizenship based on liberal ideals. Galvanized by such possibilities, the two most productive publishers of superhero comics, DC Comics (creator of Superman, Batman, and Wonder Woman) and Marvel (creator of Captain America), reinvented the superhero as a biological misfit and social outcast whose refusal or failure to conform to the norms of social legibility provided the ground for a new kind of political community.

This new generation of heroes challenged dominant assumptions in three key arenas of postwar cultural and political life. First, postwar superheroes upended the assumed relationship between scientific enhancement of the body and liberal citizenship. Simultaneously made superhuman by scientific interventions on the body, yet physically and symbolically shattered by such experiences, postwar superheroes were as damaged and vulnerable as they were powerful. By making vulnerability the ground upon which unexpected forms of solidarity might flourish, superhero comics reorganized the dominant narrative of liberal progress that associated science with man's mastery over nature and the body; according to these new stories, it was the *failure* to manage the consequences of scientific and technological innovation that laid bare the instability and unpredictability of the human. Second, these vulnerable figures overturned traditional hierarchies of gender and questioned presumptions about the physical superiority of the virile white male body. In the 1960s and 1970s male superheroes were repeatedly depicted as physically and psychologically unstable beings, their bodies seeming to switch genders through an array of anatomical metamorphoses or appearing incapable of performing the proper sexual functions of heterosexual masculinity. Unlike earlier depictions of the rigid male body struggling to secure its boundaries from perceived hostile forces, a new generation of superhero comics presented the unpredictable transformations of the male physique as a far more pleasurable and liberating form of embodiment than traditional models of sex and gender could ever conceive. These texts also showcased the development of empowered female superheroes, using the ecstatic visual cultures of women's and gay liberation to depict the exercise of superhuman powers as an expression of liberated female sexuality, pleasure, and agency.

Both the qualities of bodily vulnerability and gender instability constituted the postwar superhero as a figure in continual *flux*, visualized on the comic book page as constantly moving among different identities, embodiments, social allegiances, and psychic states.[12] At first glance the extraordinary physical malleability (and sometimes *literal* flexibility) exhibited by postwar superheroes—such as Mr. Fantastic's seemingly limitless physical pliability—might appear an expression of what some cultural critics have called neoliberal flexibility. Neoliberalism describes a shift in the ideological and political structure of capitalism in the late twentieth century—the same period as the superhero's reinvention—that involves the increasing imposition of market demands on all aspects of American culture, politics, and social life. Under neoliberalism formerly vilified or outcast social identities—for instance being gay or lesbian—have been revalued on the basis of their profitability, both as new target markets for consumer products and as sites of cultural expertise that aspiring entrepreneurs can claim "insider" knowledge about on the basis of their own racial, gendered, or sexual identity. This accelerated diffusion of market demands into private life has encouraged the development of the "flexible subject," a social type who exhibits the capacity to flexibly adapt every aspect of her identity to accommodate the demands of neoliberal capital and its periodic crises, including recessions, market fluctuations, and increased economic risk.[13]

Rather than performing flexibility, I argue, the monstrous powers and bodies of postwar superheroes exhibited a form of *fluxability*, a state of material and psychic *becoming* characterized by constant transition or change that consequently orients one toward cultivating skills for *negotiating* (rather than exploiting) multiple, contradictory identities and affiliations. Fluxability identifies one mode of being, fictionally depicted in the superheroes' many mutated or transitional forms, that exists in tension with neoliberalism's co-optation of oppositional identities. The visibly unruly and in flux bodies of superheroes like the Hulk, the Fantastic Four, and the mutant X-Men not only identified them as social deviants but also made them notoriously bad laborers, neither capable of holding down steady jobs nor interested in conceiving of their ethical service to the world in economic terms. The postwar superhero's fluxability attenuated the figure's potential as an effective laborer and also came to describe a form of material existence in which one's relationship to the world and its countless others was constantly subjected to questioning, transformation, and reorganization. This fact defines the third intervention of the postwar superhero: its generative engagement with the production of alternative alliances across difference at local, global, and cosmic scales.

Specifically, postwar superhero comics depicted the social communities and solidarities produced by a new "mutant generation" of heroes as the ground upon which progressive social transformation could take place. If cold war political rhetoric touted the hyperindividual, heterosexual, and presumably middle-class citizen as the antithesis of the communist subversive, superhero comics presented such individuals as narcissistic, alienated, and potentially destructive of social community. Against this self-centered figure of liberal politics, superhero comics celebrated the production of implicitly queer and nonnormative affiliations that exceeded the bounds of traditional social arrangements such as the nuclear family and the national community. Whether willfully choosing alternative solidarities or unwittingly thrown into relation with a host of mutated or monstrous others, postwar superheroes produced complex and internally heterogeneous communities of fellow travelers—often brought together under the rubric of the superhero "team" or chosen "family"—who sought to use their powers for shaping a more egalitarian and democratic world. Like the bodies and identities of the superheroes, aliens, mutants, and outsiders that composed their ranks, these alternative solidarities were depicted as being in constant flux, expanding, retracting, and transforming their stated values on the basis of unexpected encounters with a wider world.

Few superheroes exemplified these transformations more than Marvel Comics' Incredible Hulk (1962). Bombarded by radiation rays during the testing of a "gamma bomb," the shy, gentle scientist Bruce Banner is unwittingly transformed into a giant green monster with mammoth strength and invulnerability. As the Incredible Hulk, Banner is a physical powerhouse of unparalleled magnitude, yet in mutated form, he recurrently loses control of his emotions, destroying everything in sight during bouts of uncontrollable rage. The Hulk was a material expression of Banner's repressed psyche, manifesting at moments of extreme emotional distress. The competing halves of Banner's identity would have public ramifications as well: as a respected scientist for the military-industrial complex, Banner is an asset to national security. Yet as the Incredible Hulk, he is a violent threat to the American people, making his alter ego a target for the U.S. military. In the Incredible Hulk comic book, creators linked scientific interventions on the body to biological and psychic instability, depicting the superhero's body as a vulnerable, porous surface always on the verge of radical transformation and consequently threatening the very definition of citizenship as the mutual recognition between individual subjects and a governing state.

At the same time, just as Steve Rogers's transformation into Captain America was gendered masculine, his enhanced body expressing virility and strength, Banner's mutation was troubled by an excessive and unstable performance of gender. On the one hand, the Hulk's physical appearance as a muscled green giant and his outbursts of violent rage identified him as hypermasculine; on the other, Banner's vulnerability to science and his subsequent emotional struggles to control his unpredictable abilities indicated a newfound association between the superhero and those traits commonly associated with femininity, including fragility and emotionality. In figures like the Hulk, comic books presented what appeared to be physically masculine bodies failing to live up to the norms of proper gender and sexuality or else threatening the boundaries between male and female, invulnerability and vulnerability, human and inhuman. At every level these were figures in flux.

As the superhero evolved from a rigid representation of law and order to a dynamic figure of flux negotiating multiple identities and affiliations in the postwar period, it straddled overlapping, and often competing, commitments to liberal and radical political ideals. On the one hand, superhero comics continued to espouse a liberal belief in individual freedom and political choice, remained committed to science and reason as avenues for human progress, and endorsed human rights discourse, which confers political recognition on the basis of a universally shared humanity among all people. In its increasingly radicalized form, however, the superhero comic book expanded who counted as legitimately "human" within liberal thought by valuing those bodies that were commonly excluded from liberal citizenship, including gender and sexual outlaws, racial minorities, and the disabled. It highlighted human (and nonhuman) difference as the defining feature of all social creatures rather than their universal sameness, while also suggesting the need for a political common ground that would bind people across multiple identities and loyalties. I identify this project as radical because it actively undermined the philosophical basis of liberal thought—namely the concept of a universally shared humanity underpinning each individual's claim to political rights—while also promoting collective freedom above the securing of individual rights and privileges. The tension between these various political impulses—to endorse human rights while undermining the basis of the human, to value scientific discovery as the basis of progress while questioning the very idea of objectivity, to embrace cross-cultural solidarity while taking pleasure in difference—would form the conceptual ground upon which postwar superhero comic books would develop their greatest adventure stories.

In shifting the creative weight of superheroic fantasy from a focus on individual power and agency to bodily transformation and the question of collective belonging, postwar superhero comics contested and imagined alternatives to the cold war political logics of containment and integration. Recent scholarship in cold war cultural history has shown how containment—the political policy of halting the global spread of communism through economic and military coercion—existed alongside competing ideological formations. In *Cold War Orientalism*, Christina Klein has argued for a more complex reading of containment as a political policy and cultural ideology that worked in tandem with a policy of global *integration*, which saw Americans' active engagement with foreign cultures as an avenue for promoting U.S. interests abroad. Like containment, the policy of integration worked through cultural formations such as Hollywood musicals, popular travel memoirs, and foreign aid campaigns to encourage Americans to see themselves as civilian ambassadors to the U.S. government and supporters of anticommunist ideals abroad.[14]

Alternatively scholars like Julia Mickenberg and Cynthia Young have shown how, for a variety of left-wing activists and intellectuals, culture became an avenue for performing radicalism during a period of intense political repression.[15] In her cultural history of children's literature during the cold war, Mickenberg uncovers a diverse network of left-wing artists, intellectuals, and activists of the 1930s Popular Front era who rerouted their political energies toward the field of children's publishing after World War II. These Old Left writers, artists, editors, and librarians produced and circulated stories with egalitarian political messages for a new generation of American youth who would become the political activists of the New Left in the 1960s. Similarly Young narrates how an emergent Third World Left deployed a variety of cultural and intellectual forms—including film, literature, and scholarly research—to forge links between racial and class minorities in the United States and colonized peoples across the globe by identifying their shared experiences of poverty, social inequality, and political violence.

The New Mutants contributes to this body of work while focusing greater attention on the fantasy content of cold war popular culture. I seek to uncover the radical political possibilities contained in a fantasy form that was not produced by self-proclaimed left-wing activists or artists but rather emerged as the product of an ongoing negotiation between competing liberal and radical visions among creators and readers of comic book texts. To capture the cultural and political work of postwar superhero comics, I forward a model of world making that treats comic books "as a form of politics, as a means of reshaping individual and collective practice for specified interests."[16] World making describes instances when cultural products facilitate a space of public debate where dissenting voices can reshape the production and circulation of culture and, in turn, publicize counternarratives to dominant ideologies.[17] I am drawn to the concept of world making because of its dual reference to the aesthetic production of imaginative worlds and political practices that join creative production with social transformation. Michael Warner and Lauren Berlant identify world making as a practice engaged by sexual minorities and other social outcasts to create forms of culture, as well as public spaces, that offer recognition to nonnormative social relations and hail audiences commonly ignored by mainstream mass-media forms. Warner and Berlant posit that the term "world . . . differs from community or group because it necessarily includes more people than can be identified, more spaces than can be mapped beyond a few reference points, modes of feeling that can be learned rather than experienced as birthright." They continue, "The queer world is a space of entrances, exits, unsystematized lines of acquaintance, projected horizons . . . alternate routes, blockages, incommensurate geographies."[18] José Esteban Muñoz adds to this description social practices and performances that "have the ability to establish alternate views of the world" that function as "critiques of oppressive regimes of 'truth' that subjugate minoritarian people."[19] These definitions of world making underscore the importance of both social *and* creative practices in the construction of alternative ways of life for a variety of marginalized groups and point to the kinds of open-ended political projects that take flight in directions that are clearly incommensurate with, or actively resistant to, dominant social formations.

Berlant and Warner's description of the "queer world" as a "space of entrances, exits, unsystematized lines of acquaintance [and] projected horizons" beautifully captures both the aesthetic and symbolic thrust of post–World War II superhero comic books, whose visual elaboration of new heroic identities and alliances, lush fictional worlds, and enchanting phenomena would break the traditional aesthetic borders of the comic strip form, while offering readers "alternate routes" for imagining left-wing politics during the cold war and after. World making in postwar superhero comics involved a conceptual, narrative, and visual scaling upward of the superheroes' orientation from the local frames of city life and national affiliation, toward an expansive idea of "the world" as the object *at stake* in a variety of superheroic endeavors. As political theorist Ella Myers elaborates, "To say . . . that the world is 'at stake' in politics means that although the specific motivations and sentiments that inspire collective democratic action vary widely and produce outcomes that are uncertain, an underlying impulse, the 'wish to change the world,' is shared by even the most divergent democratic actors."[20] With the birth of a mutant generation of superheroes in the early 1960s, the formerly touted values of the superhero comic book, including law and order, nationalism, and virile masculinity, were increasingly sidelined in favor of producing imaginative fictional universes infused with a democratic political orientation toward the world. I call this ethos a "comic book cosmopolitics."

Comic Book Cosmopolitics

I use the term *comic book cosmopolitics* to describe the world-making practices of postwar superhero comic books. Unlike the liberal spirit of World War II comics, which championed individual freedom and the defense of a national community against outside threats, the cosmopolitan ethic of postwar superhero comic books valued the uncertainty of cross-cultural encounter and the possibilities afforded by abandoning claims of individualism in exchange for diverse group affiliations. This ethic was both an aesthetic and a social achievement. It was formed in the mutual transformation of the creative content of superhero comic books *and* the changing values of an emergent participatory reading public that actively conversed with comic book creators about the formal and political content of the fantasy worlds they produced.

By attaching the label of *cosmopolitanism* to the American comic book, a medium commonly associated with "nonrealist" juvenile entertainment, I aim to relocate a seemingly apolitical form of mass culture within a genealogy of American political and intellectual thought. Following David Hollinger, I understand cosmopolitanism as an ethos that "promotes broadly based, internally complex, multiple solidarities equipped to confront the large-scale dilemmas of a 'globalizing' epoch while attending to the endemic human need for intimate belonging." Expanding on the ethical implications of Hollinger's description, Amanda Anderson elaborates that cosmopolitanism "aims to articulate not simply intellectual programs but ethical ideals . . . for negotiating the experience of otherness. . . . Although cosmopolitanism has strongly individualist elements (in its advocacy of detachment from shared identities and its emphasis on affiliation as voluntary), it nonetheless often aims to foster reciprocal and transformative encounters between strangers variously construed."[21] Postwar superhero comics facilitated such "transformative encounters between strangers variously construed" on multiple levels. They depicted expanding casts of superhuman characters "negotiating the experience of otherness" within a vast cosmos, while fostering "ethical ideals" of democratic debate between creators and readers about the aesthetic and political content of superhero stories. These varied scales of engagement produced countless opportunities for developing multiple, "internally complex" solidarities—between and among comic book characters, readers, creators, and various political visions—that embodied a cosmopolitan willingness to be transformed by encounters with new worlds, bodies, ideas, and values.

Comic book cosmopolitics was cultivated in three ways. First, as the superhero came to embody a model of universal citizenship, the visual locus of superhero comic books dramatically expanded. Where once superhero comics focused on the happenings of local city life, depicting the crime-fighting exploits of urban vigilantes, now they presented the superhero as a freewheeling adventurer within a vast web of relations between human and nonhuman actors across the cosmos. This expansion of the visual field of superhero comics took advantage of the comic book medium's vast representational capacities, captured in the conceit that *whatever can be drawn can be believed.* As a low-tech visual form requiring only pencil and paper, comics allow for the visual depiction of extraordinary scales of existence and embodiment without the need for costly technical special effects. With the advent of global satellite imaging technology, technical innovations in film and television media, and the emergence of new discourses of globalism in the 1950s and after (including postwar internationalism, cold war geopolitics, and environmentalism), comic book creators began to exploit the capacity of their medium to represent grand totalities in such figures as the world, the universe, and the cosmos.

Corollary to the expansion of comics' visual scale, editors at DC and Marvel Comics reconceptualized their individual publishing houses as overseers of distinct fictional "universes" inhabited by particular cadres of superhuman characters. They encouraged readers to see each of the company's superheroes as inhabiting the same unified social world rather than characters isolated in their own discreet stories. This diverged from the comic book publishing model of the 1930s and 1940s, in which complete, bounded stories were narrated in the space of a single issue so that on-again, off-again readers could follow the plot of a given serial regardless of which issue they purchased. By the late 1950s comic book publishers found themselves catering to a regular reading audience who wished to follow multi-issue story lines and see character development over time. The trademarking of distinct DC and Marvel universes boosted sales by luring readers with the promise of various character crossover stories. Yet it also expanded the "worldliness" of comic book content by encouraging creators to depict individual superheroes' unfolding interactions with countless other figures who populated their daily lives, interactions that now took place across vast geographical terrains on Earth and beyond.

As these fictional worlds took shape, superhero comics became less about common crime fighting and more about the unpredictable encounters between an expanding cohort of superhumans, aliens, cosmic beings, and an array of fantastical objects and technologies. As a result, cross-cultural *encounter* rather than assimilation became the primary site of political world making in the superhero comic book, offering an alternative to the one-sided model of cultural tolerance promoted by the cold war logic of integration. If the goal of cold war integration was a stable postcommunist world dominated by American cultural and economic values, the open-ended serialized narratives of postwar comics, as well as the increasingly complex fictional worlds they produced, promised indefinite instability. Each new issue of a series offered creators an opportunity to critique, reimagine, or wholly transform the narrative and visual trajectory of previous stories so that narrative outcomes were always unpredictable and provisional. This fact was redoubled in the sequential character of comic book art, which became a formal tool for underscoring the transformative and unpredictable nature of the superhero's body.

In the post–World War II period, comic book creators began to underscore the serial visuality of comics—its use of sequential images unfolding across space to depict change over time—as a formal corollary to the superhero's unstable anatomy. They experimented with the visual layout of sequential images to depict bodily flux as a visual effect of transition between panels on a page. What would appear as an ordinary human body in one panel might appear in the next as a body in flight, as invisible, aflame, shape-shifting, encased in metal, or altogether *not there.* The visual instability of the superhero's body across time and space negated the figure's previous iconic status as a seemingly invulnerable masculine body by proliferating countless permutations of the superhero that refused to cohere into a unified image or physiology.[22] Such bodily fluxing and its articulation to the cosmopolitan ideal of unpredictable, worldly encounter became both a central "problem" of superhero stories—requiring superheroes to negotiate their bodily transformations and encounters with similarly mutant, nonhuman, or hybrid beings—as well as a site of cultural and political investment for a new generation of comic book readers.

The emergence of a participatory reading public as a fixture of postwar comic book culture would form the second foundation of comic book cosmopolitics. In the late 1950s DC Comics editor Mort Weisinger began including a letters page at the end of the company's best-selling title, *Adventure Comics*. There Weisinger published short letters from readers across a wide demographic spectrum that commented on the company's creative productions, including praise and criticism of various story lines, the aesthetic details of specific issues, and suggestions for new characters. The popular response to these letters pages was so powerful that both DC and Marvel instituted regular letters pages in all their best-selling comic book titles. By offering readers the possibility of greater interaction between characters and increasingly elaborate fictional worlds, creators put themselves in the position of having to respond to a growing audience demand for *more* innovations in comic book storytelling.

By the mid-1960s these print forums had produced an affective counterpublic (which included the institution of fan clubs and comic book conventions) where readers could voice their relationship to the characters and worlds they followed monthly while democratically debating the comics' content. Just as fictional superheroes were encountering a cosmos filled with alien life in a spirit of cosmopolitan engagement, so too the heterogeneous members of a growing postwar readership were using a popular media form to engage one another across race, class, gender, generation, and geographical space. As I show in chapter 3, while a majority of letters across titles focused on aesthetic concerns, some of the most acclaimed comic book series of the period, particularly *The Fantastic Four*, became famous for printing letters that directly addressed the relationship of superheroes to contemporary political concerns, including civil rights and race relations, the women's movement, and the Vietnam War. Consequently superhero comics became an evolving creative site for exploring questions of cultural difference, social inequality, and democratic action that would form the basis of a comic book cosmopolitics.

The alignment of a new reading generation's emergent political investments with the superhero's increasingly cosmopolitan outlook on the world was underwritten by a third, and final, transformation in comic book culture: the medium's resurgent investment in the liberal values of antiracism and antifascism alongside its absorption of the more radical politics of New Left social movements. Though few comic book creators voiced commitments to radical political ideals—many even politically conservative—the generation of writers, artists, and editors who helped forge the industry in the late 1930s was deeply invested in liberal egalitarian values. These primarily Jewish creative producers were shaped by the dual experiences of being second-generation immigrants as well as witnesses to, and sometimes active military participants in, the battle against Nazism. These experiences led them to espouse the ideals of religious and ethnoracial tolerance, as well a broader commitment to universal political freedom and equality. Writing in his monthly editorial, "Stan's Soapbox," in December 1968, Marvel Comics editor Stan Lee proclaimed:

> Let's lay it right on the line. Bigotry and racism are among the deadliest social ills plaguing the world today. But, unlike a team of costumed supervillains, they can't be halted with a punch. . . . The only way to destroy them is to expose them—to reveal them for the insidious evils they really are. . . . Although anyone has the right to dislike another individual, it's totally irrational, patently insane to condemn an entire race—to despise an entire nation—to vilify an entire religion. . . . Sooner or later, if man is ever to be worthy of his destiny, we must fill our hearts with tolerance.[23]

By the late 1960s this commitment to liberal tolerance had become a defining value of superhero comics. In its most progressive iterations, this antiracist and antifascist worldview intersected with and helped theorize an emergent radical sensibility among postwar youth that combined liberal ideals of political freedom with a powerful critique of the interlocking oppressions of race, class, and gender and the government institutions that underwrote the violent conflicts of a global cold war.

The young readers who galvanized this increased radicalism in comic book content were growing up in a world where the rhetoric of civil rights and anticolonialism was in ascendancy, offering a utopian political alternative to the cold war's rigidly antagonistic view of the world divided between a capitalist United States and a communist Russia. An increasingly international readership hailing from every major demographic welcomed the superhero comic book's expanded visual scope and its attendant ideal of universal human (and "inhuman") equality. Frustrated with the normalizing social expectations of 1950s America, these readers also valued the superhero's physiological nonconformity with proper humanity. Consequently they facilitated the invention of an array of new figurations of the superhero, including aliens, cyborgs, and mutants, while encouraging the demographic diversification of comic book characters.

From the production side, the diversification of superhero comics through the introduction of racial minorities and women to previously white, male-centered superhero stories was ostensibly a *liberal* response to the traditional homogeneity of comic book content. It was also a transformation conditioned by economic demands to appeal to a more diverse readership. From the perspective of readers, however, the demand for greater representational diversity was less about the mere visibility of minorities in comics and more an appeal to creators to develop stories and worlds that explored the cultural politics of identity. As a generation attuned to the emerging cosmopolitan visions of the New Left, and later black power, Third World movements, and women's and gay liberation, many readers and cultural critics of comics understood that *differences* (whether of race, class, sex, or gender, geographical location, ability, or religious orientation) were not only sites of political oppression but potent cultural resources for articulating new forms of social and political affiliation, questioning the limits of democratic inclusion, and developing new knowledge about the world from the position of the outcast and the marginalized. An increasingly politically minded readership took seriously the idea (presented by superhero comics themselves) that the internal heterogeneity of the fictional universes of Marvel and DC Comics could facilitate interactions between differently situated characters that might foment debates about the political possibilities, pleasures, and limits of cultural differences. The very fact that superhero comics were conceptually obsessed with phenotypic and physiological difference, expending vast narrative and visual space depicting new species, bodies, abilities, and identities, meant that the introduction of previously unrepresented differences (whether real-world ones like race or fictional categories like mutation) demanded a substantive recalibration of the social relations between characters, the visual depiction of new distinctions, and a language with which to discuss such differences.

This approach to difference dovetailed with the values of women of color feminism and other radical critiques of race in this period, which "were fundamentally organized around *difference*, the difference between and within racialized, gendered, sexualized collectivities."[24] As Roderick Ferguson and Grace Hong elaborate, "The definition of difference for women of color feminism . . . [was] not a multiculturalist celebration [or] an excuse for presuming a commonality among all racialized peoples, but a cleareyed appraisal of the dividing line between valued and devalued, which can cut within, as well as across, racial groupings."[25] Comic book readers were surprisingly adept at articulating these ideals in their own words. They demanded that creators value commonly devalued identities and bodies in comics (including women, people of color, and the working class) and that the fictional narratives of these characters honestly dramatize the uneven social value attributed to different kinds of superhumans within their distinct fantasy worlds based on the magnitude of their abilities, specific form of mutation, or level of social standing. Readers understood, for instance, that the introduction of an African female superhero, Ororo Monroe (Storm), in the pages of the popular *X-Men* (1974) series might force writers to address the distinctions between African and African American experiences of race, *as well as* the gendered dynamics of a black woman superhero capable of controlling the elements working alongside predominantly white, male teammates whose powers were largely extensions of physical strength; similarly, when creators introduced the first African American superhero, Luke Cage, in his own series, *Luke Cage: Hero for Hire* (1972), as an economically struggling private detective, readers lauded the series for taking seriously the race and class implications of hero work (including the expense of costumes, travel, and headquarters space) especially for inner-city minorities. Readers' willingness to embrace the liberal project of representational inclusiveness in comics, then, was conditioned by a more radical investment in comic books as sites of political world making where the presence of diverse actors in expansive fictional universes of encounter, conflict, and negotiation could provide substantive creative responses to social difference.[26]

One of the most radical outcomes of this attentiveness to difference within a cosmopolitan frame was to facilitate the reinvention of the superhero as a distinctly "queer" figure. I invoke the term *queer* to describe how postwar superheroes' mutated bodies and alternative kinships thwarted the direction of heterosexual desire and life outcomes and cultivated an affective orientation toward otherness and difference that made so-called deviant forms of bodily expression, erotic attachment, and affiliation both desirable and ethical. The postwar superhero comic's embrace of indefinitely unfolding narratives with no predetermined outcome, its unraveling of the traditionally gendered physiology of the white, male superhero, and its centralizing of cross-cultural encounter and mutually transformative engagement popularized a mode of storytelling that was largely uninterested in traditional heterosexual reproduction, family forms, or gender norms. Even when comics told stories of superheroes getting married or having children, these narratives were shot through with contradictions about the supposed social normalcy of such practices. The weddings of superheroes were attended by motley crews of alien, mutant, and cyborg guests dressed not in formal wear but in flamboyant superhero costumes, and when superheroes looked forward to child rearing, they fretted over the queer potential of progeny born from nonhuman parents.[27] Instead of solidifying a "straight" future organized by the nuclear family and the promise of heterosexual reproduction, postwar superhero comics framed the proliferation of difference, its ceaseless alteration of the social world, and the pursuit of ever more complex forms of affiliation and collective action *across* all manner of cultural and geographic divides as the goal of a comic book cosmopolitics.

Taken together, the expanding visual horizon of the superhero comic book, the emergence of a participatory reading public, and the alignment of comic book content with the egalitarian ideals of left-wing political projects constructed the parameters of comic book cosmopolitics. I locate the political productivity of comics—understood as their capacity to imaginatively innovate and make public aesthetic and social responses to the limits of contemporary political imaginaries—in the generative relationship between comic book producers, an emergent countercultural readership, and the expanding visual and narrative content of comic book texts. Yet I place my greatest analytical emphasis on the actual visual and narrative content of superhero comic book texts themselves. This content, and the broader cosmopolitan aspirations it articulated, was the common object of concern that brought creators and readers into dialogue in the first place; it was also the material outcome of their various engagements with each other and the wider cultural and political contexts within which they articulated their distinct positions. Taking a dual-pronged approached, I conceive of comics as historically constituted objects emerging from distinct social and material conditions—including shifting economic demands, the biographies of different creators, demographic transformations in readership, and new printing technologies—while also seeing their rich narrative and visual content as producing imaginative logics that offer ways of reconceiving, assessing, and responding to the world that are *not* reducible to any single historical factor. In other words, I never assume that the "meaning" of a given comic book text, story, character, or fictional event can be deduced from a single biographical element of a creator's life, or by laying bare the economic conditions that encouraged a specific creative decision, or by making an abstract reference to a historical event that took place shortly before a story was scripted. Rather, following Foucault, I see the interpretive possibilities of texts (not their ultimate meaning, but what people *do* with them) as emerg-

"I invoke the term *queer* to describe how postwar superheroes' mutated bodies and alternative kinships thwarted the direction of heterosexual desire and life outcomes and cultivated an affective orientation toward otherness and difference that made so-called deviant forms of bodily expression, erotic attachment, and affiliation both desirable and ethical."

ing within a field of dynamic interactions and antagonisms between competing actors who exercise power in different ways that ultimately shape and proliferate *multiple* meanings and interpretive possibilities around a text.[28] Consequently my method for analyzing comics involves a form of close reading that centralizes questions of literary scale to bridge the distances between the historical and the imaginative valences of comic book content.

In her essay "The Scale of World Literature," Nirvana Tanoukhi conceptualizes scale as "the social condition of a landscape's utility." By "landscape" Tanoukhi means the field of social and aesthetic relations that surrounds the production of and composes the creative content internal to a given literary text. Tanoukhi theorizes scale not merely as geographical or historical distance but as the *conceptual distance* that must be traversed by a reader in order for a particular element of a text (including characters, themes, tropes, or literary and visual techniques) to have meaning or use to them in varied contexts.[29] This understanding of scale allows us to consider, for instance, what conditions enabled readers to take up the visual depiction of the mutant (or genetically outcast) superhero as a figure for Third World politics or internationalism or any number of cosmopolitan political projects attuned to the relationship between marginalized identities and broader scales of affiliation beyond the nation. From this perspective the categories of world making (as a creative practice) and comic book cosmopolitics (as an ethos) can be understood as tools or *metrics of scale*. Each offers a framework for analyzing how a local, material, worldly object like the superhero comic book aspired to broad scales of conceptual and political experience, what I am labeling a cosmopolitics, through both shifting conditions of production and innovative aesthetic practices. To analyze superhero comic books this way is, in a sense, to aspire to the world-making possibilities of comics themselves, but with critical attention to how those possibilities were historically produced and articulated, taken up by various actors, and revised over time. The basic fact that so many readers and cultural critics were able to make political meaning out of the fantasy content of superhero comic books suggests the capacity of these texts to elicit imaginative acts of scale making from its audiences, ones specifically oriented toward a cosmopolitan ethos, *despite* the numerous economic, social, and political constraints on the production of comics themselves.

A variety of business histories of both Marvel and DC Comics have shown how, since the 1960s, economic demands to maintain operating budgets, pay salaries, make profits, and increase market share have placed incredible pressure on creators and editorial management to produce salable comic book content.[30] While taking into account the economic pressures that mediated the relationship between creators and readers, I narrate a different story that explores how the social conditions of comic book production and circulation from the 1960s onward helped produce figures and stories that often exceeded, contested, or altogether repudiated the mandates of profitability at both Marvel and DC Comics. The postwar superhero's fluxability was one such figure, an imaginative tool for thinking outside the framework of economic profitability that also encouraged the sale of comics. The fluxible superhero was not innocent of economic interests, but neither were his meanings reducible to them.

Because comic book production in the 1960s was less constrained by corporate demands and underpinned by the basic need of creators to make a living wage, I approach this period as one of relatively unrestrained creative innovation when the economic interests of creators dovetailed with the political radicalization of a growing countercultural audience. By the mid-1970s and early 1980s, Marvel and DC would become fully corporate ventures (owned by Cadence Industries and Warner Communications, respectively) with increasing investments in making comic books profitable to publishers, CEOs, and shareholders. This transformation attenuated open-ended dialogue and creative experimentation between readers and creators but also heightened tensions between a new generation of creative talents and their corporate employers. Rather than reducing all comic book content to corporate pandering, then, these constraints added another dynamic variable to superhero comics' production that encouraged innovative creative responses to corporate economic pressures. Because of this, in later chapters I analyze how the political and visual content of superhero comics since the mid-1970s became an index of the shifting scales of negotiation among creators, fans, and a newly appointed corporate management within an increasingly profit-driven industry. As I discuss in chapter 5, this included a bold critique of corporate capital lobbied by writers and artists in the pages of mainstream comics as a response to the economic devaluation of their artistic labor in the 1970s. Simultaneously the aesthetic innovations that creators used to articulate their economic frustrations—including recasting the superhero as an icon of working-class virility—provided readers with a new set of conceptual tools for scaling downward from the cosmic worldviews they had become accustomed to and addressing the daily living conditions of racial minorities, the working class, and the homeless. Both a product of dynamic dialogue and contestation *and* a figure mediated by the vicissitudes of the mass entertainment market, the comic book superhero would come to articulate a variety of potential solutions to the impasses of contemporary social politics within the constraints of industry realignments.

If bridging the conceptual distances between the fictional world of superhero comics and the political world was the central project of a comic book cosmopolitics, then the vehicle for this work was undoubtedly fantasy. The capacity to invent and depict a near-limitless range of fantasy figures, scenarios, and worlds was an imaginative skill that creators and readers both exercised but that comic book texts visually manifested and circulated to mass audiences. It was fantasy that made the scale-making aspirations of superhero comics both possible *and* pleasurable, displaying the worlds that might unfold from a cosmopolitan view of life, while imbuing those worlds with endless desire.

2.4 Discussion Questions

1. Define "liberalism" and "democracy."
2. Describe the "superhero's dual relationship to individual agency and public life" and the tensions that arise from these relationships.
   a. Give two to three examples of superheroes who navigate liberalism and democracy that Fawaz highlights in the excerpt.
   b. Analyze two to three superhero examples of your own that are not previously mentioned or discussed in Fawaz's work.
3. Analyze the differences between superheroes of the Golden Age and superheroes of the Silver Age, using Fawaz's ideas about liberalism and democracy.
4. Define and unpack the "three key arenas" in which Silver Age superheroes "challenged dominant assumptions of postwar cultural and political life" (9).
5. Define "flux." How does it apply to the superhero's "identities, embodiments, social allegiances, and psychic states" (10)?
6. What is "fluxability"? Give one superhero example from the text, and provide one superhero example of your own that is not mentioned.
7. What is "world making"? How has it guided Fawaz's methodology and analysis?
8. Define "comic book cosmopolitic." Discuss the three ways in which it was cultivated in superhero comics.
9. How did the "participatory reading public" shape content in comics and bolster interaction between readers and creators about current events and politics?
10. Reread and analyze Stan Lee's monthly editorial "Stan's Soapbox" from December 1968 (20). What do you notice and observe about Lee's stance and word choice?
11. What is Fawaz's analytical approach to comics? Why did he choose this method?

2.5 Reading: "The Difference a Mutant Makes"—*Los Angeles Review of Books* Article

by Ramzi Fawaz

Like any good origin story, I've told this one a thousand times: The first comic book I ever read was *X-Men* #80, the 35th anniversary issue of America's most popular comic book series, which, for over three decades, had narrated the lives, loves, and losses of a band of mutant outcasts gifted with extraordinary abilities because of an evolution in their genetic makeup. It was 1998. I was thirteen years old, and the cover of this single comic book issue was a young gay boy's dream: a shiny pink hologram with a tower of dazzling disco-attired superheroes exploding before one's eyes. Growing up in a queer family, sibling to a gay brother, and bullied to tears on a daily basis for my own exuberant gayness, the words "A team reunited . . . a dream reborn" emblazoned on that cover spoke to me of the promise and possibility of queer kinship and solidarity in the face of all odds.

Above all, what struck me about that cover was the sheer variety of characters depicted—how could a man of made of steel, an intangible woman, a white haired weather goddess, a butch teen girl with bones sticking out of her skin, and a teleporting blue elf be any kind of team? Who were these people, I wondered, and what kind of dream did they share?

Like so many readers of the X-Men over the decades, no character drew me in more than the weather goddess Storm, a Kenyan immigrant to the U.S., the first black woman superhero in a mainstream comic book, and by the 1990s, the X-Men's team leader. In that same anniversary issue, at a low point in the team's battle with an imposter group of X-Men, Storm rallies her bruised and beaten comrades by reminding them that what defines their bond is a set of shared values, a chosen kinship maintained through mutual love and respect, not by force or expectation. With my budding left-wing consciousness on one side, and my attachment to queer family on the other, I fell in love with this fictional mutant goddess and her team: this was the kind of community I longed for. How did it come to be that a thirteen year old, Lebanese-American, suburban gay boy found common cause with an orphaned, Kenyan, mutant, immigrant X-Man?

"How did it come to be that a thirteen year old, Lebanese-American, suburban gay boy found common cause with an orphaned, Kenyan, mutant, immigrant X-Man?"

If one were to try and explain this question by turning to recent public debates about superhero comics, we might put forward the answer: "diversity." Yet this term and its shifting meanings—variety, difference, or representational equality—would have rung false to my thirteen year old ears. It was not simply the fact of Storm's "diverse" background as Kenyan, immigrant, woman, or mutant that drew me to her, but rather her ethical orientation towards those around her, her response to human and mutant differences, and her familial bond with her fellow X-Men. These were qualities significantly *shaped* by her distinct differences, but not identical to them. This was not any traditional idea of diversity then, understood as the mere fact that different kinds of people exist. Rather what Storm and the X-Men embodied was true *heterogeneity*: not merely the fact of many kinds of people but *what those people do in relation to their differences*. As I became a dedicated comic book fan, I realized that every issue of the *X-Men* was both an extended meditation on the fact that people are different from one another, *and* that this reality requires each and every person to forge substantive, meaningful, intelligent responses to those differences.

As a teenage reader, I simply took this fact for granted as part of the pleasures of reading superhero comics. As a scholar years later, I came to realize that the ability to respond to differences and forge meaningful relationships across them was a capacity, a super-power if you will, that comics could train their readers to exercise, an imaginative skill fit for a truly heterogeneous world. It was this realization that led me to write *The New Mutants: Superheroes and the Radical Imagination of American Comics*, in which I ask the question: What is it about the visual and narrative capacities of the comic book medium, and the figure of the mutant, cyborg, or "freak" superhero in particular, that has allowed so many readers to develop identification with characters across race, class, gender, sexuality, ability, and cultural origin?

Recent public dialogue about the rapidly diversifying ranks of superhero comic books has overwhelmingly celebrated the increased racial, gender, sexual, and religious variety of America's greatest fictional heroes. Yet every time a news outlet lauds the major comics companies for introducing a gay superhero, or a Pakistani superhero, or a classically male superhero replaced by a powerful woman, the historian in me thinks, "But comics were doing that in 1972, so what's the big deal now?"

Certainly, one potentially distinct element of today's push for diversity is the range of "real-world" or identifiable differences comics are willing to name and represent on the comic book page. But in writing *The New Mutants*, I came to the conclusion that without an underlying democratic ethos or worldview, such real-world differences have little meaning. In *The New Mutants*, I argue that cultivating egalitarian and democratic responses to differences became the sine qua non of American superhero comics from the 1960s through the early 1990s.

I call this vision a "comic book cosmopolitics," an ethos of reciprocal, mutually transformative encounters across difference that infused the visual and narrative content of comics for nearly three decades. In the 1960s and 1970s comic book series like the *Justice League of America*, the *Fantastic Four*, and the *X-Men* provided readers an exceptionally diverse range of new characters and creative worlds, but most importantly, modeled what it might look like for those characters to bridge divides of race, species, kin, and kind for their mutual flourishing and the good of the world. What "doing good for the world" meant or could mean was the question that motivated these characters to engage one another, forge bonds, disagree, and take collective action. Today's celebratory proclamations about the internal diversity of American comics ignores the fact that by 1984 Marvel Comics alone had Kenyan, Vietnamese, Native American, Russian, American working-class, Jewish, and Catholic superheroes, and even a pagan demon sorceress at the helm of one of its main titles.

What distinguished these earlier figures from their contemporary counterparts were the seemingly endless dialogues and struggles they engaged to negotiate, respond to, rethink, and *do something* with their differences as a matter of changing the world. It was this negotiation within the context of characters' *actual* diversity that allowed readers like me, and thousands more, to identify with a vast range of people who were, at least on the surface, radically *unlike* us.

In a recent op-ed for the *New York Times*, "That Oxymoron, The Asian Comic Superhero," columnist Umapagan Ampikaipakan makes the counterintuitive claim that the push for racial diversity in contemporary superhero characters, rather than reflect the progressive evolution of the superhero, might actually "dilute" the fundamental purpose of the figure to function as a universal fantasy of belonging. The more specific or particular the superhero gets, he suggests, the less the character speaks to all kinds of readers.

As a child growing up in Kuala Lampur, Ampikaipakan explains that even thousands of miles away from U.S. culture, he found himself identifying with the misfit and freak Spider-Man. It didn't matter that Spider-Man and so many of the superheroes in the Marvel Universe were white. Rather it was the message these comics carried about the value of being a freak or an outcast that translated across both actual and virtual distance.

In the face of much public celebration of comic book diversity, Ampikaipakan's argument is compelling because it refuses a reductive understanding of identity politics, namely that seeing oneself or one's own particular identity reflected back in any given character is the only possible way that one can feel invested in them or their creative world. This argument is both undoubtedly correct, yet severely misguided.

The mistake Ampikaipakan makes is not to claim that readers have the capacity to identify with a range of characters regardless of their social identity, but in his failure to stress that *it is difference and distinction itself* that has made the superhero such a durable fantasy to so many readers globally, not the figure's empty universality or the flexibility of whiteness to accommodate a variety of identifications. The fact that superheroes *highlight* (rather than overlook) the social, cultural, and biological differences that shape humankind, that makes identifying with them possible—this is why one superhero is never enough. Superheroes proliferate because no matter how many there are, they can never quite capture the true heterogeneity of everyday life. The attempt to do so is what keeps us reading.

We should not settle for the mere representation of more diverse characters, as though the very existence of a female Pakistani Ms. Marvel alone were an act of anti-racism, or anti-sexism; these latter categories describe not a representation or image, but an ethos, a worldview and way of life—this ethos is what Ampikaipakan was drawn to in reading *Spider-Man*. It was an underlying ideal of celebrating outcasts, misfits, and freaks—a democratic investment in all who did not fit into the model of "normal" American citizenship—that defined Marvel Comics in the 1960s and 1970s, and that shaped readers' relationship to characters like Spider-Man and his universe of mutant, alien, and superhuman friends, all of whom we grew to love *because of* their particularities, differences, and distinctions, not their imagined universality. As readers, we must demand that the depiction of more diverse characters be motivated by an ethos attentive to human heterogeneity, its problems and possibilities; these character must be placed into dynamic exchange with the world around them, rather than merely making us feel good that some more of us are now included every once in a while.

Take for example the dramatic creative decision by writer Matt Fraction to relocate the X-Men from their long-standing home at the Xavier Institute for Higher Learning in Westchester, Massachusetts, to San Francisco in 2008. With this momentous move to one of America's most recognized gay holy lands, it seemed as though the X-Men series had finally made explicit its long-standing symbolic association between mutation as a fictional category of difference, and gayness, as a lived form of minority identity; and yet, in the handful of years that the X-Men resided in San Francisco between 2008 and 2012—where they lived as billionaire jet-setters buying property in the Marin headlands at the height of a national recession no less—never once did they address the city's massive housing crisis, increasing rates of violence towards the city's queer and minority populations, or the shifting status of HIV. Did the X-Men even deign to go to a gay club in their five years in the Golden Gate City? Did the team's one putatively "out" character, Northstar, claim any solidarity with the city's queer community? I'm afraid not.

The series capitalized on its symbolic gesture of solidarity with minorities, queers, and misfits, but it jettisoned its earlier substantive engagement with the problem of difference: back in 1979, when Storm visited the slums of Harlem and witnessed the reality of youth homelessness and drug abuse, she was forced to contend with the realities of inner-city African American life from the perspective of a Kenyan immigrant who experiences blackness differently than African Americans and the working poor; and in the early 1990s, with the invention of the fictional mutant disease the Legacy Virus, the X-Men series used fantasy to address the AIDS crisis by thinking through the kinds of solidarities mutants and humans would have to develop to respond to a genetic disease ravaging the mutant population.

In today's comic book pages, is there a single X-Man with HIV? Now that Iceman is out of the closet, will he go on PrEP, the HIV prophylactic? And as a former lady's man, will his sexual health be an issue at stake in the series? The likelihood that Bobby Drake's gayness will either be treated substantively, or have a meaningful effect on the social fabric of the Marvel Universe, seems very low in today's creative environment, where the mere "outing" of characters as exceptionally diverse in their identities is presupposed as an act of social benevolence on the part of writers and artists.

My point here is not that superhero comics need greater realism in their storytelling or should be more "true to life." Rather, superhero comics are one place where fantasy and creative worldmaking can run up against the specificities of our everyday lives, so that "real life" is presented to us anew or opened up to other possibilities. Mutation and gayness, for instance, are not the same thing. But they resonate in surprising ways.

The imagined category of mutation sheds light on the workings of a real-world social identity like gayness, or blackness, but it also reveals the limits of analogy because all of these categories are never quite identical. The ability to distinguish between the places where differences overlap and where they don't is a political skill that fantasy can help us develop. It demands we not only see where solidarity can be forged, but also figure out what to do when sameness no longer holds true, or our differences overwhelm the ability to forge meaningful bonds.

What I was doing that summer day when I read my first issue of the *X-Men* was figuring something out not only about myself, but about my relationship to the world around me as someone who fundamentally understood that I was different, but didn't yet know how to respond to *being different*. This is the true gift that superhero comics have given to American culture in the 20th century, but it is a creative offering increasingly taken from our grasp.

When Marvel Comics reached a creative level of near maximum mutant heterogeneity in the X-Men series around 2005—a moment of incredible promise when mutants no longer appeared as minorities but a significant portion of the human population—Marvel spun out a barrage of storylines from "E is for Extinction" to "House of M" that depicted the mass slaughter of the majority of the world's mutants by members of their own kind. The X-Men have been living in the shadow of genocide ever since: shot down by ever-more efficient mutant killing robots, murdered and harvested for their organs, nearly eliminated from history by time-traveling mutant hunters, and now subject to M-Pox, another genetic disease threatening to wipe out the mutant race. In a sense, Marvel could not face the complexities of the world it had created, and decided to obliterate it instead: in so doing, fantasy truly became a reflection of our violent post-9/11 reality.

> "My point here is not that superhero comics need greater realism in their storytelling or should be more "true to life." Rather, superhero comics are one place where fantasy and creative worldmaking can run up against the specificities of our everyday lives, so that "real life" is presented to us anew or opened up to other possibilities. Mutation and gayness, for instance, are not the same thing. But they resonate in surprising ways."

Contrast the exuberant, bubble-gum pink cover of the first X-Men comic book I ever read, with the most recent issue I picked up: in the renumbered *Uncanny X-Men* #1 (2013) written by Brian Michael Bendis, the cover presents us a picture of mutants at war. There is a revolution afoot, but it is led by a single male figure, the famed character Cyclops reaching out to the reader from the center of the page with his army of followers, merely black and white outlines in the background. That army is composed of some of the most complex characters to ever grace the pages of the X-Men series, yet here they have been flattened to ghosts haunting the background of the X-Men's former dream.

The X-Men now appear as a leather-clad, armored military unit, not a high-flying, exuberant, queer menagerie. At the center, Cyclops's hand reaches out to us not in a gesture of solidarity but as a claw, perhaps ready to grip our throats. In this new chapter of the X-Men's history, mutants are presented as divided over the right path towards the preservation of the mutant race. But instead of rich, textured disagreements the characters appear merely as ideologues spouting flat and rigid political manifestos. There is no space for genuine debate, or loyalty amidst disagreement, or even the notion that more than one dream could exist side by side among companions. As Alex Segade has recently argued in a brilliant *Art Forum* article on the *X-Men*'s decades long mutant mythology, the recent introduction of increasingly "diverse" cast members to the series has come at extraordinary costs, including the mass deaths of entire swathes of mutants round the world.

In the *X-Men*, fantasy—that realm meant to transport us to a different world—has become the ground for narrating the collapse of all visions of hope, social transformation, or egalitarian action: in Bendis's epic narrative the original five teenage members of the X-Men are teleported to the present only to see that their youthful dreams of peaceful relations between human and mutant kind have resulted in death, destruction, and seemingly endless violence.

When I recently caught up on Bendis's *X-Men* plot about time traveling mutant teenagers, it made me wonder what my thirteen year old self would have thought about *his* future had these been the comic book issues he first encountered in the summer of 1998. But I'm lucky they weren't. In the face of the kinds of violence and death-dealing that recent comics present, I remember that there are other uses for fantasy, because it was the X-Men series itself that first showed me it was possible. Today, as years of reading, thinking, and writing about superhero comics come together with the publication of *The New Mutants*, I look back at that first cover image of *X-Men* #80 with a mix of longing and hope: I wonder now how a team can be reunited, and how new dreams can be born.

2.6 Discussion Questions

1. What are Fawaz's ideas about the term "diversity" as it dominates discourse regarding representation in comics in the late 2010s? How does he experience and analyze this term?
2. Define the term "ethos." How does Fawaz use the concept of "democratic ethos" throughout his essay?
3. In response to the contemporary comic book industry's push for diversity, Fawaz writes, "In writing *The New Mutants*, I can come to the conclusion that without an underlying democratic ethos or worldview, such real-world differences have little meaning." Unpack Fawaz's sentiment regarding the differences between "diversity" and "an underlying democractic ethos" behind these superheroes.
4. Fawaz writes: "As a scholar years later, I came to realize that the ability to respond to differences and forge meaningful relationships across them was a capacity, a super-power if you will, that comics could train their readers to exercise, an imaginative skill fit for a truly heterogeneous world. It was this realization that led me to write *The New Mutants: Superheroes and the Radical Imagination of American Comics*, in which I ask the question: what is it about the visual and narrative capacities of the comic book medium, and the figure of the mutant, cyborg, or 'freak' superhero in particular, that has allowed so many readers to develop identification with characters across race, class, gender, sexuality, ability, and cultural origin?" Analyze his argument, then answer this question: What evidence does Fawaz provide throughout his essay for this argument?
5. How does Fawaz compare the ethos of Marvel in the 1960s and 1970s to the ethos of Marvel today? What examples does he use?
6. What are Fawaz's critiques of Umapagan Ampikaipakan's *New York Times* op-ed, "That Oxymoron, The Asian Comic Superhero"?
7. What does Fawaz argue in regard to the relatability of superheroes in response to Ampikaipakan? What is the ethos, or "underlying ideal," he emphasizes in superhero comics?
8. What are Fawaz's observations of the transformation of the X-Men from the 1960s until today in regard to his concept of "comic book cosmopolitics"?

2.7 A List of Further Reading

Gateward, Frances K., and John Jennings. *The Blacker the Ink: Constructions of Black Identity in Comics and Sequential Art*. Rutgers University Press, 2015.

Hatfield, Charles. *Alternative Comics: An Emerging Literature*. University Press of Mississippi, 2005.

Smith, Matthew J., and Randy Duncan, eds. *Critical Approaches to Comics: Theories and Methods*. Routledge, 2012.

Tabachnick, Stephen, ed. *Teaching the Graphic Novel*. The Modern Language Association of America, 2009.

History and Background

3

3.1 An Introduction

The purpose of this chapter is to get you acquainted with the history of comics. This is by no means an exhaustive history of comics. There are several textbooks on the market that dive into the histories of the "Big Two" publishers (Marvel and DC), comics, and manga in the United States and around the world. This chapter seeks to highlight comics histories that are often erased, untold, or buried in the footnotes. It also includes an expansive array of interviews from editors who have collaborated to create anthologies that will prove significant in comics history, to historians and comics scholars who have shed light on comics work from underrepresented communities.

Betsy Gomez's work with the Comic Book Legal Defense Fund is illuminated in this chapter as she reflects on the legacies of Fred Wertham and the history of comics censorship and its pervasiveness in schools today. This chapter continues with a Spotlight on the amazing online Cartoonists of Color Database and Queer Cartoonists Database founded by cartoonist MariNaomi; an interview with Keith Sicat, who directed a documentary on the history of Filipino comics, also known as komiks; and an interview with cartoonist and historian Fred Van Lente, who reinterpreted the emergence of the comics industry in the United States, in addition to the origin stories of major creators and figures, such as Stan Lee, through the comics form.

There are interviews with notable historians and comics scholars whose work strives to reconsider the history of comics and American history: Dr. Frederick Aldama, author of *Your Brain on Latino Comics*

Learning Objectives

- Define patterns in the history of comics, particularly in the United States, and compare them to significant historical trends and events.
- Describe and analyze scholarly and creative work by featured historians, editors, scholars, and comics creators.
- Assess the influence of Art Spigelman's graphic memoir, Maus, and how comics in general were received and studied after its publication.

Learning Outcomes

- Examine the history of comics censorship in the United States and its legacy and influence on comics publishing trends.
- Evaluate underrepresented histories in comics, in particular Latinx, Asian American, and African American representation, in addition to Philippine komiks.
- Act as historians by researching a lesser-known comic, trend, or historical figure/creator from an underrepresented community.

and *Graphic Borders*, who illustrates the multitude and flexibility of Latinx comics creators' work and has written volumes dedicated to their work; and Dr. Deborah E. Whaley, who writes about her experience of centering Black women in comics in her book, *Black Women in Sequence: Re-Inking Comics, Graphic Novels, and Anime.*

Keith Chow and Jeff Yang, who coedited a series of groundbreaking anthologies, *Secret Identities: The Asian American Superhero Anthology, Shattered* (the follow-up to *Secret Identities*), and *New Frontiers*, a graphic novel anthology inspired by the life and work of George Takei who (best known for his role as Sulu in *Star Trek* but is socially and politically active in the Asian American community), are interviewed to discuss their formative work.

Ryan North, creator of *Dinosaur Comics*, traces the origins of his immensely popular webcomic that utilizes clipart, and he emphasizes his insistence on making comics despite his lack of drawing abilities: "I'd wanted to do a comic but couldn't draw and didn't realize that 'comic writer' was a thing: I thought everyone wrote and drew their own comics. So *Dinosaur Comics* was a way to get around the 'can't draw' limitation by only having to get images set up once, and then I could recycle them."

The chapter ends with an exercise that invites students to research comics creators who are traditionally considered marginalized and underrepresented and to write a profile based on their findings. The goal of this particular project is to push students to read outside of their comfort zone, to discover work that they haven't yet encountered, and to highlight a creator's work that might have been historically overlooked.

Key Terms

- The Comics Code Authority
- Genre
- Intersectionality
- Komiks
- Webcomics

3.2 Interview with Betsy Gomez, Editorial Director of the Comic Book Legal Defense Fund (CBLDF)

Below is an interview with **Betsy Gomez,** *who is the editorial director for the Comic Book Legal Defense Fund, a nonprofit organization dedicated to defending the First Amendment rights of the comics community. In this interview, she discusses the legacies of censorship and the Comics Code Authority in the comics industry. Gomez manages the editorial content for cbldf.org and CBLDF's print publications, including CBLDF's quarterly news magazine,* CBLDF Defender. *Gomez is the editor of CBLDF's book about the women who changed free expression in comics,* She Changed Comics. *With an extensive background in educational publishing, Gomez has worked as a content developer and editor for several companies, including Houghton Mifflin Harcourt and Pearson Education, among others. She began volunteering for CBLDF in 199 and joined the CBLDF staff in 2011. Gomez was introduced to comics in college and since then has been an advocate for the medium. Her work with CBLDF combines her love of the medium with her passion for the right to read.*

Can you describe the cultural, social and political climate during the rise of comics censorship and the Comics Code Authority? What made this era ripe for the rise in popularity of Fred Wertham's *Seduction of the Innocent,* which argued that comics turned kids into "juvenile delinquents"?

In the late 1940s and early 1950s, nearly everyone in the country read comics regardless of age or gender. Prior to World
War II, superhero comics were immensely popular, but in postwar America, readers were losing interest in superheroes. The comic companies turned to other genres to boost sales. Crime and horror comics, many of which featured outlandish plots, colorful and frequently violent artwork, and mature themes, came to the fore.

Fredric Wertham, a respected psychologist who had done commendable work on behalf of impoverished populations and children of color, kicked off his attack on comics in "Horror in the Nursery," a profile by writer Judith Crist that ran in the March 27, 1948, issue of *Collier's*. Wertham argued that comics were "definitely and completely harmful," and he described several crimes involving juveniles, alleging that the crimes were inspired by comics. The article itself was illustrated with garish photos of child models acting out some of the crimes.

Wertham published several sensationalist articles in the following years and even organized a symposium, "The Psychopathy of Comic Books," that targeting the format. A forerunner to *Seduction of the Innocent* entitled "What Parents Don't Know About Comic Books" ran in the November 1953 issue of *Ladies Home Journal*. Claiming to reveal the "startling truth about the 90,000,000 comic books America's children read each month," Wertham used to article in his ongoing bombardment of the medium, claiming that comics would make even the most innocent children into hardened criminals.

Comic Book Legal Defense Fund logo.

Wertham hit a nerve. Groups around the United States organized to take on the scourge of comic books, passing laws and even burning the offending publications. This was happening just three years after the end of World War II, during which Allied forces took on an enemy renowned for burning books. The resulting moral panic goaded the federal government into taking action. On April 21–22, 1954, Senator Estes Kefauver led the Senate Judiciary Committee's Subcommittee to Investigate Juvenile Delinquency in hearings about the supposed link between comics and crime. Wertham was the star witness.

Comics didn't lack a defense during the hearings: Bill Gaines, publisher for EC Comics (the home of some of the most popular crime and horror titles) spoke on behalf of the four-color, saddle-stitch newspaper pamphlet that dominated the proceedings. But, for various reasons, Gaines was not the best spokesman, and his testimony ultimately added fuel to the anti-comics movement. After a deluge of bad press, compounded by an angry public and the threat of regulation by the government, the comics industry was backed into a corner. They responded by establishing the Comic Magazine Association of America, which instituted the Comics Code Authority, leading to decades of self-censorship by the industry.

What was the purpose of the Comics Code Authority, and how did it change the landscape of comics at the time? Particularly, how did censorship at this time affect comics that were aimed at mostly girls and women as their audience?

In October 1954, the Comics Code Authority adopted the Comics Code, a set of standards the regulated what could be depicted in comics. In particular, the Comics Code specifically regulated the portrayal of crime, horror, and sex in comics. Comics that complied with the code bore the CCA Seal of Approval, a requirement for any comics publisher that wished to make it to newsstands—comics that lacked the seal would not be distributed.

Prior to the code, the comics industry spanned most creative genres. But the code effectively destroyed crime and horror comics—amongst the code's more draconian regulations were rules that would not even allow the words "horror" or "crime" to appear on the cover. The code also neutered jungle girl and Western comics, and because of Comics Code regulations about sex and relationships, the romance genre—which was particularly popular with the female audience—was also decimated. The only genre that survived the Comics Code more or less intact was superhero comics, which appealed in particular to younger male readers. To survive, many of the comics publishers turned almost exclusively to superhero comics.

Ultimately, the CCA led to the loss of jobs for hundreds of comics creators, the shuttering of several comics publishers, and the distillation of the number of titles on newsstands—by some accounts, the number of titles released monthly was only a quarter or so of the number released prior to the code's implementation.

Women creators, who were already dealing with a loss of opportunity in the medium due to the return of men from World War II, were further impacted by the regulation of comics. In the early 1950s, there was something close to parity in terms of readership and gender, but in the intervening years after the institution of the Comics Code, female readership dropped, and the opportunities for women in mainstream comics were relatively limited until fairly recently.

What are the legacies of the Comics Code Authority, and what are the effects of the Comics Code Authority in the comics industry today? How did it affect comics creators?

The Comics Code Authority was officially disbanded in 2011, and the copyright and trademark for the Seal of Approval were transferred to CBLDF as a means to raise money to fight censorship. While many publishers had left the seal behind years earlier, the effects of the code are still felt now.

Some genres, such as romance and westerns, have yet to see success comparable to the pre-code era. Horror found a way to survive the code in magazines, which were not regulated by the CCA. Despite a brief upsurge in horror comics during the late 1980s and early 1990s that coincided with the success of horror movies, the genre has only really picked up steam in the last decade or two, driven in part by the success of imprints like Vertigo and comics like *Hellboy* and *The Walking Dead* (to name just two).

This isn't to say that comics have been only superhero comics since 1954—but creators have had to find ways to work within the bounds of and around the code. The mature topics of the underground comix movement in the 1960s and 1970s were created in direct contravention of the Comics Code, and creators had to develop novel ways to distribute their books because they were too controversial for the typical newsstand (and lacked the Seal of Approval). These creators turned to non-traditional outlets, like headshops, independent bookstores, and even porn stores, to sell their work. But after decades of self-censorship, comics had become so sterilized that many wrongly believed comics were only for children. Upon encountering the decidedly mature content of undergrounds, some people in power tried to prosecute booksellers for obscenity.

In the 1980s, mainstream comics themselves began to mature with its core constituency —still mostly male but no longer young. Creators like Alan Moore (*Watchmen*) began to deconstruct the format and to develop more sophisticated storylines, as did Frank Miller (*The Dark Knight Returns*) and Neil Gaiman (*The Sandman*). Their work brought renewed attention to the medium from academic and literary circles and helped catalyze the inclusion of comics in library collections. But the misconception that comics are for kids (and even a mistaken belief that comics *aren't* for kids that resulted from the maturation of mainstream comics) leads to challenges to the format. Further, we continue to encounter the idea that comics aren't "real" literature—a common refrain even in the 1950s and one that is often played when addressing any pop culture that is popular with younger enthusiasts (for example, it is reflected in contemporary attacks on video games and rap music).

Can you talk about the role that the Comic Book Legal Defense Fund plays in defending comics and combating censorship?

CBLDF was established in 1986 to help protect the First Amendment rights of the comics community. At the time, the fund was called upon to protect the manager of a comics store in Lasing, Illinois, who had been arrested for the display of obscene materials after police officers had raided the store and seized several titles for mature readers. The fund paid for his defense.

Today, CBLDF continues to provide legal representation when the need arises, but our work has diversified to include referrals, advice, education, coalition work, and more in defense of the First Amendment. We help individuals and businesses who are being criminally prosecuted, and we help educators and libraries gather resources to defend graphic novel challenges. We are the first line of defense when authorities intimidate individuals or businesses about the comics they read, make, buy, or sell. We also sign on to legal briefs opposed to unconstitutional legislation that would restrict the rights of the creative community, and we engage in educational outreach through presentations around the country and publications like our quarterly news magazine *CBLDF Defender*, our *Banned Books Week Handbook*, *She Changed Comics*, and more.

In a panel at Geek Girl Con, you spoke about a trend that the CBLDF observed about contemporary bans and challenges of comics and other books, a majority of which reflected the experiences of people of color, women, LGBTQ people, and other underrepresented communities. Can you reflect more on this trend?

Books that incorporate diversity are more likely to be targeted by censors, and those attacks are happening with greater frequency. In particular, the recent attempts to ban comics have frequently been due to the depiction of LGBTQ characters and the depiction of religions other than Christianity. For example, the American Library Association recently released their annual list of the ten most frequently challenged books. The top two books were comics: *This One Summer* by Jillian and Mariko Tamaki and *Drama* by Raina Telgemeier. The former has been challenged for LGBTQ content, but interestingly, the only reference is oblique; the book is generally challenged for its depiction of teenage pregnancy and profanity (often under the umbrella of "unsuited for age group"). Challenges to the latter can almost exclusively be attributed to the inclusion of LGBTQ characters.

Other comics that have been attacked for LGBTQ content include Alison Bechdel's *Fun Home*, Neil Gaiman's *The Sandman*, and Howard Cruse's *Stuck Rubber Baby*.

Marjane Satrapi's acclaimed *Persepolis* has been challenged on multiple occasions. While many of those challenges are for violent images and profanity, some of them are notably for the depiction of Islam. Ironically, Satrapi doesn't depict the faith in the most favorable light, but for some, the mere suggestion of Islam is enough to make a book a tool of "indoctrination."

We haven't had to deal with many overtly racist or sexist attacks on comics, but some attacks have targeted books that bring racial and gender diversity to classrooms and libraries. The critically-acclaimed comic collection *Palomar* by Gilbert Hernandez was called "child porn" by a parent in Rio Rancho, New Mexico. On its face, the challenge did not appear to be racially motivated, but *Palomar* reflects the Chicano background of its creator and would undoubtedly engage diverse students.

We've also helped other books from racially motivated bans: In 2012, the Tucson Independent School District dissolved their acclaimed Mexican American Studies program in response to a state law that specifically targeted the program for fomenting "racial hatred." Subsequently, several books by Mexican American and Native authors were banned. CBLDF defended the books and filed an amicus brief challenging the constitutionality of the law. (That case is still working its way through the court system).

The gender of the creators and characters of books isn't always considered a diversity issue, but when it comes to comics, women, transgender, and nonbinary creators and characters are still underrepresented (but that is changing very quickly). The depiction of female nudity, sexuality, and coming of age are frequent targets of would-be censors, as is the depiction of LGBTQ and nonbinary characters. Of the comics that have been included in ALA's ten frequently challenged books lists since 2011, more than half have been created by women or have focused on female characters. While gender likely does not play a direct role in the challenges, censorship attempts disproportionately impact comics created by women and featuring female primary characters.

There is plenty of comics scholarship on the Comics Code Authority and Wertham's influence. Has this focus created erasures in other parts of comics history that specifically affect cartoonists of color, LGBTQ cartoonists, women cartoonists?

I think there have been erasures of the roles diverse populations have had in comics, but I don't think that's due scholarship on Wertham and the CCA. I think it's more a component of the monoculture that existed in mainstream comics for the last several decades. But the culture of the industry itself is shifting and diversifying very quickly right now. The creators of comics and the characters within comics are increasingly diverse, and I think that will drive interest in exploring the history of marginalized populations within the community.

There are more and more epigraphs on the contributions of women, people of color, and LGBTQ individuals to the medium. Further, people are also exploring the impact of the medium in cultures outside the United States. In my research and encounters with academia, I've encountered individuals who are investigating the history of comics in the Arab-speaking world, comics in India, and more. As more diverse populations engage with, make, and teach with comics, I think we'll see those gaps in the history of the medium close.

3.3 Spotlight on MariNaomi, Cartoonist and Founder of the Cartoonists of Color Database and the Queer Cartoonists Database

You created the Cartoonists of Color Database (CartoonistsofColor.com) Queer Cartoonists Database (QueerCartoonists.com), which are incredible resources for publishers, bookstores, other cartoonists, and media platforms. What inspired you to start the databases? Can you share any stories about how others have used them?

"I created the Cartoonists of Color database when I was researching people of color in comics, and realized there was pretty much no information about that subject on the internet. I take for granted that the internet is such a wealth of information, when in reality it's missing so much, and a lot of what's there is bullshit. So once I realized there was a need, I knew I had to fill it.

Once I figured out the mechanics of the database, I knew I also wanted to make one for queer creators. But I was nervous about that, as I didn't want to force anyone out of the closet. My way around that was to only enter people I found in

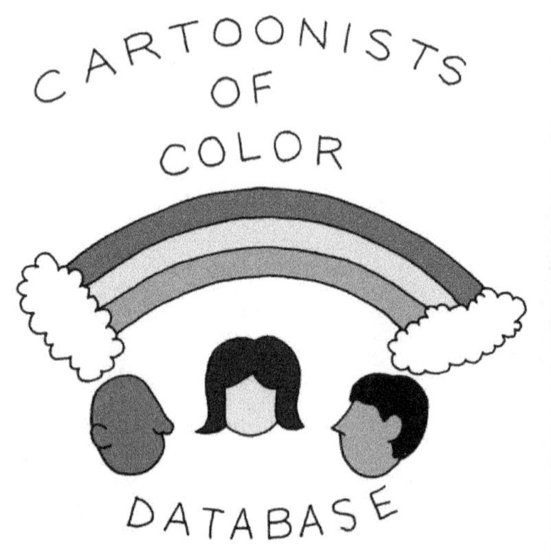

Cartoonists of Color Database and Queer Cartoonists Database logos.
Artwork by MariNaomi.

queer anthologies, and then let new additions add themselves (instead of how it works on the Cartoonists of Color database, where anyone can add anyone). So far, this has worked out without problems arising.

The response has been pretty great. I've heard from individuals who got paying gigs, gallery shows, etc. I've heard of bookstore owners using the databases to research what books to carry. From what I've heard, teachers use it, librarians, people looking to diversify their panels and conventions, and on and on. It's a good thing it seems to be working, because maintaining the databases is a lot of work! And it's a labor of love, so the only thing I get out of it is the hope that it's making a difference. ”

3.4 Activity: Students as Historians—Creator Profile

Instructions: Research a creator from a traditionally marginalized and underrepresented community. (Visit MariNaomi's fantastic databases, CartoonistsofColor.com and QueerCartoonists.com, for an excellent head start on your research.) Then, write a 1,000-word profile of your chosen creator and be sure to cite your sources.

You may search on this creator's website, if he/she has one; academic journals and databases; and magazine articles/blogs. Read three to four examples of his/her work; then, use the following questions to guide your research.

1. How did this creator become familiar with comics?
2. How did this creator get started with his/her/their career?
3. Who are his/her/their influences?
4. Does this creator seek to resist stereotypes about the communities he/she/they comes from in his/her/their work? If so, how?
5. What challenges has this creator encountered in his/her/their work?
6. What are this creator's artistic, stylistic, and thematic concerns or interests?
7. What patterns do you observe in his/her/their work?
8. Which techniques does this creator use (see Chapter 1: Reading Comics)? Discuss their use of panels, color, format, etc.
9. Why must readers learn and read more about this creator?

3.5 Reading: Making Comics Respectable: How *Maus* Helped Redefine a Medium

by Ian Gordon

Over the last twenty years comic books have undergone a substantial change in terms of types and content available and in their critical reception. The genesis of this shift can be traced to certain events in the production and distribution of comics. For fans of superhero comic books the key moments include Alan Moore and Dave Gibbons's *Watchmen* (collected in 1987) and Frank Miller's *Batman: The Dark Knight Returns* (collected in 1986). For others, including the great mass of non-comic-book readers, the publication of Art Spiegelman's *Maus* (collected in 1986 and 1991) and the critical response to it is the singularly most important phenomenon in the reevaluation of comic books.

As Joseph Witek prophesied in 1989, *Maus* has changed forever "the cultural perception of what a comic book can be and what can be accomplished by creators who take seriously the sequential art medium" (97). This chapter discusses this process with particular emphasis on public and academic discourses on the status and nature of comic books in the wake of *Maus*. *Watchmen* and *The Dark Knight Returns* reinvented comic books for superhero fans—*Maus* reinvented comic books for non-comic-book readers.

One reason comic books enjoy a newly found respectability is that they are no longer a mass medium with numerous genres of stories printed on cheap paper sold in pamphlet form. Superhero comics are virtually the sole survivor of the vast array of comic book genres available from the late 1930s through to the 1980s—and the characters in these titles are probably more familiar to mass audiences through movies and computer games than comics. In search of respectability, at the end of the 1980s the industry and the media heralded the transformation of comics into graphic novels—books sold in bookshops rather than on newsstands.

As indicated in the introduction, scholars have taken issue with the periodization of the term and even whether it is semantically accurate; many graphic novels, of which *Maus* is the prime example, are simply not novels at all. But *graphic novel* is the catch-all designation given to a range of innovative work, perhaps not generally associated with comic books, that have received critical attention from academics and the quality press. Indeed, to complain about the term graphic novel as applied to a comic book, say like *Maus*, on the basis that they lack the qualities of novels is akin to noting that not many comic books, *Maus* included, are funny.

This shift in terms is rather mild when compared to the shifts in form experienced by comic book characters most likely to appear in movies today. For every blockbuster superhero film there seems to be a quirky, offbeat independent film based on a comic book. Academics studying comics have mostly gone beyond earlier studies that labeled them worth studying for providing a funhouse mirror on American culture or somehow being representative meta-narrative texts. An array of scholars now account for the formal properties of comics, their impact on national and international cultures and societies as constituent and active phenomenon, and as a literary genre. In short, the medium has been transformed and artists receive critical acclaim.

This chapter unpacks this development in four sections: an overview of the development of comics that led to the production of *Maus*, a discussion of why *Maus* had such an impact, an analysis of the changing view of comics in the press, and an examination of the blossoming of academic work on comics art.

From Wertham to *Maus*

In the 1950s, Fredric Wertham and others attacked comic books as a cause of juvenile delinquency and other behavior deemed abnormal. Wertham's campaign promoted the view that comics were for children, though he specifically excluded comic strips

Ian Gordon, "Making Comics Respectable: How Maus Helped Redefine a Medium," *The Rise of the American Comics Artist: Creators and Contexts*, pp. 179-193.

from his onslaught because he said their presence in newspapers ensured they were subject to editorial control and thus primarily aimed at adults. To be sure, newspaper readership surveys supported Wertham's view of comic strips as material read by adults—but then why were comic books seen as children's material rather than as a form with readership among all ages?

Viewing comic books as a children's genre lumped together Archie comics, superhero comics, Harvey comics, Dell comics (including the licensed Disney characters), and the horror and crime comics that EC and other companies produced. Viewed by critics as a genre, rather than as a medium with many genres, comic books were reduced to a childish level just at the time the medium showed potential to develop critical new forms. It was their unsuitability for children that made many of the EC titles stand out as examples of the potential of the medium. The imposition of the Comics Code then delayed the maturing of the form alongside the maturing of the great mass of comic book readers: adolescents and service personnel from the war years. It is also fair to say that broad social transformations such as the baby boom, the suburbanization of America, and the advent of television mitigated the appeal of a form born in the Depression and that found its widest popularity during the hardship of war. But these developments also contained the seeds of a transformation of comic books that occurred in the 1960s.

The rebirth of superhero comics is a familiar enough story to comic book aficionados—and there are two versions of the tale, depending on one's allegiance to which publisher: Marvel Comics or National Periodical Publications (later DC Comics). In the DC version, in 1956 Julius Schwartz introduced the Flash, a new version of the 1940s character, and started a superheroes revival. In the Marvel version, Stan Lee, facing the impending closure of Timely/Atlas/Marvel in 1961, or perhaps his own departure from the industry, decided to do the sort of story he really wanted to do. Copying the success of DC's The Justice League of America, Lee created the Fantastic Four with Jack Kirby.

The history of superhero comics is important to understanding the changing attitudes to comic books for numerous reasons including the role of organized fandom, the longevity of the characters and their appeal across generations, and the political economy of the industry. But the tale of comic book history and the long march to respectability requires some acknowledgement of the immense popularity of other comic books. In the absence of longitudinal studies of comic book (and comic strip) readership it is difficult to offer an overview of the impact and role of particular comics in shaping comics readers, but as John Jackson Miller has shown, for many years the leading comics by sales figures (at least as reported by the companies in their annual statement required for special mailing rates) were Dell Comics's *Uncle Scrooge* (1960 and 1961) and Fawcett's *Dennis the Menace* (1963). In 1969 *Archie* sold more than any other comic book. The point here is that comic book reading was more likely than not an eclectic enterprise with the same people reading a range of comic books no doubt cycling through different types and genres and gradually leaving behind younger genres for perhaps the relatively more mature superhero comic books of Marvel and DC, or other comic-type fare.

The original *Mad* comic book, with its satires of comic book superheroes, and other subjects, illustrated that comics were a medium. The sort of satire in *Mad* and the later magazine version took the comics art form back to the satirical and caricature forms from which it in part derived. It put the *comic* back in comics art. *Mad*'s place in a historical narrative of the developing respectability of comics might at first seem odd. I think my own experience of a broad diet of comics material that included *Uncle Scrooge*, Harvey comics, *Archie*, DC, Marvel, *Beano*, *Dandy*, *Mad*, and many other titles may have been atypical, but only for Americans by the inclusion of the two British titles. In any case *Mad* founding editor Harvey Kurtzman drew an association between *Mad* and the underground comix that began in the 1960s at the level of creators (Kurtzman 1991, 58–59; see also Witek 1989, 45).

It is more than likely that readers too followed a similar trajectory. Comix played with the form in ways that comic books simply did not. To be sure comix contained virulent racist and sexist images, such as Robert Crumb's Angelfood McSpade, which was both. Crumb has described this work as humorously poking "at the spot people are most uncomfortable with" and suggested that such images stemmed from a consciousness broken from its "social programming" by LSD (Crumb 2005). Whatever Crumb's explanation for his work, the underground comix broke through all sorts of programming and opened spaces for experiments with the form.

Art Spiegelman responded to the "flaming promise of Underground Comix." He contributed work to several comix, including one of the funniest, *Young Lust*, a parody of romance comic books. With fellow *Young Lust* artist Bill Griffith, the creator of Zippy the Pinhead, Spiegelman tried to realize the potential of comix in a more professional publication, *Arcade: The Comics Revue,* which Print Mint published for seven issues between 1975 and 1976. By 1980, though, that moment had "fizzled" out, and as Spiegelman puts it, comix "were stereotyped as dealing only with sex, dope, and cheap thrills . . . [and] got stuffed into the back of the cultural closet along with bong pipes and love beads."

Spiegelman moved back to New York City in 1976, where he met Françoise Mouly, and in 1980 they published the first issue of *Raw,* a graphix magazine. *Maus* first appeared in serialized form in *Raw*, commencing with the second issue in December 1980. Pantheon published volume one of *Maus* in book form in 1986. For the book Spiegelman reworked his illustrative style, reducing his more elaborate looking art in the serialized form to the deceptively simple appearance of funny animal comics (Spiegelman and Mouly 1987, 6–8).

The Power of *Maus*

The infantilization of the form between Wertham's campaign and the advent of comix lasted fourteen years or so, about the time for a generation of comic book readers such as Spiegelman to reach a maturity of sorts (he was twenty in 1968). Spiegelman's trajectory from suburban Rego Park, through youthful rebellion, to a hard-won adult relationship with his father is present in *Maus* and that narrative, especially the latter part, drives the story forward. As Witek suggests, *Maus* is as much autobiography as biography. Indeed the publisher denoted the work as "Holocaust/Autobiography" on the inside cover of the second printing of the first edition of volume one, but this categorization may well refer to the father's story.

Whatever the case, it is in this intersection of autobiography and biography that *Maus* becomes history, and not just a history of the Holocaust. Looking at *Maus* in 2008 it seems to me that one reason it resonated so well with Spiegelman's contemporaries, alongside Spiegelman's creative allegorical and metaphorical forms of Nazi/Cats and Jews/Mice, was that it offered the possibility for those of the generation who participated in a youthful rebellion of the 1960s to reconcile themselves with the world of their parents. Trying to understand a parent by recovering their experience of war has become somewhat of a calling for Americans who in the years since *Maus* have anointed their parents, in the words of Tom Brokaw, "The Greatest Generation." A comic book about the horrors of the Holocaust and its effects on survivors such as Vladek and his son Art provided a symbolical form through which to patch up generational conflict. That may seem a lot of freight for a comic book to carry, but no more than bearing the weight of the Holocaust on the backs of comic mice.

Maus is, as Joshua Brown noted in his insightful review, "an important historical work" with "a unique approach to narrative construction and interpretation." It is a work based on oral history and a work that reveals the processes of creating history from oral accounts (Brown 1988, 98). Moreover, *Maus* appeared at a moment when interest in the Holocaust as a topic of historical inquiry and memorialization was at a crescendo in America that translated (for example) into the creation of the United States Holocaust Memorial Museum, which opened in Washington, D.C., in 1993.

Maus as history is wonderful because it literally shows us how history is produced in a dialogue with the past and how historical narratives and interpretations are created through processes of selection and editing to convey the best sense of what happened. It deals with the issues of memory as a reliable source of evidence. Brown finds *Maus* "a successful work of history because it fails to provide the reader with a catharsis, with the release of tension gained through the complacent construct of 'knowing' all" (98). But *Maus* gained attention initially because of Spiegelman's representational strategies.

Adam Gopnik in a long essay in the *New Republic* remarked that people knew of *Maus* as the "Holocaust Comic Book" and its fame rested on drawing characters as animals. Gopnik labeled Spiegelman's choice as "a peculiar, idiosyncratic convention" suggesting that "there isn't any allegorical dimension in *Maus,* just a convention of representation." Gopnik took issue with those who saw *Maus* as trivializing the Holocaust through these representations and also with those who saw Spiegelman as overthrowing the tyranny of comics in favor of comix.

> "*Maus* as history is wonderful because it literally shows us how history is produced in a dialogue with the past and how historical narratives and interpretations are created through processes of selection and editing to convey the best sense of what happened. It deals with the issues of memory as a reliable source of evidence."

For Gopnik, Spiegelman had reconnected with and resurrected "the serious and even tragic possibilities of the comic strip and cartoon," a form that in Gopnik's account could be traced back to about 1600 or so in Italy. Gopnik argues that Spiegelman draws his characters more as though they are wearing animal masks, rather than anthropomorphic characters. And he argued that *Maus* drew "its power not from its visual style alone, but rather from the tension between the detail of its narration and dialogue and the hallucinatory fantasy of its images" (Gopnik 1987, 29–34). Some of *Maus's* impact lay in the way readers had to confront the issue of how we look at and depict race/ethnicity/nationality visually; describing just how this process worked engaged many early reviewers of the book.

Joshua Brown thought readers of *Maus* would decipher the characters as humans wearing animal masks (metaphorically if not literally in the illustrations) and that Spiegelman had been purposively disruptive in this representation. Hitler described Jews as a different species and Spiegelman forces us to confront that particular racial rhetoric by recognizing his cats, mice, and pigs as humans. Joseph Witek understood *Maus* as firmly in the tradition of funny animal comics, starting with *Felix the Cat* and most famously Disney's animated characters. For Witek the animal metaphor worked simply "as a premise to be absorbed and then put out of mind," or in Spiegelman's words, "shucked like a snakeskin" (Witek 1989, 112). Writing in the *American Quarterly* in 1991 I saw Spiegelman's technique as more allegorical in that the metaphor was not so easily "shucked." I read the Nazi/Cats as cats who dressed like humans and who had forced the Jews to live like mice (Gordon 1991, 341–46).

Fresh from working as a teaching assistant to Rabbi Abraham J. Karp in his History of the Holocaust class at the University of Rochester, my reading Nazis as cat-like came easily, and I think I was probably not alone in that reaction. On the other hand, reading the Jews as having the characteristics of mice did not come so easily. For a start the central protagonists, the characters whose stories we follow and by the author's intention are meant to identify with, are Jew/Mice. But the metaphor is more easily shucked because *Maus* is biography and autobiography, and the reader is constantly pulled back to a narrator represented as a mouse.

Cats play with their prey. It is in their nature, just as it was in the nature of Nazis—being a Nazi required a commitment to an ideology that denied some humans their humanity. The most basic of human instincts is to survive, just as Jews did everything they could to survive the genocide unleashed by the Nazis. Gopnik says the cat metaphor lets the cats, the Nazis, off too easily, from the question of how could they do it? But I think the binary at work here—the Nazis were cats and the Jews were struggling to survive as people—suggests the simple answer to the question: cats are amoral and Nazis were amoral, which is to suggest that evil is often as Hannah Arendt wrote: banal.

Gopnik wondered if perhaps such horror could only be presented in masks (Gopnik 1987, 33). For his part Spiegelman drew his masks in an extraordinarily simple fashion avoiding a "cute pudgy little mouse character with big, round, soulful eyes" because he wished to avoid unnecessary pleas for sympathy (Spiegelman qtd. in Brown 1988, 108). The power of *Maus* lay then not in pleas for sympathy, but in the depiction of the struggle for survival against an amoral, methodically brutal killing machine and in showing the cost of surviving for Vladek and those around him.

A quick guide to the impact of *Maus* can be had from doing a search of the Lexis database. From the publication of volume one in 1986 to 1997 the book has 772 citations. For the next ten years to January 2007 there are 2053 hits. From January 2007 to September 2008 there are 445 mentions. The book has only grown in reputation, and any mention of graphic novels (just call them what they are: comic books) is incomplete without a tip of the hat to *Maus*.

For instance, a long piece in the *Washington Post* in August 2008 extolled the virtues of comic books through self-described lifelong prose guy Bob Thompson's discovery of their many virtues—and he duly gave *Maus* credit for starting a graphic novel boom. Moreover, the article was accompanied by a three-page comic (retrievable as jpg files from the website), one of which depicted Thompson's visit to Spiegelman and Mouly's loft residence, where *Maus* was born (Thompson 2008). On September 18, 2008, the *Wall Street Journal* ran an item including a short interview with Spiegelman about his reissued book *Breakdowns*, and over half the piece concerned *Maus* (Trachtenberg 2008). Two days earlier *The Times* (of London) carried an article by Ken Russell, the director of such films as *Women in Love* and *Tommy*, on a forthcoming festival of comics at London's Institute of Contemporary Arts under the heading "How the mighty *Maus* fuelled my flights of fantasy." To be sure the mouse of the title was Mickey, but Russell in his 1,000-word brief about the importance of comics dutifully gave two paragraphs (about twenty percent) to *Maus* and labeled Spiegelman a genius (Russell 2008, 18).

Museums and the Media

In the first ten years after Pantheon published the first volume of *Maus* it was not immediately apparent it represented a transformative moment. To many critics and commentators it indeed looked like the exception that proved the rule that comics were not only (by and large) junk: only a rare genius like Spiegelman could pull off a work of quality in the medium. Writing in the massive catalog to accompany the *High & Low: Modern Art and Popular Culture* exhibition at the Museum of Modern Art in Manhattan (MoMA) in 1990, Adam Gopnik (with Kirk Varnedoe) described *Maus* as a "singular" achievement (Varnedoe and Gopnik 1990, 385).[1] Singular though Gopnik thought Spiegelman's work in the 1980s, the exhibition and the catalog contained a section on comics that examined the form from the Swiss originator Rodolphe Töpffer to Robert Crumb.

"Comics," a seventy-two-page chapter in the catalog, gave comics the sort of respect they seldom receive at the hands of art critics. Gopnik described them as "not a precursor of modern art but another kind of modern art" and one that shared "many of the same motives, forms, and dreams" (Varnedoe and Gopnik 1990, 152). Gopnik stressed both the accomplishments of outstanding artists such as George Herriman, Winsor McCay, and Crumb, but also pointed to the broader relevance of comics as an important optimistic counterbalance in modern art to the tendency to present modernity's destructive and alienating side.

Gopnik wove a tale showing the common response to modernity and artistic sensibilities of (say) Herriman and Juan Miro, the rise of comic books, the delirious ride they took through grotesque and kitsch stylings, and the impact this had on modern artists like Andy Warhol and Roy Lichtenstein. In Gopnik's hands the pleasure given by comics alleviated the mass commercial nature of the form and the tendency to leveling kitsch. His argument is enlightening and one not much examined by those who study comics. But in the exhibition, which I viewed in early 1991, placing comics side by side with, for example, Miro and Lichtenstein, tended to reduce the complexity of Gopnik's argument to "gosh gee these comics must have something going for them since great artists were either inspired by them or copied them more or less wholesale."

The interpretation tended to wash out and comics became curios of childish popular culture that somehow touched more rarefied levels of culture. Spiegelman responded to the exhibition with a scathing pictorial review, "High Art Lowdown," published in *Artforum International* (Spiegelman 1990, 115). Spiegelman took the curators to task for their "myopic choices," exclusions, and arbitrary organizational principles. In a 2002 interview Spiegelman recounted that these comments, which he regretted were all negative, led to MoMA contacting him, resulting in an exhibition of his work there in 1992 and eventually in the 2005 *Masters of American Comics* exhibition at the Hammer Museum and the Museum of Contemporary Art in Los Angeles.

The *Masters of American Comics* exhibition was curated by John Carlin and Brian Walker with an accompanying volume from Yale University Press. Although this exhibition and volume greatly improved on the MoMA effort, it still valorized the efforts of a few creative geniuses, all of whom were men. In a complex and difficult media like comics, which sometimes is produced by individuals and other times by collaborative teams, singling out individuals in some ways engages in the same sort of marketing of artists as name brands that many art critics such as Graham Bader have criticized MoMA for doing in the *High Low* exhibition (Bader 2004, 109–12). But to be fair, the exhibition dealt with the complexity of comics as an art form, a creative medium, and a commercial undertaking in ways that no previous major exhibition had even broached (Fischer 2007, 730–32; Rhode 2007, 732–38).

Treating comics as childish remains the most common media trope. As comics researcher Gene Kannenberg Jr. writes, journalists and/or sub-editors often seem incapable of producing a story on comics without a condescending headline along the lines of "Pow! Zap! Wham!: Comics Aren't just for Kids Anymore" (Kannenberg 2008, 8). Two types of articles tend to appear under these sorts of headlines: pieces that track the rise of graphic novels and pieces that discuss the increasing number of superhero-comic-book-based movies and the lucrative profits to be had. The first usually start with *Maus* and track through a series of graphic novels such as Marjane Satrapi's *Persepolis*, Chris Ware's *Jimmy Corrigan*, and for good measure something by Will Eisner and Ben Katchor.

The second type approaches comics as idea generators for blockbuster movies, generally starting with Tim Burton's 1989 *Batman* (which incidentally does not hold up as well as Richard Donner's 1978 *Superman*) and work their way forward. In these accounts comics get some respect through backhanded compliments. The bottom line for respect in such articles is, well, the bottom line.

"Comics Boom!: Magazines earn megabucks through TV, film, retail sales," a cover story by David Liberman that ran above the fold in the "Money" section of *USA Today* in July 2008, is fairly typical of the way the press reports the business of comics. Replete with a dramatic splash headline featuring the Hulk crashing through a wall, the "comic" and "boom" of the headline are rendered comic-book style. But the report is all business, noting that the second Batman movie directed by Christopher Nolan, *The Dark Knight*, took a record $158 million in box office receipts in its opening weekend in the USA.

Overall comic book-based movies were on track in 2008 to best the 2007 record of $925 million in ticket sales, which amounted to ten percent of that year's box office receipts. Time Warner licensing resulted in retail sales of $6 billion for products carrying images of Superman, Batman, and other non-comic-book characters in 2007. Marvel characters did $5.5 billion worth of licensing sales. Against these figures the $700 million sales of comic books in 2007—up about $60 million from 2006—makes the other efforts look like a tail that is wagging the dog.

The article offers the now standard interpretation of comic books' role in this generation of profit in a succinct, sound bite-worthy quote: "'Comics are a low-cost laboratory, with instant feedback, for what's happening in pop culture,' says Milton Griepp, publisher of ICv2, a website that tracks comic publishing." There is nothing particularly new about this sort of reporting since such articles have appeared regularly in the press since the success of the 1989 *Batman* movie and the accompanying licensing bonanza (see Kleinfield 1990, 1). The April 27, 1992, edition of the television show *Entertainment Tonight* reported Batman merchandise from the first film garnered sales of over one billion dollars worldwide by spring 1992.

Comics, then, fit into a corporate business plan as generators of licensed characters that produce super profits. Time Warner President Jeffrey Bewkes may have told the *Wall Street Journal* that the notion of synergy was "bullshit," but as far as comics goes, synergy has fertilized a rich vein of profit (Karnitschnig 2006, A1). And as both Connie Bruck and Gerard Jones have shown, the profitability of licensing comic book characters was part of the appeal to Steve Ross when he put together the Warner side of the Time Warner corporation between 1967 and 1969 in part through the purchase of DC (then National Periodical Publications) in 1967 for $60 million, a deal which included the associated company, the Licensing Corporation of America (Anon. 1967 and 1968; Bruck 1994; Jones 2004). It is a simple enough equation: with greater profitability comes greater respectability.

Academics and Comics Art

Much of the early quality academic work on comics can be traced back to Austrian-born and British-based art historian E. H. Gombrich, whose 1960 book, *Art And Illusion: A Study in the Psychology of Pictorial Representation*—derived from a series of lectures for the

Smithsonian Institution in 1956—called for a critical inquiry of the form. Ellen Weise's 1965 edited volume, *Enter: The Comics,* which brought together the Swiss Rodolphe Töpffer's *Essay on Physiognomy* and one of his comics albums, *The True Story of Monsieur Crépin,* for the first time in English, was an initial response to Gombrich. David Kunzle, self-consciously following Gombrich's call, published the first of his two-volume history of the comic strip, *The Early Comic Strip Narrative Strips and Picture Stories in the European Broadsheet from c. 1450 to 1825* in 1973 (Kunzle 2007, ix). The second volume, *The Nineteenth Century,* followed in 1990. Kunzle's work set a benchmark in analytical and descriptive depth, but for a good many years Americans interested in comics did not take up his work or his methodology, which carefully placed technical and stylistic developments within a broad cultural matrix and offered a history of the form that explained why these developments happened.

But America did produce some early scholarly work of comics criticism. Arthur Asa Berger published his *Li'l Abner: A Study in American Satire* and followed up in 1973 with a series of essays in *Comic-stripped American.* Berger's work focused on how comic strips demonstrated American traditions of satire and caricature. Much of his argument was a plea to take comics seriously since they mirrored society's concerns and interests.

Other early academic work included Ariel Dorfman and Armand Mattelart's 1975 *How to Read Donald Duck: Imperialist Ideology in the Disney Comic.* Originally issued in Chile in 1971, this volume's highly polemical analysis of the Chilean versions of Disney comics made the none-too-subtle observation that comic book stories, even satires like Scrooge McDuck, proffered ideological positions. The book presaged a debate that became familiar enough among scholars of comics and other media about just how a cultural form infused its readers with a particular ideology. Elsewhere in academia around this time (circa the early 1970s) Donald Ault, a Blake scholar, was making waves through his courses at Berkeley that examined comics as part of a literature curriculum. Other academics with an early interest in comics included the Temple University communications professor, John Lent, and Faulkner specialist M. Thomas Inge.

In the late 1980s, Seetha Srinivasan at the University Press of Mississippi set up the Studies in Popular Culture series with Inge as the general editor. Witek's *Comic Books as History* was the first book in this series that focused on comics (Heer 2008). In an essay for the *American Quarterly* I discussed Witek's book side by side with Kunzle's second volume. It may seem at first an odd juxtaposition, a work on twentieth-century American comic books with a foot in the comix camp, and a volume decidedly about nineteenth-century European comics art. But as it turns out, not so much so, because such a discussion marked a stage in the development of a comics studies field.

I hasten to add that the review editor of the journal, Charles Bassett, proposed the essay to me as I was searching for an opportunity to review Kunzle's book. Though not giving Witek nearly enough credit for the merits of his work I concluded the *American Quarterly* piece by suggesting that the comics form after a century of mass acceptance might be "about to receive the critical attention it deserves" (Gordon 1991, 341–46). Witek's book marked the beginning of some respectability, however attenuated, for academics who first and foremost study comics. Witek, too, was probably the first academic to build a successful career mostly around the study of comics, moving his way from a PhD under Ault at Vanderbilt through to being a full professor at Stetson University.

The somewhat older David Kunzle had been a working academic since the mid-1960s when he arrived at UCLA in the art history department and was perhaps protected from lowbrow accusations by the reach of his learning, his British accent, and Gombrich's reputation. As far as respectability went, Kunzle had the advantage of studying comics art unencumbered by associations with mass media or popular culture. At the same time Kunzle demanded that the material he studied be viewed as comic strips, which called into question the then popular and accepted notion of comics as a distinctively American art form.

I mean no disrespect to either of my colleagues, nor to suggest fundamental disagreement between them, when I say that they represented positions around which a field of comics scholarship grew. The University Press of Mississippi has continued to bring out a steady stream of works on comics and, as Jeet Heer has written, transformed "comics studies, hitherto and [sic] inchoate body of critical writing, into a coherent field" (Heer 2008). In addition to the many fine books published by Mississippi, other academic presses such as Duke, Chicago, Yale, and the now defunct Smithsonian Institution Press also published works on comics.

Conclusion

Given the boom in academic work on comics it is surprising that there is no English-language, single-authored monograph on *Maus*. Pierre-Alban Delannoy published a work in French in 2002 and Ole Frahm a work in German in 2006. In 2001 the Belgian Leuven University Press published the English-language volume *The Graphic Novel*, edited by Jan Baetens from papers delivered at a conference of the same name, and many of its chapters dealt with *Maus*. In 2003 the University of Alabama Press published *Considering* Maus: *Approaches to Art Spiegelman's "Survivor's Tale" of the Holocaust*, edited by Deborah R. Geis. These few volumes suggest a paucity of works on *Maus*, but there are, however, numerous journal articles and book chapters that discuss *Maus* in the context of the Holocaust, history, memory, trauma, and the formal properties of comics. The issues to hand in most of these pieces, even in two of the best by James E. Young and Marianne Hirsch, mostly expand on the concepts raised by Brown, Witek, and Gopnik in the 1980s (Young 1998, 666–99; Hirsch 1992–93, 3–29).

Maus may have shifted many attitudes toward comic books, but much of the academy still drags its heels. The March 2008 issue of *PMLA* contained an article by Hillary Chute titled "Comics as Literature?" that begins:

> Comics—a form once considered pure junk—is sparking interest in literary studies. I'm as amazed as anybody else by the comics boom—despite the fact that I wrote an English department dissertation that makes the passionate case that we should not ignore this innovative narrative form. . . . The field hasn't yet grasped its object or properly posed its project (Chute 2008, 452–65).

Chute's tone in framing her article belies much of the work that has shaped scholarship of comics and the quality and thoughtfulness of her own writing. Her piece goes on to discuss much of the scholarship on comics, but she overlooks several key scholars such as Witek and—surprisingly—Charles Hatfield, whose book, *Alternative Comics: An Emerging Literature* (2005), conveys in the title its importance to an author trying to discuss comics as literature. But she does of course discuss *Maus* at length. Indeed Chute is working with Spiegelman on his forthcoming *MetaMaus*.

Maus has made comics respectable. Those who study comics are slowly being admitted to the academic party, but sometimes comics scholars have to suitably humble themselves before being accepted in the VIP lounge of journals like the *PMLA*.

NOTES

1. The authors divided the chapters and Gopnik was responsible for the chapters cited here.

WORKS CITED

Anon. 1967. 'Kinney Plans to Acquire National Periodical in Exchange for Stock.' *Wall Street Journal*, 24 July.

———. 1968. Kinney National Acquisition. *Wall Street Journal*, 27 Mar.

Bader, Graham. 2004. "High and Low." *Artforum International* 43(2): 109–12

Brown, Joshua. 1988. Of Mice and Memory. *Oral History Review* 16: 98.

Bruck, Connie. 1994. *Master of the Game: Steve Ross and the Creation of Time Warner*. New York: Simon & Schuster.

Carlin, John, Paul Karasik, and Brian Walker, eds. 2005. *Masters of American Comics*. New Haven: Yale University Press.

Chute, Hillary. 2008. 'Comics as Literature? Reading Graphic Narrative.' *PMLA* 123: 452–65.

Crumb, Robert. 2005. "'I'll never be the same.'" *The Guardian*, 10 Mar. http://www.guardian .co.uk/books/2005/mar/10/robert-crumb.comics [accessed 10 June 2008].

Fischer, Craig. 2007. "Masters of American Comics—Two Reviews." *International Journal of Comic Art* 9.1: 730–32.

Gopnik, Adam. 1987. "Comics and Catastrophe." *New Republic*, 22 June, 29–34.

Gordon, Ian. 1991. "'But Seriously, Folks . . . : Comic Art and History.'" *American Quarterly* 43: 341–46.

Hatfield, Charles. 2005. *Alternative Comics: An Emerging Literature*. Jackson, MS: University Press of Mississippi.

Heer, Jeet. 2008. "The Rise of Comics Scholarship: the Role of University Press of Mississippi." *Sans Everything*, 2 Aug. http://sanseverything.wordpress.com/2008/08/02/ the-rise-of-comics-scholarship-the-role-of-university-press-of-mississippi/ [accessed 30 Aug. 2008].

Hirsch, Marianne. 1992–93. "Family Pictures: *Maus*, Mourning, and Post-Memory." *Discourse: A Journal for Theoretical Studies in Media and Culture* 15(2): 3–29.

Jones, Gerard. 2004. *Men Of Tomorrow: Geeks, Gangsters, and the Birth of the Comic Book.* New York: Basic Books.

Kannenberg, Jr., Gene. 2008. *500 Essential Graphic Novels.* New York: Collins Design.

Karnitschnig, Matthew. 2006. "That's All Folks: After Years of Pushing Synergy, Time Warner Inc. Says Enough." *Wall Street Journal,* 2 June, A1.

Kleinfield, N. R. 1990. "Cashing in on a Hot New Brand Name." *New York Times,* 29 Apr., 1 [Section 3].

Kunzle, David. 2007. *Father of the Comic Strip: Rodolphe Töpffer.* Jackson, MS: University Press of Mississippi.

Kurtzman, Harvey. 1991. *From Aargh! To Zap!: Harvey Kurtzman's Visual History of the Comics.* New York: Prentice Hall.

Rhode, Michael. 2007. "Masters of American Comics—Two Reviews." *International Journal of Comic Art* 9(1): 732–38.

Russell, Ken. 2008. "How the mighty *Maus* fuelled my flights of fantasy." *The Times,* 16 Sept., 18.

Spiegelman, Art, 1990. "High Art Lowdown." *Artforum International* 29(4): 115.

Spiegelman, Art, and Françoise Mouly. 1987. "Raw Nerves." *Read Yourself Raw,* ed. Art Spiegelman and Françoise Mouly, 6–8. New York: Pantheon.

Thompson, Bob. 2008. "Drawing Power." *Washington Post,* 24 Aug. http://www.washingtonpost.com/wp-dyn/content/story/2008/08/22/ST2008082201503.html [accessed 1 Sept. 2008].

Trachtenberg, Jeffrey A. 2008. "King of Cartoons." *Wall Street Journal,* 18 Sept. http://www .wsj.com/article/SB122166625405548219.html [accessed 18 Sept. 2008].

Varnedoe, Kirk, and Adam Gopnik. 1990. *High & Low: Modern Art and Popular Culture.* New York: Museum of Modern Art.

Witek, Joseph. 1989. *Comic Books as History: The Narrative Art of Jack Jackson, Art Spiegelman, and Harvey Pekar.* Jackson, MS: University Press of Mississippi.

Young, James E. 1998. "The Holocaust as Vicarious Past: Art Spiegelman's *Maus* and the Afterimages of History." *Critical Inquiry* 24(3): 666–99.

3.6 Discussion Questions

1. Gordon writes: "Viewed by critics as a genre, rather than as a medium with many genres, comic books were reduced to a childish level just at the time the medium showed potential to develop critical new forms" (181).
   a. Define terms "genre" and "medium."
   b. What is the difference between considering comics a "medium" as opposed to a "genre"?
2. Why were comics considered childish? What are the implications behind this assumption?
3. Define the term "respectability" and how it applies to comics.
4. How does Art Spigelman's graphic memoir *Maus* use history and autobiography?
5. According to Gordon and the scholars he cites, how does *Maus* depart from its predecessors in terms of tone, subject matter, and style?
6. How would a satirical publication such as *MAD Magazine,* which pokes fun at superheroes and other comics subjects, help to develop "respectability"?
7. What are "underground comix"? Research this topic and give examples of these comics. What are their subject matter and concerns?
8. Gordon offers different interpretations for the use of animal figures in *Maus* from his own work and the work of other scholars. For example, "Gopnik argues that Spigelman draws his characters more as though they are wearing animal masks, rather than anthropomorphic characters" (184). After

reading *Maus*, how did you interpret the use of animal figures assigned to groups of characters, like the Jewish communities; Art and his father, Vladek, as mice; and the Nazis as cats?

9. What was the reception for comics at museums? What were some of the conflicts in displaying or curating exhibits on comics?
10. Gordon details the incredible profit margins made from superhero movies and states that "... with greater profitability comes greater respectability" (189). Discuss the implications behind this quote. How does commerce affect the "respectability" of comics?
11. Describe the development of the study of comics in academia, according to Gordon. What does respectability of comics in academia produce?

3.7 Interview with Keith Sicat, Director of *Komikero Chronicles*

Keith Sicat is an independent filmmaker and comic book creator who has screened his films in local and international film festivals. He was heavily involved with painting and photography before falling in love with cinema. Under the Kino Arts banner, he has a total of twelve features under his belt as a director, writer, or producer, including award winners *Rigodon*, *Ka Oryang*, *The Guerrilla is a Poet*, and *Woman of the Ruins*, their subjects ranging from social-realist documentaries to gothic fiction. A number of the films screened in museum spaces such as the Ayala Museum, Lopez Museum, Smithsonian Institute (Washington, DC), and Museum of Modern Art (MoMA, New York). He served as head of concepts for animation firms in the Philippines, culminating in the first Philippine-Japanese anime coproduction, *Barangay 143* with TV Asahi, which is due for release next year. He is constantly developing new documentaries and fictional feature films.

In this interview, Keith Sicat dives into his filmmaking process regarding his documentary, Komikero Chronicles, *which outlines the history of Filipino comics (also known as komiks) and showcases interviews with various Filipino cartoonists and their work.*

Promotional film poster for *Komikero Chronicles*.

Can you please describe *Komikero Chronicles*? What inspired you to embark on documenting the lives and work of Filipino cartoonists and the history of komiks in the Philippines?

Komikero Chronicles is my take on an advocacy film channeled through my inner ten-year-old. I remember being enthralled by comics from the get-go, tracing drawings as a very small boy, but ironically, my interest in Filipino artists happened only once I was transplanted to the United States.

It was strange because although I did have a sense of cultural identity instilled in me, the "colonial mentality" did manage to seep in, manifesting in how American culture and norms were perceived as having better quality than those of Filipino origin. So I was elated when my mom mentioned to me that the artists whose illustrations I obsessed over in the pages of *Conan* magazines were Filipino; it gave me an immense sense of pride.

“Imagine my surprise when my research led me to discover that the first documented Filipino comics-creator was our very own national hero Jose Rizal!”

That pride continued when I noticed that some of my favorite artists working in the superhero genre also sported Filipino surnames—with specific cultural nods like drawing an X-Men character to sport the Filipino flag on a leather jacket—that sense of my culture having been legitimized in a global context was exciting.

Being a fan—boy with a fondness for visual storytelling, I naturally gravitated to the more involved world of comics—traveling to different cities to attend conventions and meet my heroes was how it started—but my exposure to Filipino komiks was quite limited.

It was only years later, after I had returned to the Philippines from living over a decade in the west—and attended the first Komikon, where I saw and met some great artists—did my education on Pinoy komiks begin.

Somehow, I chanced upon the online Philippine Komiks Museum of artist Gerry Alanguilan. His work in mainstream American superhero comics is well known, and he had now embarked on working on his own idiosyncratic, Pinoy stories. And his devotion to the history of the medium is unending!

Due to Mr. Alanguilan's Herculean efforts in reintroducing old Filipino artists into the public consciousness (including the formidable task of restoring one of the classic stories of Francisco Coching), I started to learn about the history of the medium within the Philippine context.

Imagine my surprise when my research led me to discover that the first documented Filipino comics-creator was our very own national hero Jose Rizal! When I discovered that, I immediately thought, "How would my ten-year-old self react to that mind-blowing fact?" And so my journey in making *Komikero Chronicles* began—so that I can share with the current and future crops of ten-year-olds the amazing history of this artistic medium.

Which komiks were crucial in your development as a filmmaker and in starting a project like *Komikero Chronicles*? How did these particular komiks spark your imagination?

I think every single graphic illustration I was exposed to informed my filmmaking. This is why whatever the project, even if documentary, has a very strong visual sense. I cannot help but process stories in a visual manner.

There are quite a few things I learned from comics that translate to cinema, not just visually in terms of composition, but even abstract storytelling techniques.

1. *Acting/Performance*—the illustrations, expressions, and even physicality of the bodies are very evocative of the drama, tension, or humor in a scene.
2. *Blocking and Mise-en-Scène*—the reason why an artist positions his figures within a frame to tell a story is the equivalent of choosing an angle and lens when shooting with a camera. The reason why the artist dresses them in such attire, places the characters or setting in a particular location, the way in which all those elements are rendered through line work or color; all of these decisions point towards a specific consciousness directing the manner in which the story is told.
3. *Editing*—Juxtaposition and joining of elements is how cinema is put together in the edit. The progression of images (and sound in cinema), their reason for being placed in that order, is of utmost importance; I daresay what makes cinema is the ability to manipulate and sculpt time. Beyond the literal linear progression, in comics, abstractions can even be clearly articulated; a master storyteller can show the passage of time within two or three panels even without words, same with showing flashbacks and flash-forwards in how panels interact. So even if comics don't sculpt time the way cinema does, their languages are quite similar.
4. *Economy in Storytelling*—Much like the power of a few panels conveying concepts, the art of the illustrator in choosing *what* few frames to illustrate, *what precise moments* to use to tell the story, is a masterful lesson in packing the most narrative punch within a limited space. Again to compare to cinema, an action scene may take numerous shots (or in animation, numerous shots and even more numerous drawings/still images), but in comics, a whole scene can be conveyed in a few panels. In that sense, the way comics can articulate ideas economically is almost poetic.

How does the history of Filipino komiks respond to the histories of colonialism and imperialism in the Philippines? How have Filipino cartoonists, writers, and artists responded to these histories and other current events through the medium of komiks? How have audiences and critics reacted?

How artists respond to historical and political ideas is as varied as the number of artists tackling those issues—and perhaps even the manner in which these are discussed can vary from the overt to those that may even be executed subconsciously.

If we look at the history of komiks as an offshoot from cartooning—of which political cartoons are a major part—then we can say that komiks dealt with these issues of colonialism and imperialism at the outset. There is a collection of banned cartoons, dating from the days of the Philippine-American War at the end of the nineteenth century showing the atrocities, horrors, and absurdity of the imperialist project.

In a more literal sense, the likes of Francisco Coching, some of whose stories seem to be heavily inspired by Rizal's novels, you can see how the revolutionary-as-hero tropes begin (see *Barbaro* and *El Indio*). In fact, the whole genre of tulisan stories (the outlaw heroes) manifests as the revolutionary zeal that seems imbedded in the DNA of komiks creators.

Comedy was also used as a way to discuss and poke fun at America's cultural influence in the 20th Century, best illustrated by *Kenkoy*—the lead character of which hilariously spoke in phonetic "Americanese," or mish-mash English/Tagalog neologisms.

Perhaps one unique trait in Filipino komiks is the wholesale acceptance of strong female characters. This is less a direct discussion on colonialism and imperialism towards its more patriarchal cultural tenets.

> "If we look at the history of komiks as an offshoot from cartooning—of which political cartoons are a major part—then we can say that komiks dealt with these issues of colonialism and imperialism at the outset."

In the U.S., the superhero must be embodied by an all-powerful man, a good specimen of which is *Superman;* whereas no one batted an eyelash that the Philippines' equivalent came in the Amazonian shape of *Darna*. The fact that creator Mars Ravelo had many strong women characters (and in turn, weak male characters—see *Bondying*, the tale of the adult male who still acts like a baby) alludes to the Philippines' inherent matriarchal society, even if hidden under the veneer of pure machismo.

How has the medium of komiks affected your own style and vision as a filmmaker? Has it had an impact on your methods for visual storytelling in any way?

A strong graphic sensibility comes with everything I choose to film. That starts with framing and extends to production design, to the colour palette, textures, and silhouettes.

Silhouettes is a specific one because all the strong comics artists use these distinct shapes to their advantage—often you can tell who a character is, their emotional state, their personality, all from their silhouette.

I know that has directly affected the way a cast is selected and the way wardrobe affects their physical forms.

The discipline of shot selection owes a lot to my exposure to comics as well. My first professional job was as a storyboard artist in New York City, and my love for sequential storytelling served me very well in that regard.

To this day, I storyboard key sequences. They need not be all complex action set pieces or scenes with complicated requirements like those with VFX. Sometimes I also do it for quiet, dramatic scenes if the blocking and composition can imbed another idea into the scene. This is even more important if the scene is not dialogue heavy. The visuals have to carry much more narrative weight for ideas to be conveyed.

Was there anything surprising in the process of making this film?

There were quite a few surprises in making this film; the most exciting history-geek-wise was getting the chance to go into the vault of the National Library to see Rizal's old notebooks filled with sketches (apparently, he was a doodler during class), the first Filipino komiks, *Pagong at Matsing*, and even his others, such as his emulating the German comic *Max and Moritz* and even his attempt at a medical treatise in comics form while in exile in Dapitan!

Another discovery was that Filipino cinematic auteur Lav Diaz (the man behind eight-hour-plus epics) wrote komiks for years in the eighties. I know that was a revelation to many who only see him as this uncompromising cinematic force. So to see him recall his comedic komiks going by such titles as *Rambo Gid* and *Pinoy Ninja*—and even his stint doing smut komiks at the height of martial law—was quite a trip.

This martial law angle was quite the revelation. It never occurred to me that the entry of so many Filipino artists into the mainstream American comics scene (via Marvel and DC Comics) was a direct result of the clampdown on media during martial law.

The dictatorship actually started this exodus of our best talents. And for those whose nationalistic views made them scoff at the idea of working in America, such as the legendary Francisco Coching, he decided to quit creating komiks altogether because the government was giving him notes on his creations. The last straw was their demand that he change one of his titles to a more "acceptable" type. And so, the country—and the world—was robbed of further stories from this master; it made him stop sharing his gift.

And then, to show the absolute deviousness of the dictatorship, the proliferation of smut, or bomba komiks, was encouraged and backed by the administration itself—even if such material was illegal. Again, much like how bomba films were used in cinema, the bomba komiks served as a way to distract the masses from the abhorrent, abusive policies of the Marcos regime. And for quite a while, it worked!

Continuing with the dovetailed relationship of komiks and cinema, it was also a revelation to see some of the classic films based on komiks. Some of the dramas were helmed by the likes of Lino Brocka; Celso Ad Castillo also did his *Pedro Penduko* (Celso Ad Castillo even ventured into writing komiks), and of course many superhero films were made much like today, best exemplified by the *Darna* films. But one film that astonished me because of its sheer cinematic craft, was based on a work by Francisco Coching—it was the film version of *El Vibora*—directed by none other than National Artist for Cinema Ishmael Bernal! Yes, the man behind *Himala* and *Manila By Night* directed a komiks-based epic adventure picture. It is still a regret that *El Vibora* couldn't be included in the documentary, but to have seen it as part of my research was a gift.

What were some of the challenges in documenting this history and making *Komikero Chronicles* in general?

The first hurdle was getting it greenlit! I had been developing and pitching the film for about three years until the *CineTotoo Film Festival*, under the aegis of the GMA Network, came in and gave grants for documentary features—the first of their kind.

Much like how the medium of komiks is maligned by the arts and general public as being a "low" form of artistic expression, I think most grant-giving bodies felt the same way about the topic. *Why would this "low" form of art be worthy of a documentary*? So it's a big thanks to *CineTotoo* and its festival head Joseph Israel Laban who saw its worth and took a gamble.

Another big challenge was logistical—how to shoot and get all the archival material in the extremely tight schedule and budget. I know a number of fellow documentary filmmakers who dismissed the idea of producing a film for such a small sum and such a rapid pace, but the desire to get the film made and share my enthusiasm for the medium and its history superseded all doubts.

What would you like audiences of your documentary to take away from the film?

It's enough for me to share the fascinating history and the political implications of such a special art form with people. If they catch a bit of the complexity—how our historical situation from the Philippine-American War onwards through martial law affected the medium and, in so doing, affected many lives and our very cultural fabric—then that is icing on the cake.

What trends do you currently see in komiks in the Philippines?

Local komiks is quite an exciting world. You have multiple strains going—multiple schools of thought—which for me means a healthy milieu of creative spirits. In addition to the superhero-based titles that will always be there and the humor-based stories from Pol Medina Jr. (*Pugad Baboy*) and Manix Abrera (*Kiko Machine*), you have more idiosyncratic creators such as Mervin Malonzo creating these highly artistic works like his *Tabi Po* series and his Rizal adaptation *Ang Subersibo*, to a lot of young artists drawing inspiration from Japanese manga. In fact, this manga-fication of Filipino artists is a story that is still in the making, and maybe deserves a critical treatment in a few years.

There's also a good mix of hybrid genres exploring themes of history and traditional folk mythology. Historical pieces like *Mactan 1521*, myth-based stories like *Skyworld*, the fantastical-meets-slice-slice-of-life works of Arnold Arre, allegorical tales like *Elmer* by Gerry Alanguilan, and the paranormal detective stories of *Trese* from writer Budjette Tan and artist Kajo Baldisimo are all available in bookstores and comics specialty shops.

Are you reading any exciting, innovative Filipino komiks that you'd recommend?

Ever since I discovered Mervin Malonzo during the shoot of *Komikero Chronicles* (where he was debuting the first issue of *Tabi Po*), I've followed much of his work, including his science fiction contribution *Terrorium*. A large part is his art—which, because of his fine art background—has a depth and aesthetic sophistication most other artists don't have; put together with his keen interest and knowledge of history and local mythology, it is really inspiring. And anyone with the drive to interpret Rizal for a new generation deserves applause. For other titles, there's the political-satire-as-horror series written by fellow filmmaker Mike Alcazaren; his zombie tale *Patay Kung Patay* has some biting insights—as it should!

I also personally love Rob Cham's silent graphic novels *Light* and *Lost*. They are such sensitive works with gorgeous art—really strong and emotive.

Filipinos have never been lacking in creative talent, and we are all the better for these brave, persevering souls who continue to share their gifts!

3.8 Interview with Fred Van Lente, Author of *The Comic Book History of Comics*

Fred Van Lente is the #1 New York Times—bestselling, award-winning writer of comics like *Archer & Armstrong* (Harvey Award nominee, Best Series), *Action Philosophers!* (American Library Association Best Graphic Novel for Teens), and *Cowboys & Aliens* (with Andrew Foley), the basis for the feature film. His many other titles include *Weird Detective*, *The Comic Book History of Comics*, *The Incredible Hercules* (with Greg Pak), *Taskmaster*, *Marvel Zombies* and *The Amazing Spider-Man*. He lives in Brooklyn with his wife, the playwright Crystal Skillman, and some mostly ungrateful cats.

In this interview, Fred Van Lente unpacks his process with nonfiction comics, particularly The Comic Book History of Comics, *which narrates and illustrates the historical origins of comics in the United States.*

Where did the idea for *The Comic Book History of Comics* come from? What fascinates you about the history of comics?

Ryan Dunlavey and I got our start in nonfiction comics with the surprise success *Action Philosophers,* which started out more or less as a lark. Once we realized there was an audience for this material, we cast about what we could do as a followup, and we realized there was never a history of comics in comic book form. I was always interested in that story—I had volunteered a lot for this organization, the Museum of Comic and Cartoon Art, which was trying to get a comics museum set up in New York City, and had learned a lot there. So it ended up being a kind of no-brainer.

In the introduction of *The Comic Book History of Comics*, Tom Spurgeon wrote: "*The Comic Book History of Comics* abandons the idea of One Great Narrative—that a truth is out there to flatter whatever present we choose to embrace." Can you describe your methodology in making sure a variety of perspectives on the history of comics was presented in your book? What is the danger of "One Great Narrative"?

As humans, our minds have a narrative bent—partly that's just a simplification and oversimplification of reality, to force our world to be logical, manageable. We do that with our day-to-day experience as well as history. But that's not accurate, when you're trying to look at history, which should be a pseudoscientific enterprise, where evidence has greater weight than theory or opinion. So really, it sounds corny—or maybe artsy-fartsy?—but you just assemble as many facts as you can and let them shape the narrative. And when you do that, it's never neat—unlike a fictional story, there's no necessary ending or conclusion that follows from the beginning.

An issue of *The Comic Book History of Comics* by Fred Van Lente and Ryan Dunlavey.

There's a lot of false starts and dead ends. So that's why *Comic Book History* is sort of structured the way it is, in these little mini-essays focusing on specific topics. The early ones have that throughline of Jack Kirby's life, and he is very important, but he's not the end all or be all for the entire medium.

Can you talk about your research process for *The Comic Book History of Comics?* What were the challenges and successes of this particular process?

I did a little bit of everything. I had been interested in comics history for a long time and accumulated a lot of material for a prose biography of Jack Kirby, research that wound up in my and Crystal Skillman's play *King Kirby*. So a lot of magazine articles and photocopies pages from books (this was the late nineties) gave way ultimately to obscure blogs and corners of the internet. One of the greatest research libraries in the world is free to everyone at the New York Public Library, so I made a lot of use of that. Some of the figures in the book were some of the most interviewed people in the world, as much as some presidents, I'd wager, so I had a lot of people's own words to use—for me, like most historians, I think, it's always best to use the direct testimony of people who were living through these events in real time.

What was your collaboration process like with Ryan Dunlavey on *The Comic Book History of Comics?*

We've been working together for a long time. We agree on a project together, and I go off and research and script it, find as much picture and photo reference I can for it, and then he draws it, tweaking stuff here and there, and now he letters it, too. We don't talk a whole lot to each other during the process anymore. . . . It is like we're sharing a brain! It's definitely been the best collaboration of my creative lifetime.

This textbook examines the global history of comics in the beginning chapters. Are there any influential moments, movements, texts, or figures in comics history that have influenced you and your work in any way?

I think for me, being a teenager in the late 80s, I was that generation that experienced the advent of *Dark Knight Returns* and *Watchmen* in real time. They were the real gamechangers that both revolutionized the superhero genre and first made people look at comics more quote-unquote seriously, along with *Maus,* which came out at the same time. I remember I got *Watchmen* for Christmas—this was the first time it was published in book form—and I just sat on the couch in my jammies and robe and read it all in one sitting. I was fourteen or fifteen or so. So instantly I wanted to be Alan Moore.

This was, of course, before I realized it was much better to be Fred Van Lente, but everyone goes through that period, when you're learning how to become and be yourself.

Which lesser-known historical figures, events, movements, moments, or texts did you encounter in your research that comics readers, students, and scholars need to be more aware of or learn more about? Why?

Rodolphe Töpoffer, the Swiss pioneer of graphic novels, was largely unknown to me. That was a cool find. And I think, more than anything else, what struck me was that we set out to do this book as a *general* history. Most comics history is written by fans, and most fans prefer to stay in their individual silos—they write about underground comics, or Batman, or the Golden Age, or what have you. We wanted to show all these things really informed each other, and that was the assumption going in. So I was very surprised when, once we started researching all of this, to see how interconnected it was. How Harvey Kurtzman influenced Alan Moore, how *Archie* influenced *Young Romance,* and on and on and on. Rather than any one thing it was the connection *between* things that really surprised me.

3.9 Interview with Dr. Frederick Aldama, Author of *Your Brain on Latino Comics, Multicultural Comics, and Graphic Borders*

Dr. Frederick Luis Aldama is University Distinguished Scholar, Arts & Humanities Distinguished Professor, and University Distinguished Teacher at The Ohio State University, where he teaches Latino and Latin American literature, comic books, TV, and film in the departments of English, Spanish/Portuguese, and film studies. He is the author, coauthor, and editor of thirty-four books. He is creator of the first documentary on Latinx comics, based on his Eisner-nominated and International Latino Book-finalist, *Latinx Superheroes in Mainstream Comics.* He is designer and curator of *The Planetary Republic of Comics*—a fully searchable website with thousands of entries on comics and creators from around the world. He is founder and director of the Ohio Education Summit Award, Columbus Council Award, and Obama White House Hispanic Bright Spot-winning LASER/ Latinx Space for Enrichment & Research. He was recently inducted into the Academy of Teachers and the National Cartoonists Society.

He is editor and coeditor of eight academic press book series that include: Latino and Latin American Profiles (University of Pittsburgh Press), Latino Cultural Studies (Routledge), Global Media & Race (Rutgers), and Latinographix (Ohio State University Press), a trade-press series that publishes Latinx graphic fiction and nonfiction. He is coeditor of the following book series: Latinx Pop Culture (University of Arizona), Global Latino/a Americas (The Ohio State University Press), Cognitive Approaches to Culture (The Ohio State University Press), and World Comics & Graphic Nonfiction (University of Texas Press). He sits on the board of journals such as *Narrative,* the *Journal of Narrative Theory,* and *INKS: The Journal of the Comics Studies Society.*

Your Brain on Latino Comics by Frederick Luis Aldama.

He sits on the board for the *New Suns: Race, Gender, and Sexuality in the Speculative* (OSU Press) and is a member of the standing board for the *Oxford Bibliographies in Latino Studies.*

How did you develop your work as a scholar, writer, and editor of essays about comics?

I knew already while in the English PhD program at Stanford that I wanted to systematically study comics—especially Los Bros Hernandez. However, I also knew that a dissertation on comics wouldn't get me a job. This was the mid- to late 1990s. Cultural studies was on the rise. It provided a recognizable scholarly platform for those of us who wanted to work on other cultural phenomena than literature. However, I knew that a dissertation (or even part of a dissertation) on Latino/a comics wouldn't get my foot through the door of a job. Even with the great strides forward that we've made, there's still a tremendous amount of prejudice against comics studies in the academy today. Of course, my students write on comics—and TV, film, literature, you name it—but not entire dissertations. And, when they go for campus visits to give talks, I encourage them to enact a form of subterfuge: to stick to a chapter on alphabetic literature, and not pull out the one on comics.

I knew I wanted to write on comics, but knew too that I had to get a job—and tenure. So, once I got both (CU Boulder) and advanced to full professor (The Ohio State University in 2005) I jumped right in and began working on what would become *Your Brain on Latino Comics* (2009). With the exception of a few scholarly pieces, including one by a fellow graduate student at Stanford, Darieck Scott (now a professor at Berkeley), who published on fandom and Los Bros Hernandez, this was terra incognita. To be honest I wasn't sure where to find the Latino comics archive. I wasn't sure if I would have enough primary textual material for a book. Both of these concerns quickly washed away. I discovered very quickly that there was a deep and wide array of Latino/a comic book creators in San Francisco, Los Angeles, Texas, Chicago, New York, and San Juan, Puerto Rico. That is, I discovered that my archive was not a special collections library somewhere. It was a living, breathing, ever-evolving entity.

I began my work. This involved lots of driving, flying, training and so on to meet with the creators and to get hands on their work. It involved lots of phone conversations and, yes, snail mail. It also involved digging back into my own issues of non-Latino mainstream and independent comics to begin to understand how these Latino creators worked within and against this history.

I knew at the time that this was going to be an important book. There was a tremendous urgency driving me to research and write *Your Brain on Latino Comics.* I knew that its publication would help lift Latino comic book narrative creations in the eyes of scholars and others. I knew that it would pave a way for others to come along and continue to deepen and widen the work. I felt like it might also become a hub for Latino/a creators to come to know of one another's work.

In 2009 *Your Brain on Latino Comics* saw the light of day. It had a quick and deep impact. The *San Francisco Chronicle* got wind of it and ran a story on it and Latino comic book creators. At my first public reading from the book at Berkeley's University Press Books, I had scholars and community members eager to learn more about Latino comics. This is where I first met Ricardo Padilla, who went on to cofound the Latino Comics Expo—a yearly event that I've been intertwined with since its inception. The researching and writing of the book brought me to all these incredible Latino creators, from Laura Molina (*The Jaguar*) and Rhode Montijo (*Pablo's Inferno*) to Javier Hernandez (*El Muerto*), Wilfred Santiago (*In My Darkest Hour*), Frank Espinosa (*Rocketo*), Lalo Alcaraz (*Migra*

> "I discovered that my archive was not a special collections library somewhere. It was a living, breathing, ever-evolving entity."

Mouse), Roberta Gregory (*Bitchy Bitch*), Hector Cantú and Carlos Castellanos (*Baldo*), and so many more. Like adding hot water to my Top Ramen, the scholarship brought me deeply into the Latino comics fold.

I knew more had to be done, not just in the area of Latino comic book creations, but also those otherwise swept to the margins: Asian American, Native American, African American, Filipino American comics. I began work with scholars on the collection that would be published as *Multicultural Comics: From* Zap *to* Blue Beetle (2010). I haven't stopped since, not only publishing scholarly books on Latino comics—and world comics generally—but also in choosing to create venues for scholars and practitioners. To legitimize the study of comics in the academy and to ensure that Latino creations were seeing the light of day, with my former graduate student, Christopher González, I launched the scholarly book series, World Comics and Graphic Nonfiction. The scholarly book series has grown to be one of the most robust in the University of Texas Press catalog. All along I knew that something also had to be done to clear pathways for the Latino creators. In 2015 I launched the *Latinographix* trade-press series with Ohio State University Press. This series has swiftly become a hit with the press—and readers across the country. Following in the footsteps of Alberto Ledesma's best-selling and award-winning *Diary of a Reluctant Dreamer* (2017), I published the *New York Times*–lauded *Angelitos* (2018) by Ilan Stavans and Santiago Cohen. And, my edited collection *Tales from la Vida* brings together over eighty original contributions by extraordinary Latinx creators. Their short visual-verbal narratives spring from autobiographical experience and showcase the huge variety of styles and worldviews of today's Latino comic book and visual creators. Eric J. García's *Drawing on Anger: Portraits of U.S. Hypocrisy* (2019) reconstructs and critiques moments in US history, including the disappearance of forty-three Mexican students, genocide and torture in Iraq, femicide along the U.S.-Mexico border, anti-immigration laws, global imperialism, and the conquest of the Americas.

Finally, with the field of Latino comics so robust today I teamed up with Ricardo Padilla (of Latino Comics Expo) and John Jennings to create SÕLCON: Brown and Black Comics Expo. Every fall, dozens of Latino and African American creators convene at The Ohio State University to affirm our communities and our shared histories and struggles. I bus to campus dozens of K–12 students of color learn how to create their own stories in comics, animation, zine, and flip-book forms.

I should add that the field of Latino comics has grown exponentially. Not only in its scholarly study, but also in the number of creators out there making comics. And, unlike the moment when I first began to do my research in the area, today there's much more gender parity.

I pinch myself constantly. This is the time to be working in the field—working to shape a field that is growing rapidly and with great vitality.

Where did your research interests in comics come from?

Ever since I was a kid I'd been particularly taken by the way visuals in comics could tell, or rather *show* a story. Those spinner racks at my local 7/11 and Circle K would keep me pretty busy. And when

I had a quarter or two, I could actually take one home to relish on my own time. It was a way for me to visualize a superheroic life beyond my proximate present—one filled largely with anxiety about money (single mom), language (told not to speak that "dirty Mexican"), and body (awkward and that, unlike my Anglo peers', would never turn golden in the sun). I intuited then what I know intellectually now: a creator's careful *geometrizing* of story could be transformative.

Of course, it would take decades before I would have the time, space, and cultural capital (as a professor) to be able to carefully study just how comic book narratives work. Had I dedicated my early life to drawing, I likely would have figured this out earlier. Indeed, it was the careful study of *Archie* comics and the work of Steve Ditko and Jack Kirby that led Jaime and Gilbert Hernandez to know how to give shape to their *Love and Rockets* stories. They figured out the power of comic book narrative storytelling early on—and through the actual doing of comics. I had to wait decades before I could also figure this out.

Which comics were crucial in your development as a scholar? Why?

This is going to sound very lowbrow, but honestly it was the DC and Marvel comics—and arguably more the Marvel. I say this not only because they were the ones I could get my hands on as a kid—and thus in many ways they formed my aesthetic tastes and choices as an adult—but because in terms of visual shaping devices and geometric design, the good DC and Marvel comics are the bedrock of comic book storytelling. I don't spend time on comics that don't *move* me at the visual level. If they don't have energy at the visual level, then I tend not to want to read or study them. Of course, there's the important moment in comics when someone like Jaime Hernandez came along and combined the countercultural worldview embodied in the underground and alternative comics (R. Crumb, Spain Rodriguez, Art Spiegelman, for instance) with the dynamism of the superhero storytelling mode. There's the moment when Gilbert Hernandez brought the complexity of a novel like *One Hundred Years of Solitude* into his multilayered, multi-character populated *Heartbreak Soup*.

We see this further refined and deepened in the work of all those I study in my books, including the superlative work of Latinas such as Cristy C. Road with her *Spit and Passion*, Kat Fajardo with her *Gringa!*, Kelly Fernandez's *The Ciguapa*, Liz Mayorga with her *Monstrous*, Crystal Gonzales with her *In the Dark*, Grasiela Rodriguez with her *Lunatic Fringe*, Jules Rivera with her *Misfortune High*, Vicko Alvarez with her ScholaR Comics series, and Lila Quintero Weaver with her *Darkroom*, among many others. These are comics at their best. These are the ones to which I choose to dedicate my time and energy to deepen our understanding of how the visual *and* verbal shaping devices can and do *make new* our perception, thought, and feeling about the world we live in and actively transform.

How did you specifically start focusing on documenting the histories of Latino creators, comics, and representation particularly in your book *Your Brain on Latino Comics*?

As I mentioned already briefly, the research was not in library catacombs. It was getting out and meeting the living, breathing creators. And, as I met and learned of one creator, another would pop on the radar and another and another in an ever proliferating string of new encounters. This is also

> "Ever since I was a kid I'd been particularly taken by the way visuals in comics could tell, or rather *show* a story. Those spinner racks at my local 7/11 and Circle K would keep me pretty busy."

why I chose to structure *Your Brain on Latino Comics* in three sections that included a history of representation, a formulation of a theory for reading these comics, and interviews with the actual practitioners. The real pearls of insight come from the creators themselves. They are the ones doing this every day—and many while holding down nine-to-five jobs. They are the ones who have been systematically studying the creation of comics since day one. They are at once the archive—a living breathing one at that—and they are the true scholars of the form.

Your book *Graphic Borders,* which you coedited with Christopher Gonzalez, is an anthology of scholarly essays that explores various Latino creators like Gilbert Hernandez, Los Bros Hernandez (of Love and Rockets), and Lalo Alcaraz, in addition to topics such as otherness, anti-assimilation, *luchadores*, and Latino Spider-Men, like Miles Morales. These essays demonstrate the sheer variety of concerns and aesthetics of Latino creators. From your previous books, *Your Brain on Latino Comics* and *Multicultural Comics: From Zap to* Blue Beetle, until your new books and in this current moment, what changes and/or phenomena have you noticed in Latino-created comics, scholarship, and/or readership?

Indeed, from my first forays to the publication this October of *Latinx Superheroes in Mainstream Comics* (2017) much has changed *and* much has stayed the same. First, as I mentioned, I still advise my students who work on Latino comics to also be sure to include work in the same traditional field of alphabetic literature; I want them to get jobs, and while many departments want someone now who can teach comics, they still need PhDs to teach bread-and-butter courses on literature surveys. And, with Diamond monopolizing distribution of in print comics, it's still difficult for Latino creators to get their comics out there in ways that would allow them to make some kind of living. This said, there's much that has changed, including, importantly, as I already mentioned, the wonderful and wondrous wave of Latina comic book creators. When I first wrote *Your Brain on Latino Comics* there were less than a half-dozen or so Latinas creating comics, including Roberta Gregory (yes, she's Latina). Today, Latina comic book creators might even out the number of Latinos. And, also, back when I wrote *Your Brain* there was only one self-identified LGBTQ Latino comic book creator, Ivan Velez—at least that I knew of. Today, there are dozens of out Latinx creators. It's still a challenging time, both within the academy and for Latino creators, but it's also a tremendously optimistic and exhilarating time.

How do you confront the erasure of people of color, women, and/or queer communities in the history of comics in your work?

From the moment you open the first page to the closing of the last in *Latinx Superheroes in Mainstream Comics* I study the simultaneous move to make visible and erase Latinx identities and experiences. It's an uneven history, too. Certainly, the general trend has been to increasingly over time make visible Latinx subjects in ways that reflect our complexity regionally, sexually, socioeconomically, and politically. So today, for instance, Marvel's lesbian America Chavez gets her own series run and is created by a queer Latinx author. And, DC's recent *Teen Titans* series features Miguel Jose "Bunker" Barragan as gay without much ado. However, there have been moments in early mainstream comic book history when we've seen the creation of some of the most incredibly vital Latino characters like George Perez's White Tiger in the 1970s. And, in the late 1990s, Joe Quesada introduced the world to one of the most extraordinary Latina characters, the deaf mestiza Echo. That's what I mean by uneven history. We've seen great strides forward in general in terms of the creation of intersectional identities and experiences that have been punctuated in earlier epochs by flashes of sophisticated brilliance. As far as work today by Latinx creators, it's mind bogglingly rich and variegated when it comes to intersectional identities and experiences. We have LGBTQ comics. We have Blatino comics. We have Mexipino comics. Take a quick glance at the thirty-five-plus creators that I interview in *Latinx Comic Book Storytelling: An Odyssey by Interview,* and you'll see what I'm talking about. You name the intersectional identity, and we have it—and we are recreating these experiences right, left, and center. It's a mind bogglingly extraordinary moment in the history of Latinx comic book creation and reception. Extraordinary!

"It's a mind bogglingly extraordinary moment in the history of Latinx comic book creation and reception. Extraordinary!"

Which narratives typically produced about comics history do you seek to resist?

Most scholars of comics put at arm's length this odd prejudice that continues to hang around the neck of comics and its study: that somehow comic books are part of an earlier, less formed part of our reading and mind development—with the novel as somehow the peak of our development. That somehow comics aren't as sophisticated a narrative form and that we grow out of it; and those like me, who continue to relish in their storyworlds, are somehow academically less advanced—intellectual simpletons.

I'm also suspicious of scholarship that tries to justify or legitimize the study of comics by yoking it to art or literary histories. That somehow, we can locate its evolution in early epochs of art or literary creation. I'm of the mind that comics are its own unique narrative form: while it clearly draws from visual art, cinema, literature, and the like, it's really its own unique storytelling phenomena. This is to say, to really understand how comics tick, we can't simply superimpose models of analysis learned in the study of art or literature or cinema. We have to develop a set of concepts and a grammar of techniques that grow from the comics themselves.

Do you teach comics in the classroom? If so, what is your approach? Which texts do you use and for what reason?

I feel very fortunate that I teach at a university that has a critical mass of scholars working on comics and that is home to the Billy Ireland Cartoon and Comics Research Library. Not only is it amazing to have colleagues to share ideas with—and of course the vast archive of the Billy Ireland—but it also means that my students have all variety of resources and support for their work; and, of course, these students come to OSU for precisely that reason. It also means that we can have courses on the books just on comics or variations like literature and comics or film and comics. On the books forever and eternity. That means I get to teach this stuff—and every year, and nearly every semester. I'm looking forward to November 2018 when the Billy Ireland will host the *Tales from la Vida* exhibit, showcasing much of the original storytelling artwork by Latino creators that makes up my edited collection.

To my earlier point about needing to develop our own vocabulary and concepts for analyzing comics, I do so in my courses by including readings directly from theorist-practitioners like Stan Lee and Will Eisner, as well as Matt Madden and Jessica Abel, among others. Of course, I include *Your Brain on Latino Comics* and *Latinx Comic Book Storytelling: An Odyssey by Interview*. But first and foremost, I include a rich array of comics—from the work of African American John Jennings to those of my Latinx compadres to Lynda Barry, Alison Bechdel, and Kelly Sue DeConnick, among many others. It's here that the students grow a critical vocabulary that enriches the complex riches held within the comic book pages.

Why is the medium of comics useful and effective in diving into issues such as race, gender, and intersectionality?

First, it's a question of materiality. What I mean by this is that a creator like Kat Fajardo or Breena Nuñez or Serenity Se or Christa R. Road can create a powerful narrative of Latina intersectional identity for those like me to engage with as long as they have access to paper, pencil, and ink—and a scanner and Internet. Of course, they are exercising a lifetime of growing extreme skills in the art of visual-verbal storytelling, but with rather inexpensive means they can effect great change in a person, in people, in the world.

Second, careful use of color, color washes, lines, geometric shapes, panels, gutter placement, and the like can and do open eyes to different ways of understanding race, sexuality, gender, and class identities and experiences. The careful composition of a panel where we only see a boot up in the air descending to an unseen person invites us to gap fill the racist violence that's about to happen against a person of color. The careful geometrizing of character and action suture us deeply into the moment in ways that has lasting effects. The careful use of diacriticals and typographic markers can indicate a character's speaking another language like Spanish even though we are reading it in English; Gilbert Hernandez has used this to call attention to a deep prejudice our society: how monolingual Spanish speakers are often misjudged as somehow less intelligent by English-only speakers.

Third, given that comics use the visual mode as the dominant ingredient in its storyworld construction, comics can actually be a wonderful way for non-English readers in the U.S. to immerse themselves in narrative worlds; my abuelita could read English, but only at a basic level; she never had a formal education. She could indulge in comic book storyworlds, even if written in English.

> "Comics is neither a European nor a U.S. cultural phenomena. It's global."

Which historical trends or events do you think more students and readers of comics should learn more about?

Students need a good, solid understanding of the evolution of comics—and from around the world. This is why I agreed to write for Routledge the book *World Comics: The Basics*. It's also why I created and curate the website Planetary Republic of Comics, with its hundreds of searchable entries on comics from around the world. In my books and curated website I want students to be able to know what has been happening in South Korea, the African and Indian continents, China, Russia, the Philippines, you name it. Comics is neither a European nor a U.S. cultural phenomena. It's global.

What would you tell students who are learning how to close read and analyze comics? Any strategies that are useful for you?

First, I provide basics in understanding the importance of geometry—and how the creators distill and reconstruct the building blocks of reality by using the principles of geometry. As I mentioned earlier, theorist-practitioners like Stan Lee, Will Eisner, Matt Madden, and Jessica Abel are excellent for providing students with the critical concepts and vocabulary. This also forces the students to slow down and really unpack all the elements used to give shape to a panel, series of panels, page of panels, etc. I usually throw up on a large PowerPoint slide a panel or series of panels for the students to analyze on the spot. This provides them with practice runs for the kind of analytic work I expect them to do in the formal writing assignments.

3.10 Interview with Dr. Deborah E. Whaley, Author of *Black Women in Sequence: Re-inking Comics, Graphic Novels, and Anime*

Dr. Deborah Elizabeth Whaley is an artist, curator, and writer. She is currently professor of American studies, African American studies, and is the senior scholar for digital arts and humanities at the University of Iowa, where she also serves as director of the graduate certificate in public digital humanities. Her research and teaching fields include the institutional history, theories, and methods of American studies, American cultural history, comparative ethnic studies, Black cultural studies, popular culture, the visual arts, and digital humanities. Dr. Whaley has published original art, poetry, as well as articles on social movements, popular culture, fine art, documentary photography, and film. She has been a resident visiting scholar at the Center for Cultural Studies at the University of California, Santa Cruz, and was a recipient of a grant from the Monroe Trotter Institute for Black Culture for her research on responses to 9/11 in Black expressive art and in the public sphere. In 2010, she was cocurator, with Kembrew McLeod, of the University of Iowa Museum of Art exhibition, "Two Turntables and a Microphone: Hiphop Contexts Featuring Harry Allen's Part of the Permanent Record; Photos From the Previous Century." Professor Whaley's first book was *Disciplining Women: Alpha Kappa Alpha, Black Counterpublics, and the Cultural Politics of Black*

Sororities (SUNY, 2010). In it, she examines the cultural practices, cultural work, and politics of the oldest historically Black sorority. Her current book project, *Black Women in Sequence: Re-inking Comics, Graphic Novels, and Anime* (2015) explores graphic novel production and comic book fandom, looking in particular at African, African American, and multiethnic women as deployed in television, film, animation, and print representations of comic book and graphic novel characters.

Cover artwork from Deborah E. Whaley, "Black Women in Sequence."

How did you develop your work as a scholar/academic in the field of comics?

I did training in cartooning as a teenager. I also do broader work on popular culture as an academic, and comics studies is a homology of my artistic and academic work and training. I regularly participate in comic art podcasts, reader and artist communities in sequential art, which maintains my grounding in the field. I am a curator, and I work with museums and art centers, which allows for an opportunity to connect with, learn from, and showcase the work of artists and writers in the field. I recently wrote the introduction to an exhibition catalogue on sequential art titled *'Toonskin*, which was curated by the artist Kenya Robinson. I am also coediting the *Keywords in Comics Studies* (New York University Press) with Ramzi Fawaz and Shelley Streeby.

Which comics were crucial in your development as a scholar? Why?

Mainstream comic titles such as *Catwoman*, Black-themed comic strips such as *Jumpstart*, *The Boondocks*, and *Where I'm Coming From*, television shows such as *Batman*, and the Marvel and DC films. All of these forms of media act as a nice launching pad to discuss identity and power.

Where did your research interests in comics come from?

My research interest in comics comes from my work as an artist, my personal readership and affinity with characters, and my academic interests in visual and popular culture.

How and why did you specifically start focusing on the histories and work of Black women cartoonists in *Black Women in Sequence*?

My goal was to fill a gap in the literature, and I felt the characters, artists, and readers deserve recognition and scholarly treatment. No substantial work on Black women in sequential art existed before my book. There are a few articles and some books that discuss Black women in comics, but these publications mostly focus on male characters. Even anthologies that had chapters on female characters left little room to explore Black women at length. Thus, I see my book as an intellectual and artistic intervention.

> "My goal was to fill a gap in the literature, and I felt the characters, artists, and readers deserve recognition and scholarly treatment."

Can you describe your research methodology for your book in addition to any challenges you encountered?

My methodology is very interdisciplinary. I did archival research, researched government archives, looked at primary materials, culled through secondary literature, interviewed artists, writers, and talked to readers. I participated in fandom events and comics chatrooms. Because a monograph on the topic did not previously exist, I had to create my own archive of textual, contextual, literary, historical, and cultural documents, too.

How do you confront the erasure of Black women in the history of comics in your work?

I counteract the erasure of Black women in comics via podcasts, museum exhibitions, art centers, classrooms, speaking engagements, comic-cons, and intermedia to showcase the work of Black women and Black female characters.

Which narratives typically produced about comics history do you seek to resist?

I do not seek to resist any particular title or form of sequential art. Having said that, I do seek narratives and images that broaden our understanding of the multiplicity of blackness.

How have Black women creators shaped the medium and storytelling function of comics?

Black women provide intersectional analysis and insights of power dynamics regarding race, gender, sexuality, ability, and class. In the last chapter of my book, I categorize several areas that Black women creators, artists, and writers are working within, including Afropunk, Afrofuturism, Afrophantasmagoria, Afrogoth, and Afroanime.

Which comics and creators do you seek to highlight in your work? Why?

Writers and artists I highlight include Jackie Ormes, Nara Walker, Leisl Adams, Rashida Jones, Afua Richardson, Barbara Brandon, Calyn Pickens Rich, Michelle Billingsly, and Ashley Woods. All of these women forge new ways of seeing nationmaking, blackness, gender, and sexuality.

Which historical trends or events do you think more students and readers of comics should learn more about?

Historical trends and events that students and readers would benefit from learning more about include the history of characters in the early twentieth century in mainstream media, the interventions of black comic artists in the early to mid-early to mid–twentieth century, and a full understanding of the breadth of creators and images today. A transnational frame in researching and learning about comics is also helpful, including work done across the African diaspora and the way blackness is deployed through sequential art throughout Asia and Europe.

What would you tell students who are learning how to close read and analyze comics? Any strategies that are useful for you?

It is a good idea for students to pay attention to formalism, visual aesthetics, captions and titles, and the narrative. Researchers and students benefit from assessing the social and historical contexts that sequential art forms reference. Also, distribution and production is key, and knowing about the artist or writer can help provide information about the artistic production.

3.11 Cartoonists on Comics History

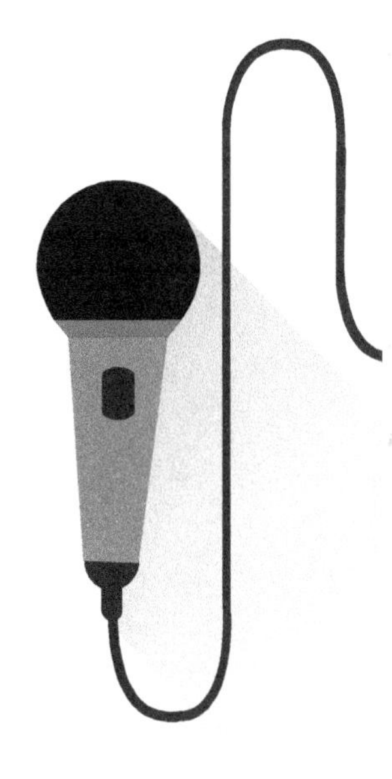

Question

Are there any influential moments, movements, or figures in comics history that have influenced you and your work in any way?

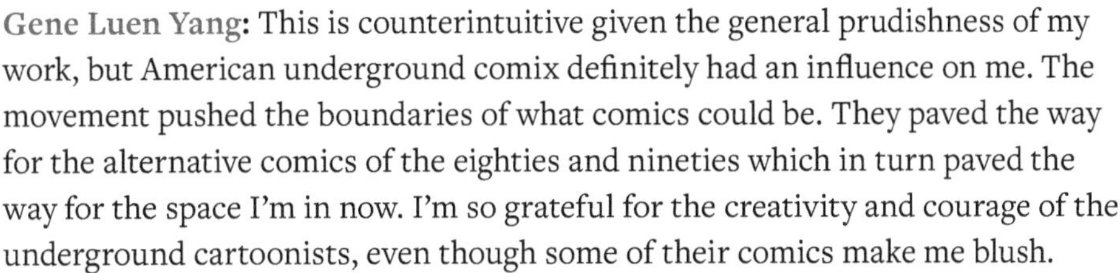

Gene Luen Yang: This is counterintuitive given the general prudishness of my work, but American underground comix definitely had an influence on me. The movement pushed the boundaries of what comics could be. They paved the way for the alternative comics of the eighties and nineties which in turn paved the way for the space I'm in now. I'm so grateful for the creativity and courage of the underground cartoonists, even though some of their comics make me blush.

Yumi Sakugawa: I think I was very aware of the time when manga and anime were becoming more mainstream in American pop culture, not an esoteric subculture, sometime in the early 2000s. I want to say it was also around that decade when I noticed that graphic novels were taken more seriously by mainstream newspapers and reviewed in book sections as legitimate works of fiction, and as a young college student figuring out how to make art and comics, I got swept into that tide and started making comics that weren't about superheroes, shoujo-manga influenced, and inspired by my favorite literary short stories. And so it was in that particular window of time I was exposed to the works of Adriane Tomine, Craig Thompson, Anders Nielsen, Esther Pearl Watson, Bryan Lee O'Malley, Jillian Tamaki—to name a few.

Sonny Liew: If you mean just from the U.S. . . . I suppose *Mad Magazine* would have been one. My dad brought home a copy one day, and I remember being completely mesmerized. The irreverent attitude towards authority, the quality of the satire I think helped shaped my own attitude towards the world.

Taneka Stotts: Jackie Ormes was the first female African American cartoonist. I did not learn this information until I was well in my years. I could blame a lot of things for this information not being readily available, but I feel this is a start as far as a figure in comics who is both influential and underrepresented.

Lucy Knisley: I really think that Bill Watterson had a major impact on the way the world relates to comics and certainly how I learned the importance of writing in comics. A lot of the newspaper comics rely on gags and familiar characters—consistency to the point of monotony—but here was an artist who would deviate wildly in style, both artistically, in format, and in the writing, in order to play with the reader. It was genius, and I am still in awe. I was also very impressed with Lynda Barry's comics, because they didn't rely on that old gag pattern, but rather seemed to me to have been written by a kid like me. It was this instinctive drawing act that all kids do to tell stories, but in published comic form. In high school, I was blown away by *Strangers in Paradise* by Terry Moore. This was a traditional floppy comic, but about this relationship between two women and their friend. I still think that was a huge and amazing deviation from what was happening in comics then and really pushed a lot of the interpersonal comics we see today into being. And of course, Allison Bechdel had a major, MAJOR impact on me when *Fun Home* came out and intricate memoir was given a figurehead in graphic novels.

“Jackie Ormes was the first female African American cartoonist. I did not learn this information until I was well in my years. I could blame a lot of things for this information not being readily available, but I feel this is a start as far as a figure in comics who is both influential and underrepresented.”
- Taneka Stotts

Leela Corman: Well, the Hernandez Brothers, first and foremost. And *RAW*, in every way. Both the American and international cartoonists they ran. I'd never seen French comics before, or African ones, for example. Phoebe Gloeckner's work hit me like an incendiary device. Later, going to France had a huge impact on me. In terms of pure art, the Belgians are kicking our asses and probably always will be. You can't beat Judith Van Istendael, for example, or Brecht Evens, or Dominique Goblet, or really any of them. There are also amazing comics coming out of the Arab world, Africa, you name it. I'm not as familiar as I should be because I spend most of my time these days working, not reading other comics. I need to remedy that!

MariNaomi: Probably riot grrl zines, although I didn't really know about the riot grrl movement at the time. Looking back, that's what seemed to be feeding the creators I admired.

Ron Wimberly: Most of my influences come from outside of comics, but I can say that Hokusai; Simplicissimus; *Métal Hurlant* and *(A Suivre)*; Shirato Sanpei and Garo; Bernard Krigstein have had significant influence on me.

Hokusai is the father of my style. He was my intro to ukiyo e, and looking at his work I first started to think about the symbol versus representation paradigm.

I forget how I found Simplicissimus . . . somehow toying around on the web—I found the Coconino Press archives, and they had a lot of work from Simplicissimus on there. The work was bold and political. It was human. The strong graphic quality of the work, no doubt influenced by the movements of the time and necessitated by the printing process . . . it was the missing link between contemporary European comics and the postimpressionists and the decadents of the last century. Also, that's where I discovered Bruno Paul. His art life empowered me; he worked in many different disciplines.

Discovering *Métal Hurlant* and *(A Suivre)* was like discovering Wu Tang. Narrative visions that somehow remain independent while adding value to each other collectively.

Shirato Sanpei, like Bruno Paul, and Bernard Krigstein made me feel like I wasn't alone in believing that creativity is a radical act. That a life of design is political.

Rafael Rosado: As a teenager I discovered underground and alternative comics like *Love and Rockets* and *Eightball*, and I realized that you could tell all kinds of stories in comics, not just superhero yarns. I'm also a great admirer of Moebius's work, both his science fiction work, and his work as Jean Giraud. I also love French comics (bandes dessinées), in particular, the "ligne claire" artists like Yves Chaland, Joost Swarte, and Serge Clerc. And I've also been influenced, on an artistic and a personal level, by Jeff Smith's epic tale, *Bone.*

Sophie Goldstein: The North American alternative comics movement that comprises the publications of Fantagraphics, Drawn & Quarterly, and Top Shelf among others has probably been the biggest influence on my own work. That's what I could find in the bookstores and libraries, years before I went to my first indie comic show. If it wasn't for those publishers, I wouldn't even know what was possible. Women are kicking butt in comics now, and some of my biggest influences now are barely older than me, like Eleanor Davis, Jillian Tamaki and Liz Suburbia.

Belle Yang: I went to Beijing in 1986 to study traditional painting. I came to recognize that Chinese paintings incorporated written characters together with images quite naturally. This is largely because the written language is comprised of picto- and ideographs. Later I learned that the horizontal Chinese scroll was not meant to be seen unrolled but revealed a bit at a time. It was a premodern form of motion picture: the scene revealed one section at a time, just like the comic book format. Certainly Speigelman's *Maus* was of utmost influence. I read him early and realized, hey, I can tell a Chinese story using comics! I only wish I had started writing and drawing *Forget Sorrow* immediately after I read *Maus*.

Danica Novgorodoff: I think I'm drawn to European authors like Joann Sfar, Emmanuel Guibert, Marjane Satrapi, Gipi, David Beauchard, Clement Oubrerie, and Marguerite Abouet because they're making adult literary work (in both fiction and nonfiction), which is a somewhat less popular form in the U.S. Authors using more experimental formats, like Richard McGuire, Anders Nilsen, and Lauren Redniss, have also very much influenced the way I think about comics, in that they're pushing literary boundaries with their work rather than just making stories "easier" to read by adding pictures.

" I rarely saw people like me on the pages of any comics, but the white-male-centric approach to so many American comics shut me out immediately. I was much more drawn to and influenced by shoujo manga because those stories respected their female characters and were usually made by women. "
- Ashanti Fortson

Nilah Magruder: I'd say Dwayne McDuffie was a huge influence. At the time that *Static Shock* became a television show, I was warring with the idea of black characters taking a central role in science fiction and fantasy. There weren't really any examples to follow when I was a kid, I didn't know about Octavia Butler or Samuel R. Delany, and I was used to black superheroes taking a backseat to their white counterparts. I was struggling to reconcile my own identity with the stories I wanted to read and to tell, and then *Static Shock* came along. That was a big push for me to embrace my skin and begin focusing on blackness in my own work.

Ashanti Fortson: I've always felt pretty disconnected from most American comics. I never read them when I was a child; in fact, I found many mainstream American comics actively offputting. I rarely saw people like me on the pages of any comics, but the white-male-centric approach to so many American comics shut me out immediately. I was much more drawn to and influenced by shoujo manga because those stories respected their female characters and were usually made by women.

Racism and misogyny are still a problem in comics today, but the ability to find amazing work online by people whose voices have been shut out of mainstream American comics is one of the best things to happen to comics.

Jenny Lin: Probably the movement of underground comics with artists who specifically worked with subject matter that was banned under the Comics Code. When I learned about this stuff while in my undergrad, I really was inspired by the really subversive content and weird unresolved narratives. I feel uncomfortable about R. Crumb now, but his work really influenced me at some point.

This lead me, later on, to be interested in Dan Clowes and Chris Ware and to especially like the works that capture a feeling of alienation and strangeness in really mundane experiences but also, with Clowes, stories such as "Like a Velvet Glove Cast in Iron," which take this reader on a really fantastical trip in such a dreamy/nightmarish satisfying way.

> "If it weren't for women like Julie Doucet and the zine movement, who fought hard to have her voice heard not only in comics—but in alternative (back when this word still meant "out of the mainstream in an anarchist punk way") and underground comics, an area where both women and queer people have a platform to be as loud and ugly as we want—I wouldn't be here."
> - Andi Santagata

Allison Bechdel has been important for me, as well, in the way that she has represented lesbian characters in *Dykes to Watch Out For* and really has them play out scenarios that reflect the time that they were created in. I love that the characters change over time or are confronted with changing politics. Also, her autobiographical works, *Fun Home* and "Are you my mother?" are really amazingly developed works on such a difficult subject matter to broach (parents and family in general). I don't feel like I work like her at all but I hugely admire her work.

I really loved reading Ulli Lust's *Today Is the Last Day of the Rest of Your Life* because it was such an ambitious, lengthy memoir. I really loved being able to immerse myself in her story and appreciated the way that she used the medium to describe such traumatic, disturbing experiences. It felt generous of her to share this.

Andi Santagata: If it weren't for women like Julie Doucet and the zine movement, who fought hard to have her voice heard not only in comics—but in alternative (back when this word still meant "out of the mainstream in an anarchist punk way") and underground comics, an area where both women and queer people have a platform to be as loud and ugly as we want—I wouldn't be here.

The underground comics movement of the seventies or eighties, starting with the birth of Weirdo comix and other underground publications, not only set the stage for the modern style of cartooning, but also proved that comics outside of the mainstream—particularly autobio—sells just as well.

The other big influence would be the life and times of Jack Kirby, which seems like a broad stroke, but is a lasting influence and cautionary tale to many young cartoonists: As you probably know, Kirby collaborated, drew, created, and wrote many heroes in the Marvel universe we're fond of—the most egregious example being Spider-Man. (Stan Lee famously asked Kirby to make Spidey "look less scary," Kirby refused, leading to the Spider-Man we know today.) Kirby, who didn't have a good contract with Marvel, ended up getting screwed out of his pay cut, losing his rights, being refused meetings with his former partner Stan, and, in a bold move by Marvel, couldn't even get some of his original art back before he died. Though many cartoonists still remember him as a tour de force, Kirby's become a cautionary tale about the industry, standing your ground, and *reading your damn contracts.*

Rina Ayuyang: I always wanted to be one of those newspaper comic strip artists, the ones who had the whole draftsman's table studio setups like what Charles Schulz or Milt Caniff had, but I think it was the alternative/indie, DIY mini-comic/zine scene that influenced the way I define and approach my comics. I especially look at the Los Bros Hernandez DIY, punk aesthetic and how they came up with *Love and Rockets* in the eighties. They made their comics their own way and created characters and stories that were unique and personal to them, but also universal. I've also been influenced by the sketchbook work (carnets) of a lot of French cartoonists like Aude Picault, Jochen Gerner and Joann Sfar.

Jade Lee: A lot of my creative influences are not strictly categorized in comics form. Some of my most longstanding sources of inspiration come from Hayao Miyazaki films, role playing video games such as *Pokémon,* and traditional Chinese brush paintings. Speaking very generally, my work is also inspired by the slice of life genre in anime and manga. I'm often interested in narratives that observe the complexities of human relationships more so than conflict-to-resolution based plot progression.

3.12 Interview with Jeff Yang and Keith Chow, Editors of *Secret Identities: The Asian American Superhero Anthology* and *Shattered*

Keith Chow is one of the editors of the Asian American comics anthologies *Secret Identities* and *Shattered* and the founder of TheNerdsofColor.org. His writing has also appeared in the *New York Times,* the *Center for Asian American Media,* and *NBC News.* Follow him on Twitter at @the_real_chow and @TheNerdsofColor.

Jeff Yang is the author of *I Am Jackie Chan: My Life in Action* and editor of the graphic novel anthologies *Secret Identities and Shattered.*

In this interview, Chow and Yang discuss their experiences with creating the idea behind Secret Identities, *the Asian American superhero anthology, and its followup,* Shattered, *and their process with editing both books. They confront issues of racism, stereotyping, erasure, or the lack of representation of Asian communities in comics and media and discuss their endeavors to create publication and community space for Asian American creators and readers.*

In the preface of *Secret Identities*, the reader encounters the comic book cover of *The Y-Men,* which features extremely Orientalist and stereotypical Asian superheroes, one of which is a character whose head is a grain of rice, and proclaims, "Special Delivery from Riceman . . . Pork-Friend Pain!" Our protagonist is an Asian American boy who is reading this comic who appears disgusted and, perhaps, shocked by this representation. He then encounters friends who, while playing make-believe superheroes, try to cast him as an Asian superhero and later, a knock-off Hello Kitty instead of his self-selected Superman.
Can you talk about your own experiences with erasure, stereotyping, and racism that propelled the development of *Secret Identities*? What other kinds of conversations did you have with each other as this book developed?

Keith Chow: *Secret Identities* came about when Jeff interviewed me for a column he was writing at the time. I used to work in marketing at Diamond Comic Distributors, the world's largest distributor of comics and graphic novels. The premise of the column was about the prevalence of Asian American comic creators and fans but stunning lack of Asian American superhero characters. Neither of us could point to an Asian American superhero we identified with—though that has changed a lot in the decade-plus since that initial conversation. The closest superhero who reflected the Asian American experience we could think of was Clark Kent/Superman—thick glasses, black hair, refugee, undocumented immigrant, transracial adoptee, a bridge between two cultures, multiple names in different languages, etc. I think we set out back in 2006–2007 to create a universe of characters that accurately reflected our lived experiences.

Cover artwork from eds. Jeff Yang, Parry Shen, Keith Chow, and Jerry Ma, Secret Identities: The Asian American Superhero Anthology.

Jeff Yang: Regarding the notion of erasure and stereotyping, I think that both of us bonded over the fact that as Asian Americans, we knew a ton of fellow Asian Americans who were comics fans—many of whom grew up reading comics to learn English or embraced comics as a means of escape from the social (and parental) pressures we faced in the real world. Superman was one mythological arc that we projected ourselves on, but there were also the X-Men, a group of "gifted" but outcast students who couldn't openly express themselves; there was Spider-Man, a science nerd from Queens who was always worried about his mother (well, his Aunt May) finding out about his extracurricular activities and who faced bullying and the challenge of overcoming his shyness and lack of self-confidence. These are classically familiar archetypes for all comics geeks, of course, but there was something particularly resonant about them for us.

Because there are so many Asian American comics fans, there are also a huge number of comics creators of Asian descent. There's a very thin line between fan and creator in the comics world. And yet, as Keith noted above, there were few Asian American representations for us to turn to "on panel." Just like with TV and movies, we had to make do with imagining Clark Kent as Clark Kang, and Peter Parker as Peter Park.

Secret Identities was our attempt to fill in that vacuum, by inviting the many creators we knew to write and draw original stories that reflected our faces, voices and realities. *Shattered* took that one step further, by exploring the negative images, often oppressive and hateful, that shape our reality—pushing back on stereotypes and caricatures of Asians with the goal of defeating them, or recapturing them.

What was your collaboration process for editing this book?

Keith Chow: Each of us had various responsibilities, whether it be outreach to artists or dealing with the publisher or press. Jerry Ma is our art director and responsible for the look and feel of the books and the universe. Parry Shen was a tremendous project manager who made sure all the trains ran on time. Comics is an inherently collaborative process—writers, pencilers, inkers, letterers, all with specific skill sets. As editors, it was our job to not only pair the right artist with his/her writer, but to ensure there was a cohesive theme to the whole book.

Jeff Yang: The most interesting thing that I think we committed to was bringing in as broad a swath of voices as we could—including many authors and artists who'd never created comics before. We found people with really interesting stories to tell, helped to shape those stories and paired wordsmiths with illustrators. That matchmaking process actually led to some amazing ongoing collaborations, such as Gene Luen Yang's partnership with Sonny Liew on *The Shadow Hero*. They first met each other and worked together through *Secret Identities*!

> “The closest superhero who reflected the Asian American experience we could think of was Clark Kent/Superman—thick glasses, black hair, refugee, undocumented immigrant, transracial adoptee, a bridge between two cultures, multiple names in different languages, etc.”

What was your publishing process like for *Secret Identities*?

Keith Chow: From the start we had a willing partner in The New Press. They weren't used to publishing comics since they were/are primarily an academic publisher, but I think the message of our book fits as comfortably on a cultural studies as in your local comic shop.

Jeff Yang: The process was interesting, in that we were creating a kind of alchemy—gathering stories and art together from all over, and then expanding on the stories with another layer: We had the conceit that all of these stories were taking place IN A SHARED UNIVERSE. We actually suggested to people connections BETWEEN stories, to weave together a continuity from unrelated tales. We thought that was important because universes can survive when individual heroes cannot.

Which narratives typically produced about comics history, creation, and consumption do you seek to resist?

Keith Chow: I think the general perception of comics creators and fans is that they are straight, white, and male. While that is definitely a segment of the population, it is not the only voice that should be heard. Comics are for everyone.

Jeff Yang: Definitely the notion that we as Asian Americans are able to render other peoples' visions, but have no imagination of our own. I think that Asian Americans have been proving that in a whole swath of other ways recently too!

What has been the reception and readership for *Secret Identities*?

Keith Chow: I think it has been generally positive. To be honest, the books are probably seen as more of an academic exercise or cultural artifact than as necessarily a commercial phenomenon. What I mean is that the books definitely serve a function in a college classroom about comics or Asian American studies because of the media message it presents. *SI* really opened the door to the idea that Asian *American* superheroes are a feasible thing.

Jeff Yang: Well, I would be less humble about the books than Keith would be! Even if they didn't sell a million copies, SI has gone through two printings, and I run into people all the time who say it's one of their favorite graphic novels . . . so that to me is plenty.

How has *Secret Identities* served as a catalyst for Asian American writers and creators to generate and publish full-length comics?

Keith Chow: Like I said earlier, in the decade since *SI* was initially conceived, you've seen a plethora of Asian American comic characters that have broken through into the public consciousness. Think Ms. Marvel or Amadeus Cho or Glenn from *The Walking Dead*. I'm not saying *SI* is responsible for that, but I think it helped. Many of the creators responsible for the rise of Asian American comics were featured in both *SI* books: Gene Yang, Greg Pak, Amy Chu, Ming Doyle, for example.

Jeff Yang: In some ways, I feel like *Secret Identities* and *Shattered* really did empower Asian American comics creators to create Asian American comics in the "mainstream" comics world—that is to say, superhero comics. Folks like Gene and Derek Kirk Kim were of course already doing Asian American stories in indie comics, but by pushing discussion about our absence in the mainstream into the forefront, I think it got editors at Marvel and DC to open their minds to the possibility of letting Asian American creators create Asian American heroes.

The first volume of *Secret Identities* was published in 2009; the second volume in 2012. What lessons did you learn about yourselves as editors and curators from the first volume to the second?

Keith Chow: I personally feel *Shattered* is the stronger book, both thematically and editorially. It helped that we went into the second book with a strongly defined vision: to deconstruct some of the most prevalent stereotypes of Asians that exist in Western fiction.

Jeff Yang: I agree with Keith—we built the world in *Secret Identities*, and *Shattered* allowed us to live in it. It was great bringing in a lot of the original creators for a second volume as well. The challenge for us was really staying close to our vision of exploring stereotypes while also expanding the mythology behind the world.

I've noticed that both volumes don't include as many women creators. Can you talk about this and other challenges you've encountered while working on *Secret Identities*?

Keith Chow: We have been dinged in the past for subtitling our books as "the" Asian American anthologies. We take full responsibility for either book not being as representative of the community as it could have and should have been. That said, we are very cognizant of how important it is to showcase the diversity of the Asian American experience and strive to be as inclusive as possible in the future.

Jeff Yang: We actively sought out as diverse a lineup as we could, in ethnicity, gender, sexual orientation; it's always been our aim to be as inclusive as possible (as it should, given that the project began with the desire for inclusion!). We've tried to increase the diversity of our creator pool with every volume, and we hope the next one gets us closer to where we ultimately want to be in that regard!

Why is the medium of comics useful and effective in diving into issues such as race, gender, sexuality, and intersectionality?

Keith Chow: The comics medium is naturally intersectional. The interaction between text and images engages the reader's brain on multiple levels. There's also a precision to sequential art that lends itself to tackling complex issues in a simpler way. Also, it's important to note that consumers of comics who are POC, women, gay, trans, disabled, etc., have *always* been around. Many of us are not new to comics, but what you're increasingly seeing are those communities finally giving voice to those issues in comics whereas before, comics creators either ignored or were oblivious of these communities. Independent press, the web, social media, crowdfunding have all democratized comics so that these voices are no longer invisible.

Jeff Yang: Comics allow you to tell both epic and intimate stories—and sometimes both at the same time. As Keith notes, the narrative power of text plus image is uniquely impactful, and together they allow you to communicate in ways that either alone sometimes cannot. Marginalized creators don't always have the resources to make movies or television about their lives and the issues that drive them, but anyone can pick up a pen.

Both of you now cohost podcasts on popular culture and Asian America (*The Nerds of Color* and *They Call Us Bruce,* respectively), in which you discuss the problematic nature of white-washing in Hollywood (for example, *Ghost in the Shell,* which stars Scarlett Johansson in the lead role written as a Japanese woman) and other troubling phenomena. You've both also showcased works by Asian American artists and writers on your shows. How else have you been centering the Asian American stories in your current work?

Keith Chow: I'll let Jeff speak to his new podcast, but I started *The Nerds of Color* because I wanted a space that could discuss nerd culture specifically through a POC lens. The mission of *NOC* is to

> "Comics allow you to tell both epic and intimate stories—and sometimes both at the same time."

provide a platform for all POC voices to comment on the culture and show solidarity among every community.

Jeff Yang: *They Call Us Bruce* began as just a way for Phil Yu (who runs the Angry Asian Man blog) and I to record the conversations we frequently had without a microphone in front of us. But it's really caught fire, and it has been both unfortunate and fortunate that there's been plenty to talk about recently (from a negative perspective, anyway!). We began bringing guests onto the show with our second episode, recognizing that there are a lot of voices beyond ours that we wanted to include. The last episode we released, featuring Sarah Kuhn (*Heroine Complex*) and Rebecca Sun (*The Hollywood Reporter*) talking about *Ghost in the Shell*, and the one we're about to release (featuring Lilan Bowden of *Andi Mack*), were particularly great from my perspective. We're doing these weekly and look forward to hopefully doing them for a long time!

3.13 Interview with Ryan North, Creator of the webcomic, *Dinosaur Comics*

Ryan North is the (*New York Times*–bestselling, Eisner Award–winning) creator of *Dinosaur Comics*, the coeditor of the Machine of Death series, and the author of *To Be or Not to Be*, the choose-your-own-path version of *Hamlet!* He has written the *Adventure Time* comic and writes *The Unbeatable Squirrel Girl* for Marvel Comics, whom you might know from their movies about an iron man.

In this interview, Ryan North shares about his process with creating, writing and publishing his webcomic, Dinosaur Comics.

Can you talk about the origins of your webcomic, *Dinosaur Comics* (which started in 2003 and is still going)? How did you discover webcomics?

I'd wanted to do a comic but couldn't draw and didn't realize that "comic writer" was a thing: I thought everyone wrote and drew their own comics. So *Dinosaur Comics* was a way to get around the "can't draw" limitation by only having to get images set up once, and then I could recycle them. Actually my initial idea was for a comic where the WORDS never changed and the picture did, but that was the exact wrong project for me to be doing, and I'm glad I thought, "Hey, what if I did the opposite though?"

Dinosaur Comics, a webcomic by Ryan North.

Which writing and drawing exercises were helpful for you as you worked on and developed your craft?

Really, writing *Dinosaur Comics* every day for a decade was the best writing exercise I could've done. It taught me to know my way around a joke, to build characters, to meet deadlines (especially self-imposed ones, as they're the hardest) and to figure out different ways to tell a story—not to mention figuring out how to write dialogue. I thought I was just writing a fun comic, but it turns out I was also improving my craft at the same time! WHO KNEW.

In *Dinosaur Comics,* you have a fixed image of two dinosaurs interacting. The height of the action/tension is the green T-Rex stomping on a wood cabin. How did you go about choosing the fixed image of the two dinosaurs for each comic strip?

So they're clipart images, but they're *posable* clipart images: I could move T-Rex's arms and legs, mouth, etc. I basically just tried to set up a visual story that seemed interesting, and then I was stuck with it. If you look at the images you can see a lot of amateurish mistakes I make (for example, the characters all stand on the panel boundaries for the bottom three panels, which is top of the list of "Things Professionals Never Do"), but it's way too late to change the pictures now. The characters in the comic came from how they appeared in the strip: T-Rex looks excited, so he's a pretty excitable

Dinosaur Comics, a webcomic by Ryan North.

guy. I couldn't write T-Rex as a depressed dude because he doesn't look it, so the art style on those dinosaur clip art images I used really determined a lot of what was to come.

You use the same image of the dinosaurs for each comic strip. How do you keep ideas for dialogue fresh?

Comics are a SURPRISINGLY flexible medium. The layout of the comic tells a visual story, sure, but add "Meanwhile, 300 years in the future:" above any one of those panels, and you completely change the story the strip is telling. That, plus the realization that I could have off-panel characters really made me realize that, even with the same pictures for each installment, there weren't too many restrictions on the stories I could tell. I can't do a reaction shot of a toaster, sure, but beyond—it's pretty flexible.

> "I thought I was just writing a fun comic, but it turns out I was also improving my craft at the same time! WHO KNEW."

Can you talk about your work on fantastic, hilarious *Unbeatable Squirrel Girl* (out of Marvel Comics and one of my favorites)? Did you pitch the idea for the return of this character? How did you go about collaborating with Erica Henderson?

Thank you! My editor, Wil Moss, emailed me and said, "If you were to write a Squirrel Girl comic, what would it look like?" which was a really terrific email to get. I put together a pitch for the kind of comic

I wanted to write and sent it off, and shortly thereafter he sent me some sketches Erica had done of Squirrel Girl. Those sketches had such verve and personality that it made writing the comic really easy—I just wrote a comic that lined up with the character Erica had already created.

Which comics are you reading now that you love?

Sex Criminals by Chip Zdarsky and Matt Fraction is—despite the title—a really heartfelt, thoughtful, loving look at relationships and humanity. *The Wicked and the Divine* by Kieron Gillen and Jamie McKelvie is also terrific: high-concept fiction with a pop-music grounding that isn't like anything I've seen before. Both are really highly recommended! And, of course, anything Jason Shiga does.

3.14 A List of Further Reading

Chute, Hillary. *Why Comics? From Underground to Everywhere*. Harper, 2017.

Goldstein, Nancy. *Jackie Ormes: The First African American Woman Cartoonist*. University of Michigan Press, 2008.

Howard, Sheena. *Black Comics: Politics of Race and Representation*. Bloomsbury Academic, 2014.

Howard, Sheena. *Encyclopedia of Black Comics*. Fulcrum Publishing, 2017.

Madden, Matt. "A History of American Comic Books in Six Panels." Matt Madden's Blog (Archive). 8 Aug 2012, http://mattmadden.blogspot.co.uk/2012/08/a-history-of-american-comic-books-in.html.

Mazur, Dan. *Comics: A Global History, 1968 to the Present*. Thames & Hudson, 2014,

Wright, Bradford. *Comic Book Nation: The Transformation of Youth Culture in America*. John Hopkins University Press, 2003.

Creating Comics

4

4.1 Introduction

> "Make a lot of comics, try everything and break all the rules!" writes cartoonist Yumi Sakugawa, "if you aren't confident in your own drawing and writing skills, I will say that authenticity and vulnerability go a very long way over technical skill. I will take a poorly drawn comic with a lot of heart over a very polished comic with no heart always. Make something that is honest and real to you, and release it into the world when you are ready. It will affect somebody out there who is meant to read your comic, and that is the whole magic of making comics for me: making a genuine emotional connection with your readers."

Sakugawa's sentiment is a very important one to remember: you do not have to be a traditionally "good" visual artist to be a great cartoonist. All you need is a willingness to experiment, explore, play and excavate your own stories. You'll also apply what you've learned in previous chapters about reading and discussing comics to your own creations.

This chapter is meant to demystify the process of making comics by learning from the variety of cartoonists featured in this book, and most importantly, by picking up a pencil and a sheet of paper to try the provided exercises yourself.

This chapter isn't meant to teach you how to draw the most realistic human figure or bowl of fruit (there are plenty of life-figure classes offered at your local community college and a dizzying selection of books on this topic), or even make an entire graphic novel, rather; it's meant for an introductory maker and student of comics

Learning Objectives

- Experiment with comics exercises that engage theories behind the composition of image and text; for example, Scott McCloud's theories on iconography;
- Analyze the techniques that professional cartoonists use in their own comics creation process.

Learning Outcomes

- Start to develop voice, visual vocabulary and style in comics;
- Collaborate with other comics students to learn about the comics-making process;
- Create comics that reflect students' narratives, interests and styles.

to experiment and play with the comics medium, that unique relationship between text and image, and to help make your stories come alive, no matter what your drawing/illustration skill set.

Discovering the "Aliveness" in the Image

In an interview in *The Comics Journal*, cartoonist and author of *What It Is* Lynda Barry discusses this idea of "aliveness" in the image:

> *What It Is* is based on something I learned from my teacher, Marilyn Frasca, at the Evergreen State College in Olympia, Wash. I studied with her for two years in the late 1970s. Her idea seemed to be that everything we call art, whether it's music or dance or writing or painting, anything we call art is a container for something she called an image. And she believed that once you understood what an image is, then the form you give it is up to you. The question "What is an Image?" has guided all of my work for over 30 years. Because of what I learned from Marilyn, there isn't much of a difference in the experience of painting a picture, writing a novel, making a comic strip, reading a poem or listening to a song. The containers are different, but the lively thing in the center is what I'm interested in. It's the living thing we activate when we read a book.

As you explore these exercises, you are encouraged to prioritize your search for "the living thing," not how "good" or "realistic" it is.

The comics exercises contained in this chapter cover elements of craft, such as iconography, characterization, dialogue, and layout. Each exercise has a set of detailed instructions, real-life examples from introductory comics students, reflection questions to spark conversation about process and craft, and a list of variations of the exercises for students to expand their exploration.

Lastly, this chapter contains interview excerpts with comics creators, writers and artists, including National Ambassador for Young People's Literature Gene Luen Yang; Lucy Knisley; Fred Van Lente; Yumi Sakugawa; Leela Corman; and Sonny Liew, who generously share their strategies with generating ideas, their experiences with persevering during the creative process, their advice for students who struggle with making comics, and their professional insight to pitching ideas to publishers.

Key Terms

- Characterization
- Dialogue
- Iconography
- Play
- Exquisite Corpse
- Self-Portrait

Materials Needed

- Pen or pencil
- Paper
- Index cards
- Crayons
- A timer
- The willingness to let go of perfection and trust the drawings that emerge

4.2 Exercise 1: Self-Portrait as Icon

This exercise is adapted from Ivan Brunetti's wonderful comics-syllabus-turned-instructional-manual, *Cartooning: Philosophy and Practice*. The purpose of this introductory exercise is to experiment with timed drawing and Scott McCloud's ideas on iconography.

Instructions

1. Divide a sheet of paper into six, equal panels.
2. Draw lines between each panel to separate them.
3. Set a timer for two minutes. In the first panel, on the left-hand side, draw your self-portrait.
4. Reset the timer for two minutes. In the next panel, draw your self-portrait again.
5. Reset the timer for one minute. Again, draw your self-portrait.
6. Reset the time for thirty seconds. You know what to do.
7. Reset the timer for fifteen seconds. Repeat your self-portrait.
8. For the sixth and final panel, reset the timer for five seconds. Draw your self-portrait as quickly as possible.

Student example

Reflection Questions

1. After completing this exercise, observe the similarities/differences among each self-portrait you've drawn under the varying time constraints.
2. Which details changed from each self-portrait? Which stayed the same? Why?
3. Brunetti writes: "As the simplest doodle emerges, when we really have too little time to think about the drawing, we get closer to the 'idea' or essence of the thing being drawn. Here we begin to see the universal, latent, symbolic, visual, mnemonic language that is comics. You will probably surprise yourself as you spontaneously create these simple icons . . . that can still convey all the essential information about something." What surprised you about your final, five second drawing? Which "essential information" did you end up conveying? (See Chapter 1 for more information on icons.)
4. Although icons can help distill "essential information," what are their limitations in representing a character, object, or idea?

Variations

1. Do the above exercise again, but this time, use another subject, such as: the Golden Gate Bridge, Godzilla, David Bowie, or Grumpy Cat.
2. Make a four-panel comic using the final version of your self-portrait as the main character. In the comic, illustrate two things: time passing and an external conflict that your character experiences.
3. Draw twelve panels on a sheet of paper. In each panel, write down a different emotion at the bottom: angry, surprised, anxious, shocked, afraid, joyful, ecstatic, etc. Draw your final version of your self-portrait so that it portrays each emotion in its corresponding panel. Use emojis as inspiration.☺

4.3 Exercise 2: A Monster's Exquisite Corpse

This exercise is an adaptation of a collaborative, French surrealist game, entitled the Exquisite Corpse, and this version requires at least two other collaborators to complete. The purpose of this exercise is to play with characterization, dialogue, and the element of surprise. By only contributing a single part to this monster's body before passing it on to others to add the rest, this exercise creates a sense of anticipation and allows participants to let go of expectations. The results are often hilarious, astounding, and they typically open possibilities for students to use these creatures in their comics.

Instructions

1. Fold a sheet of paper in thirds.
2. On the top third, draw a monster-of-your-making's head. Draw lines for the start of your creature's neck in the middle third of the page, but don't complete the drawing.
3. Fold over what you just drew (the top third of the page), then pass it along to the person on your left. You should receive another sheet of paper from your right-hand side. The top third of the paper should be covered; you shouldn't be able to see what the previous person drew.

4. On your new sheet of paper, draw this new monster's torso. Draw lines that connect the torso to the legs/bottom half of the monster, but don't finish the bottom third of the paper.
5. Fold over what you drew (the middle third of the page), then pass it along to the person on your left-hand side.
6. You'll receive a new sheet of paper from the person on your right.
7. Finally, complete the bottom third of the last monster you received.
8. When you're finished, open the folded-up piece of paper, and a new Frankenstein-like monster should emerge.
9. If you'd like to continue this exercise and play around with dialogue, you can apply the previous exercise (Character + Dialogue) to your monster, and see which bits of dialogue develop your monster's sense of character.

Student Example

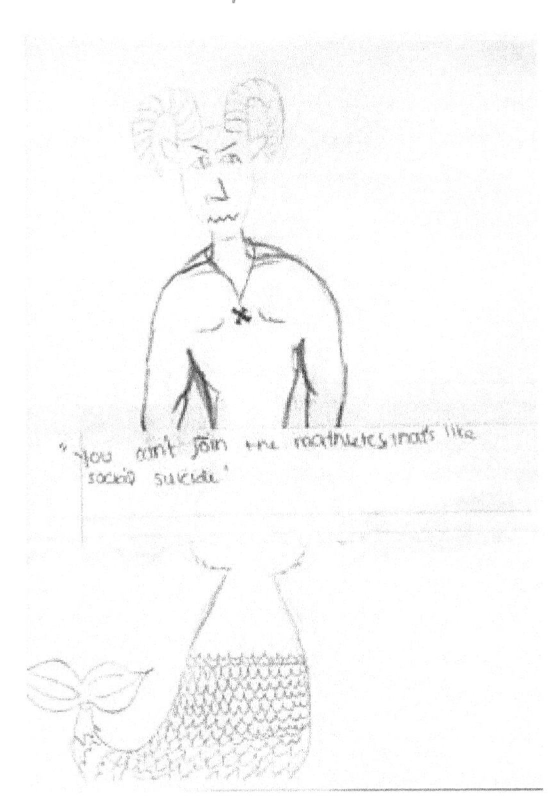

Reflection Questions

1. Describe your process of collaboration for this exercise. What surprised you?
2. Examine the results of this exercise. Based on the details that your collaborators added to this monster, what does this tell you about its character?

Variations

1. Write a biography of this monster. What is its name? What is it afraid of? What is its primary source for food? Where does it come from? What made it a monster? Based on this biography, make a four-panel comic that demonstrates its eating habits.
2. Apply the next exercise ("Character + Dialogue") to your monster, and see which bits of dialogue develop your monster's sense of character.
3. Find the lyrics to a popular song on the radio. Make a six-panel comic that uses the lyrics as captions or word balloons, and highlights this monster's morning routine.

4.4 Cartoonists on Generating Ideas

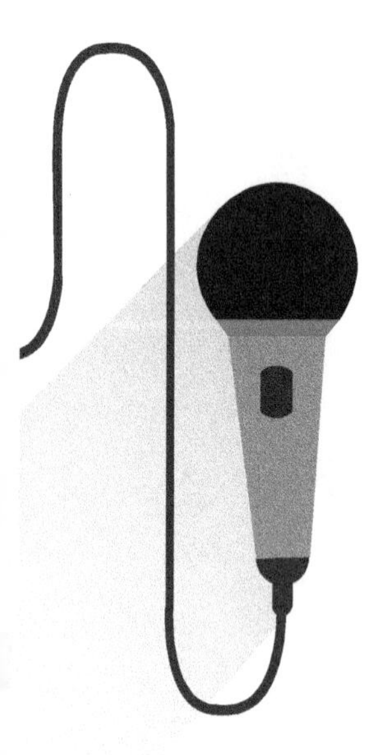

Question

Which writing and cartooning exercises were helpful for you as you worked on and developed your craft?

Gene Luen Yang: I took a figure drawing class at a local community college that was enormously helpful. That's something I need to do again. I feel rusty.

Right now, I'm doing Morning Pages, an exercise advocated by Julia Cameron in her classic book *The Artist's Way.* This is where you write three longhand pages first thing in the morning. You're not going for beauty of language. You're just trying to clear the garbage out of your mind.

Yumi Sakugawa: For books on the craft of storytelling, when I was first starting out I was very inspired by Stephen King's *On Writing*, Christopher Vogler's *The Writer's Journey*, Ray Bradbury's *Zen and the Art of Writing*, and David Lynch's *Catching the Big Fish: Meditation, Consciousness, and Creativity.* My most recent influence is probably *The Artist's Way* by Julia Cameron. So, my process is a combination of being completely loose and then being completely structured. In the beginning, I am gathering a lot of stream of consciousness ideas, sensations, feelings, memories and images. I am writing them down and sketching them out. And then I follow patterns and themes and crystallize them in multiple drafts until I feel like there is a coherent story and structure to create. I don't think there is a particular formal writing or drawing exercise I

> "I like to jot down an idea a day in my notebooks. I wrote one seven years ago about a boy working in a coffee shop and the gods he would serve coffee to. It was self indulgent and mystical. It also landed me an Eisner nomination."
> - Taneka Stotts

> "One technique I discovered that works well, as far as I can tell, for any creative endeavor, is to assemble a playlist for that specific project and play that playlist whenever you're working or thinking about that project."
> - Fred Van Lente

do other than to write a lot and draw a lot and to finish the projects I set out to finish. I do keep a regular dream journal, which I think is important for keeping my creative channels open, and there was a window of time when I did four pages of stream-of-consciousness every morning, as recommended by Julia Cameron's book *The Artist's Way.* Honestly, the most important thing I do for my writing and drawing exercise is that I meditate every morning without fail. I can't imagine being a working artist without my daily meditation practice.

Sonny Liew: In terms of learning the basics of visual storytelling, doing the equivalent of a master copies helped—taking a comic you like and doing rough thumbnails based on what you see. It's a way of understanding how the artist blocked things out compositionally, the rhythm of the panels, and more. I suppose it's similar to writers typing out the sentences of their favorites novels—you absorb the inflections and style in order to eventually evolve your own unique approach.

Taneka Stotts: I like to jot down an idea a day in my notebooks. I wrote one seven years ago about a boy working in a coffee shop and the gods he would serve coffee to. It was self indulgent and mystical. It also landed me an Eisner nomination.

Lucy Knisley: As a very young kid, I saved up and bought myself a cheapo lightbox. I would use it to trace my favorite panels from comics, illustrations from magazines and books, and drawings that my mother had made. I don't advocate dependency on tracing in finished work, of course, but I think it's important when you're starting out to see how a drawing is put together by following the line with your own pencil. I know it helped me quite a bit. As an adult, I found that the best thing to help push me to the next level was working with limitations—I often work straight-to-ink because it forces me to be less precious and dainty and to overthink my drawings. I also like the "hourly comic day" exercise, which was contrived by the very talented John Campbell, back in the day, and forces the artist to make a panel or two for every hour they are awake, usually depicting that part of their day. It's an exercise in speed and processing and forces you to interpret on the go and let go, again, of preciousness. These are the same brain muscles I use when I'm travelogueing.

Leela Corman: Hard, unrelenting work on figure drawing. Watching a LOT of films and very good episodic television. Going through a rigorous illustration/design program. Being a constant student of art of the entire world and every era. Learning how to be a good researcher. Writing individual story beats on index cards. Finding the deepest darkest portal inside myself and reaching into it repeatedly, with complete trust in what I will pull out.

Fred Van Lente: Well, I'm just going to be utterly self-serving and say I put pretty much I knew into the book Greg Pak and I did for Random House, *Make Comics Like the Pros.* That book talks about everything, from coming up with ideas to writing to page layout to coloring, inking, lettering and marketing. We poured our guts into it, and people seem to have found it useful, which is awesome.

This isn't an exercise, per se, but one technique I discovered that works well, as far as I can tell, for any creative endeavor, is to assemble a playlist for that specific project and play that playlist whenever you're working or thinking about that project. The songs in the playlist don't have to be specific to the project—like, you don't need to fill it up with scary movie themes if you're writing a horror story—but it doesn't hurt. After the repetition of this for just a few times, it becomes Pavlovian: when you play the playlist you start thinking about the project naturally. It's a great way to overcome day-to-day procrastination and writer's block. It's never failed me!

"There were no "exercises" per se. The old Nike motto, "Just do it" is also mine. There was no warm up."
- Belle Yang

Nilah Magruder: I roleplayed online a LOT. I still do a little bit. Online RP is great for learning character development and spontaneity. Drawing exercises . . . I kinda just drew everything. A lot of drawing from observation. I love those "20 character expressions" sheets, too.

Rafael Rosado: Copying the artists you admire is a great way to figure how they do things and why. My experience as storyboard artist in the animation industry has definitely been helpful in understanding pacing, acting, and staging. You also have to know how to draw all kinds of things, in different styles when you work in animation. That's worked to my advantage.

Sophie Goldstein: Now that I'm out of school (I graduated with an MFA from The Center for Cartoon Studies in 2013) I don't do any writing or drawing exercises. Occasionally I'll do a free-write, but that's generally for therapeutic reasons.

I usually advise those new to comics to start with short stories and to focus on finishing them. Produce as much finished work as you can early on. If you start with your 500-page dream-project the chances of you ever completing it are minimal at best.

Baby steps.

Belle Yang: There were no "exercises" per se. The old Nike motto, "Just do it" is also mine. There was no warm up. I began working on illustrated books after returning to California following the Tiananmen Massacre, which took place in 1989. I listened to my parents tell their stories of survival and escape from China, and I began to set them down in words accompanied by paintings. These became two prose books, each with twenty full-color illustrations: *Baba: A Return to China Upon My Father's Shoulders* and *The Odyssey of a Manchurian*.

Danica Novgorodoff: The writing aspect is very important to me. I spend a long time developing my story—character development, plot, dialogue, and so forth—before I begin to draw. In that stage, traditional writing exercises are very useful—for example, examining story arc and making sure the characters have desires, agency and conflict.

Thumbnailing has also been very helpful for me. I'm not very good at sketching quickly, but my thumbnails, illegible as they may be, contain a lot of visual information for my own reference and bridge the scary expanse between the story in my head (and in text) and a more polished comic.

Developing character sketches is a fun phase. I tend toward more realistic drawings than I think are appropriate for comics-style storytelling, and so I spend a fair amount of time simplifying and reworking in order to get to a character design that is compelling and expressive.

Ashanti Fortson: The number one most useful writing/drawing exercise that I've done is making self-contained short comics. I've made a number of short comics, either for myself or for anthologies, and each one has taught me invaluable things about how I want to tell stories and make comics. The important part is that it's short and self contained, so you can experiment as much as you want without committing to that for 200 pages.

Jenny Lin: Initially, automatic drawing or writing as a way to just get ideas out on paper and to not immediately care whether or not they made sense. I have found that process really helpful, especially if I feel stuck, to try not to censor my thoughts and just let things unfold on the page in a really rough way. To draw and write without a plan is really interesting, as a lot can come out of that. (You become inspired while drawing because the act of drawing and writing seems to activate more thinking.) I think making a lot of drawings and a lot of writing from this process is helpful.

Following this (although I find works that remain in their immediate and intuitively generated state also really interesting and important), I've found it useful to look at the stuff you have created from your automatic drawing and writing session(s) and try to think about what is happening in it, choose the parts that speak most to you, or pinpoint the overall atmosphere. You cannot keep all of what is there. It will be much more powerful if you just let yourself let go of a lot of it, just edit out and keep the essential parts that really convey the feeling of what you want rather than, maybe, the descriptive, didactic actual events and details, the more literal stuff.

I think it's also really important to try not to get too attached to all of this drawing and writing while you're still developing it. It's important with some projects to be a bit ruthless with the content and just keep paring it down until it communicates what you want (sometimes with minimal text or image).

Being aware of rhythm is also important, I find, and maybe sometimes going to extremes so that you reach some kind of tipping point with the work (a cathartic moment).

Andi Santagata: I recommend every aspiring cartoonist to go out and pick up a copy of Scott McCloud's *Understanding Comics.* No, seriously. It's an indispensable tool that breaks down your understanding of things like panel structure, the passage of time, facial expression, and color story, in the context of comics, *in* comic form—McCloud's stuff is pretty prevalent, sort of like the *Joy of Cooking* of sequential art.

Other than that—and you hear this one a lot—practice, practice, practice. Don't just practice drawing; practice making comics—put things into panels, complete a story within a set number of pages. You'll be stretching your drawing, composition, design, writing, and plotting muscles all at once, and, most publishers and editors in comics tend to ask to see your sequential work before your illustrative stuff.

"I made sure to set aside at least an hour to draw every day no matter what it was, even if it was a doodle on a little notepad." - Rina Ayuyang

Rina Ayuyang: I made sure to set aside at least an hour to draw every day no matter what it was, even if it was a doodle on a little notepad. I still do this first thing in the morning before anything else just so that I feel productive, and at the same time, it acts like a warm-up for the rest of the drawing that day. I also look at a lot of art monographs and sketchbooks by other artists and cartoonists for inspiration to see how they practice and work through their artmaking. In terms of writing, I've use a lot of techniques that Lynda Barry teaches in her writing class, which she also shares in her books on writing and creating, especially *What it Is?* Also a great book for cartooning advice is Ivan Brunetti's *Cartooning.*

Jade Lee: I'm still figuring out how to write, haha! For drawing, however, I think it's important to attend live figure drawing sessions whenever possible. Even if you're drawing very stylized characters for a fictional comic, it helps to observe and understand how the human body works first before attempting to bend the rules to achieve an aesthetic purpose. I also like to study film stills from my favorite movies or tv shows to examine how a scene is composed to achieve a specific emotional response. Focus on how color is used, where the characters are placed, how much screen space is being used and by what, what shapes surround the characters or main objects, etc. I find that this helps comic artists think of more visually interesting ways to progress their narratives.

Try it!

1. For one month, start off your day by writing "morning pages," which are three pages you write by hand. See what happens when you start the day with getting your thoughts on the page first thing in the morning. What do you observe after doing this process for a month, six months, a year?
2. For one day, make a single-panel comic for each hour that you're awake.
3. For every day of one week, make a comic using the same clipart, in the style of Ryan North's *Dinosaur Comics* (http://www.qwantz.com/).

4.5 Exercise 3: Character and Dialogue

This exercise is meant to encourage you to listen closely to the richness and "aliveness" of the conversations in the world around you in order to spark your process around juxtaposing image and text. This exercise is adapted from cartoonist and creativity instigator, Lynda Barry, and her book, *Syllabus: Notes from an Accidental Professor.*

Instructions

1. Bring a notebook everywhere you go (standing in line at the grocery store, riding the bus to school, eating dinner with friends or family) and spend an entire week recording pieces of dialogue that stand out to you. Try to collect at least twelve sentences or bits of dialogue. Write each one down on a separate small strip of paper. Examples of dialogue:
2. At the end of the week, fold an 8.5″ x 11″ sheet of paper into six panels. At the bottom of each panel, write down an occupation, or a personality type. For example, Broadway actor, comedian, feminist, backup dancer, etc.
3. Set your timer for one minute per panel and draw the character for the occupation you wrote at the bottom.
4. After you're finished with all six panels, take out your strips of dialogue.
5. Circulate and move the strips of dialogue above the characters you've drawn and see which ones "click," or elicit laughter, surprise, or shock by the juxtaposition of image and text you've created.
6. You can continue this exercise by selecting your best "match" of character and dialogue, and start a four-panel comic that introduces another character, produces conflict and expand on the conversation.

Student Example

Reflection Questions

1. How did collecting bits of dialogue affect your writing or cartooning process? What are the qualities of the dialogue you decided to record and use?
2. Describe your process of matching pieces of dialogue to the characters you drew. How did you ultimately make your decisions to match them?
3. How does the addition of dialogue change or deepen your understanding of the characters?
4. How does the dialogue change the mood of a particular character's presentation?

Variations

1. Choose one of your favorite characters with their corresponding dialogue line. Make a six-panel comic based on this character and this line. Where does this bit of dialogue lead? Feel free to introduce other characters.
2. Make a twelve-panel grid. On each panel, draw a word balloon. Then, arrange the pieces of dialogue on the grid inside the word balloons. It's up to you how you want to organize the narrative: chronologically; experimentally; imagistically; or they can be completely random. Once you've determined your organization, write the dialogue inside the word balloons. Then, fill in a character or two (or several) to match the dialogue.

4.6 Spotlight on Gene Luen Yang, Cartoonist

In *The Comics Journal*, you wrote about your fear with writing *Boxers and Saints* since it was such a huge undertaking in regards to research, storytelling, etc. You wrote: "This is a book where I kept telling myself, 'If you're going to fail, just make sure you fail big.'" Can you talk more about failure? How do you deal with it and apply its lessons in your own process as a cartoonist?

A stack of Gene Luen Yang's award-winning graphic novels.

"I am constantly fighting fear. Most of my family and friends know me as a worrier. This applies to my creative work, too. I worry about failing. I worry about making bad books. I worry about not being able to draw. I worry about everything.

As a practical measure, I meditate for about fifteen minutes every day. I read from the *Tao Te Ching*, then I read from the *Christian gospels*, then I quiet myself for a moment and try to get my mind to calm the freak down.

When I'm working, I try to focus on the joy of the process, even if the end result is a failure. Key word there is "try." I have to admit, it's difficult. But I do try to comfort myself with the thought of "failing big." If I'm going to fail, I want to fail at something I've never tried before. I want my failures to be ambitious."

4.7 Exercise 4: Making Friends with Inner Demons

This exercise is inspired by a classroom visit with Yumi Sakugawa, the author of *Your Illustrated Guide to Becoming One with the Universe* and *There is No Right Way to Meditate*, whose aforementioned work draws much from her meditation practice and spiritual ritual. After a student asked about persevering through the creative process and overcoming challenges to make and finish comics, Sakugawa emphasized the importance of play, and of not being afraid to experiment in comics. She also mentioned making friends with one's inner demons—the ones who tell you that you're not good enough, not talented enough, and other vicious things these monsters say to paralyze your creative process.

This exercise is meant for you to "make friends" with your inner demon, which will allow you to practice characterization, dialogue, and collaboration with another fellow cartoonist—you'll need at least one other person to complete this exercise. You'll also need to set a timer for each part of this exercise. The time constraints will help to get your drawings on the page and not overthink the outcome.

Materials

- A timer
- Crayons
- Paper
- Medium-tipped black markers or Sharpies

Instructions

1. Set the timer to one minute, then both partners simultaneously draw the outlines of their inner demons on separate sheets of paper. Don't fill yours in with any details, color, shading—just the outline. It should take up the majority of the space on your sheet of paper.
2. Exchange outlines with your partner. Don't critique or comment on them.
3. Set the timer for five minutes. With your crayons, fill in your partner's outline with crayon. You may add character details, such as whiskers, eyebrows, dimples, etc. Fill in the entire page, including the background, with color.
4. Set the timer for two minutes. On the back of your partner's demon, write down three questions that you should the demon would ask. These can be rhetorical questions, or questions directed at your partner. They can be as silly as: "Why are there bagpipes in the corner of the lecture hall?" or as serious as: "What are you hungry for?"
5. Exchange demons again—you should receive your original back from your partner with details, color and questions added to it. Read the questions and choose one that resonates with you.
6. On a new sheet of paper, draw four panels. In the first panel, draw your demon asking the question your chose.
7. Set your timer to ten minutes. In the four panels, make a short comic that features you and your demon discussing the question you chose.

Student Examples:

Reflection Questions

1. Describe your experience with collaborating with your partner by coloring and adding details to their inner demon.
2. What was your experience with receiving your inner demon after your partner fleshed it out with details and color? How did your inner demon's character change as a result of this process?
3. Describe your process of adding details and color to your partner's inner demon. What did you consider as you fleshed out its character?
4. When you created the four-panel comic featuring your inner demon, how did your understanding of its character change? Was it actually more encouraging than you thought? Did it reveal more of its humanity? If so, how?

Variations

1. Make a four-panel comic using another question that your partner asked.
2. Make a six-panel, silent comic that illustrates one of your inner demon's daily routines.
3. Make a six-panel comic about your inner demon, in which it reveals a secret about itself.

4.8 Spotlight on Andi Santagata, Cartoonist

Andi Santagata, Cartoonist.

"If I make you feel like you're at a high school house party hiding in the basement next to a VHS player and a cracked tube TV cause you're too anxious to socialize, I am doing my job."

What stories do you choose to tell and why?

I try to tell the stories that I'd want to read. Of course, when you're writing autobio, that changes to "telling the stories that I want to vent to my friends about, but they don't really care, so I'll write it into three panels with a joke at the end, and the internet will give me affection instead." Most of my stories in fiction take place between 1992 and 2007, as I'm trying pretty hard to capture that lost sense of teenage nostalgia from that era. If I make you feel like you're at a high school house party hiding in the basement next to a VHS player and a cracked tube TV cause you're too anxious to socialize, I am doing my job. I'm one of those people who gets the warm fuzzies thinking about death and feeling sad and stuff (to steal a line from Scott Pilgrim), so if I can elevate the "teen angst" genre into an aesthetically appealing, nuanced, and darkly funny study, I'm happy. If the world the story's set in feels nostalgic and cool and weirdly familiar, I've made a good comic, I think. I try to choose stories that would've offered me escapism and empathy, while still addressing the dark stuff, when I was a kid-slash-teenager.

Can you talk about your experiences making your autobiographical comic, *Trans Man Walking*?

Yeah! *Trans Man Walking* came out right around when America did an about-face and passed the North Carolina bathroom bill, which forces people to use the bathroom matching the gender on their birth certificate (leading to a ton of post-transition folks *following* the law and getting harassed and assaulted for *doing what it said*), and Caitlyn Jenner's transition, which, regardless of her politics, resulted in a ton of people insulting her for her audacity to come out of the closet and be herself. It was phobic, gross stuff, and I realized I had to speak up or be part of the problem, so I started jamming down my experiences and thoughts in *Trans Man Walking* on Tapastic (now Tapas.io). It's drawn entirely in Sharpie, because: A) the quickness of that medium allows me to jot down stories in a rougher, realer format and B) screw you; that's why, is a freeing place for my own expression and airing of grievances, which, I now know, allows people to understand trans issues through the lens of anecdotal comedy, a far more accessible entry point than a pamphlet and/or internet argument. There are a couple times when I have to ask myself whether something is "appropriate" or "suitable" to write about or post, but then I remind myself how much Jhonen Vasquez and Julie Doucet saved my childhood life by being honest about the screwed up things they'd experienced and felt. It's important to be visible and tell your story, even if it's a hard one to swallow, because someone else out there is almost certainly struggling with it, too.

What is your experience with self-publishing and distributing zines of your own comics? Is there a freedom to this process that you wouldn't necessarily find going through a "traditional" publishing route?

Absolutely! Self-publishing (and zines, by definition of genre, are almost unilaterally self-published) means you have 100% creative control over your final product. When you go through a traditional publisher, they decide on a number of things, ranging from marketing to pricing to cover design. For first-time cartoonists and artists putting out a book, it's also likely that you'll reach more circulation through self-publishing and distributing than trying to get picked up by a traditional publisher, through conventions, distros, social media, and writing in to get your book in zine and comic stores. You also retain full creator rights to your work and can frequently sell the book to a publisher *after* you self-publish as a zine or a mini, as well (like Luke Healy's *How to Survive in the North* or Mitch Clem's *Nothing Nice to Say*). The barrier to self-publishing that traditional publishing has a leg up on, of course, is money—you're going to have to fund your own print run. The good news is, a ton of established cartoonists already use the self-funded print run model to release comics at a profit—off the top of my head, everyone from Kickstarter darling Spike Trotman (who is a powerhouse in her own right) to established industry vet Rick Veitch (*Swamp Thing, Brat Pack*) has used the fund-your-own-print-run, sell-some-comics pipeline model.

Can you talk about your experience studying at the Center for Cartoon Studies?

The Center for Cartoon Studies is like comics Hogwarts! They offer one- and two-year certs and a Master's Degree, all of which follow along one program. It's a comprehensive course of study based around actually making, completing, publishing, and producing comics, from writing to inking to production

"It's important to be visible and tell your story, even if it's a hard one to swallow, because someone else out there is almost certainly struggling with it, too."

to bookbinding. There's a professional component, too, where the school hosts industry events and weekly talks from cartoonists currently working (this year, we had Allison Bechdel, Dash Shaw, and Jaime Hernandez, among others!). The catch (or prize) part of CCS is that it's located in White River Junction, Vermont, a rural northern town with a population of 2,000. There are sixteen people in my graduating class, but that just makes the whole place like a friendlier version of Dylan Horrocks' *Hicksville*, so I'm not exactly complaining. I personally decided to attend CCS after hitting a wall in cartooning—I'd tabled at TCAF, I'd put out some zines, I'd got good reviews, but I had absolutely no idea where to go from there. I knew I could do better, so I decided to get my Master's here at CCS—which is part comics boot camp, part comics summer camp. Your reward for knocking out your thesis is a delicious maple syrup tapping party. And, best of all, you're in good company—there's nothing like living in a colony of other cartoonists and being able to walk outside at 3 AM, waving a piece of Bristol board, and getting three different feedbacks from other insomniac cartoonists.

Which comics are you reading now that you love?

I'm really into John Allison's *Bad Machinery*—I've been a fan of his stuff since his webcomic, *Scary-Go-Round*, and it's some of the most appealing art and consistent magical-realism worldbuilding I've seen in comics! Plus, British schoolkids. I also really enjoy the art in the ongoing series *Motor Crush*, which features Babs Tarr's super smooth eighties-style sci-fi linework. On the indie side, I just finished *Megg and Mogg in Amsterdam* by Simon Hanselmann, who is probably one of the finest "underground" cartoonists of our generation. Hanselmann's probably the closest we'll get for a little while to capturing the tragedy and irony of depression in lovely, full technicolor. I also can't stop thinking about this incredible comic in *Best American Comics 2016* by Casanova Frankenstein—"The Corpse, The Ghost, and the Hollow-Weenie"—which is the closest I've ever come as an adult to feeling the same kind of wild, insane, bloodlusty anger/sadness I did when I first cracked open Jhonen Vasquez as a teenager. Seriously, those lines are mind blowing.

Exercise: Shadow Self

Comic Book Hideout owner Glynnes Pruett suggested and wrote the following exercise in relation to the idea of the "equal and opposite side of the same coin" for hero-versus-villain archetypes and development. This concept, the idea of the Shadow Self, was developed by Carl Jung. The exercise acts as a facilitator for students to conceptualize and recognize the parts of themselves and of their potential fictional hero that are negative or adverse to their heroic traits.

1. Make a list of five people you greatly admire and would enjoy spending time with. (Real people are preferable, but the selections are not the concern, they are simply a part of the exercise.) These names don't have to be written down, just thought about. Once these five people are selected, create a list of three attributes that all five of these people share. (Attributes can be anything—e.g., sense of humor, humility, kindness, honesty, etc.)

2. Ask for students to read their attributes out loud. Discuss which attributes are common among students' selections. Create a collective list of attributes that could also be considered heroic traits.
3. In equal and opposite fashion, make a list of five people you greatly despise and would *not* enjoy spending time with. (Real people are preferable, but the selections are not the concern, they are simply a part of the exercise.) Once these five people are selected, create a list of three attributes that all five of these people share. (Attributes can be anything—e.g., dishonesty, rudeness, selfishness, etc.)
4. Ask for students to read their attributes out loud. Discuss which attributes are common among students' selections. Create a collective list of attributes that could also be considered villainous traits.

Discussion

a. Are there attributes of the positive people in your life some that you see reflected in yourself? How does interacting with people who share similar traits help to exemplify the positive aspects of yourself? Do you feel that like-minded people gather around one another to promote and reward the positive behavior they see in themselves?

b. How does being surrounded by people with these positive traits affect how you view yourself and your environment? By finding and engaging with people who share these similar attributes, aren't you not only emphasizing your own positive characteristics, but also accentuating the positive characteristics of others?

c. Of the selection of negative traits, are there any in which you can see in yourself?

d. Does being surrounded by people with these negative traits accentuate the negative attributes you see in yourself? By choosing to *not* to engage with people who share these or similar attributes, aren't you not only recognizing the negative characteristics of others; but also disengaging from your own negative aspects?

By recognizing the negative characteristics we dislike in others, we can better assess and confront the negative attributes we dislike in ourselves on a fundamental level. Jung expresses this identification of the negative characteristics in ourselves as the Shadow Self. This is the equal and opposite side of our "hero's coin." We intentionally engage and befriend people who exemplify our most positive and self-affirming qualities and generally dislike people who can be described with traits that we abhor in our Shadow Selves.

Understanding the development and acceptance of our own negative personal aspects is identifying our Shadow Selves. With the knowledge of our Shadow Selves, we can be more aware of our own villainous qualities because a hero's greatest strength is overcoming their weaknesses, and a villain's greatest power often lies in exploiting their hero's greatest weakness, and vice versa.

Discussion should be engaging students to be honest and open with themselves, to feel comfortable and aware of their own positive and negative traits. Helping select traits for their fictional heroes also facilitates helping the students select positive traits they embody themselves and manifesting them in their writing.

A dynamic hero and villain interaction is as essential as creating an engaging story. By developing a balance between heroic and villainous behaviour you can manifest a worthy adversary. By your understanding and utilizing the idea of the Shadow Self, a more well-rounded and realistic hero and villain can emerge in natural storywriting.

Reflection Questions

1. After completing this exercise, were you surprised by any attributes you recognized in yourself? How can the acceptance of one's "dark side" be a tool for the growth of a person or character?
2. Which positive traits do you share with your fictional hero, and which negative traits do you share with your fictional hero? Does your hero possess traits you don't have?
3. Does your hero share these negative traits with your villain—or equal and opposite ones? Why is this balance so important in story writing and also in life?
4. Which traits does your villain have that you also possess? Does your villain possess traits you don't have? Do these traits change the way your hero and villain interact?

4.9 Cartoonists on Perseverance in the Comics-Making Process

Question

How do you get started on a project once you've explored the seed of an idea? And perhaps more importantly, how do you persevere after the initial excitement over an idea?

Yumi Sakugawa: I do a lot of stream-of-consciousness brainstorming and outlining and really terrible first drafts. Eventually, a structure reveals itself (Stephen King describes that part of the process in *On Writing* as excavating the skeleton of a dinosaur—you find one bone and then follow the rest of the structure that is already inherently there), and from there, I do a lot of thumbnails. For my last short comic story, "Ikebana," I probably drew thumbnails of that story twenty times, again and again, until I could draw the entire story from memory and everything felt right before I could start penciling. And even when I am penciling and inking, the story is still changing, and right up to the final digital edit, last-minute changes in framing or dialogue or imagery are incorporated. I think that's what keeps the initial excitement going, the fact that the core of the story keeps revealing itself throughout the creation process and can reveal hidden depths right up to its nearly finished state before it is completely finalized.

Ryan North: I think the most important thing I realized was that you don't get just One Good Idea: you'll have plenty. And so what matters is your ability to decide which idea you want to pursue and then bring them to the finish line. The trick in getting there is to keep it interesting for yourself: if I'm challenged, if I'm doing something I've never done before, then I'm really engaged in the work and can't wait to do more on it. Then it becomes fun and not work, and you're home free!

Sonny Liew: If I'm doing the writing, there'd likely be a bit of research involved—reading books, watching movies, listening to songs—trying to find the right texture and details to fill the story. The craft of storytelling is one of those things that is fairly easy to grasp but has so many hidden layers that it's always an exciting challenge to try to figure out everything, from the overall structure to individual scenes or even the panel-to-panel transitions. It's not something that I ever get bored by, though it can sometimes be frustrating when things don't quite work. Personally, I'll often go take a long walk or go for a run to clear the head and try to find new perspectives and ideas.

"I think the most important thing I realized was that you don't get just One Good Idea: you'll have plenty."
- Ryan North

Taneka Stotts: I'm a person who likes to create far too many characters than I know what to do with. I shuffle them around often, repurpose some roles, and sometimes I let them fade simply into the background. Much like the seed of an idea, I realize that not all will grow with me, bear fruit, or make it past one line scribbled in my notebook, but knowing that I put pen to paper, that I let it out of the box, helps me to continue moving forward and to allow ideas to fail. However, for the ones that do survive, I begin a cultivation project, I nurture it. I allow it to have good days and bad days, I weed it and make sure that the roots stay healthy; when it's ready I share what it has given me with others. I'm not afraid to go back and hack at the stem and allow a new growth to appear. I bet you can tell I like gardening now.

Lucy Knisley: There are ups and downs in every project. I've never made a book that I didn't loathe with a passion at one point during its creation. It helps to just keep going, because eventually you start to recognize that loathing as a normal part of things, and remember how it passed the last time this happened. The start can be the hardest part, with so much work laid before you, but I've always thought the hardest part is when a project is nearly finished but you suddenly wonder why you're even making this thing, who is gonna like it, and why did you just waste half a year of your life on it? Pushing through that is hard, but it helps enormously to have professionals in your corner, like my agent and editor, whose job it is to cheer you on through that nonsense.

Fred Van Lente: The second part is definitely the hard part. I can't tell you how many times I've started and abandoned an idea over the years, particularly when I just out of college, starting out. The key really isn't maintaining initial excitement—that will never happen. That's like expecting the feeling of love at first sight to maintain itself through a long marriage. There's one thing you can never be more than once, and that's new.

What you have to learn as a creator—and maybe I was told this when I was younger and I forgot it, but it is the sort of thing you have to learn for yourself—is that excitement won't sustain you, or the belief in a future reward—critical, financial, cultural, whatever. You have to sustain yourself. It's a grind, a daily grind, and you have to work on the idea anyway, even when you're not feeling it, even when you're down on it. With most creative works, you won't really understand what you've got until you've finished it, and then you can fix it. For the initial creation, give yourself the freedom to suck. There will be plenty of time to fix it later. But you can never fix what was never made in the first place.

Nilah Magruder: I start out by writing down everything. Thinking up characters, their personalities, subplots, conflicts. Anything that might be useful, I write down, even if I decide to drop it later. I'd rather have too much to start with than too little. From that, I try to find a single through-line, the one thread around which the story will revolve. I try to think in terms of where the characters are starting, where I want them to go, and what challenges will get them there. From there, I can start building an outline and finding some sense of structure. For a comic, I'm doing the same thing with the

> "The myth of the tortured artist working in solitude—at least for me, that's a myth. I can't do it alone; I need feedback and support."
> - Danica Novgorodoff

> "The bottom line is: If I feel that a story is worth telling, I'll finish it. If I genuinely feel, at some point, that it isn't worth telling, I'll scrap it."
> - Ashanti Fortson

art, simultaneously. Sometimes it's even an image that comes first; a character, a landscape, or simply a mood. I keep journals and sketchbooks of every scrap of detail I can dream up. You kind of hit a wall eventually as you're working; it's like you start running on level ground, and then the ground tilts, and you're going uphill. It gets tiring, you start to doubt yourself. Sometimes sharing my work with friends helps alleviate the stress of it and keep me accountable. Sometimes it's the thought of starting a blank page that is daunting. Maybe I'm unprepared, I need to gather reference or flesh out a story more. Once I'm rolling, I'm able to settle into a groove. But there's no trick to it, really. Some days, I just have to force myself to sit down and work. When I slack off, I know nothing's getting done, and I'm just creating more work for myself down the road. So I have to stay organized, keep lists and calendars, and stay on task as much as I'm able.

Sophie Goldstein: Usually I start by freewriting story ideas as they come to me, ideas for scenes or lines or characters. World-building tidbits. Then when I feel like it's percolated enough I'll sit down and outline the story and begin writing and thumbnailing the scenes. This is usually the most exciting and challenging part of the work for me. The drudgery comes later.

If I'm having trouble at any point I like to set a timer for an hour or an hour and a half. Three hours of focused uninterrupted work a day is generally enough to get a longer project completed in a reasonable timeframe.

Belle Yang: You throw every idea you have on the floor, and then you sweep away the stuff that is a dead end unnecessary, or thematically unrelated. When I worked on my three adult books with illustrations or in comic format, telling the stories of men and women who were lost in the chaos of war was urgent. I felt I was lifted by these ghosts on their shoulders and carried forth. I was seeking some form of justice and that overarching desire gave me incredible momentum. And, hey, if a publisher pays you, you've got a deadline, so that's impetus enough.

Danica Novgorodoff: I begin with the writing. And then I run the idea (or a first draft) past friends whose opinions I respect. I have a lot of good friends who are writers and artists and readers, and they are invaluable to me in the creative process. The myth of the tortured artist working in solitude—at least for me, that's a myth. I can't do it alone; I need feedback and support.

When I was working on my last graphic novel, I allowed for a lot of revision and experimentation during the drawing process. I had my basic script, but I waited to thumbnail each chapter until I was ready to draw the entire section (instead of thumbnailing the entire book in advance), just to keep a slight element of surprise for myself. I felt that if I planned each panel too thoroughly I would quickly become bored with the drawing process—which is not good when you're about to tackle a 430-page comic!

There has to be an element of improvisation at every stage. (Well, except for inking, which is basically tracing the penciled lines—and during that stage, I usually listen to audiobooks to entertain myself!)

Ashanti Fortson: I'm a pretty busy person for most of the year, so there's often some amount of time between each step of a personal project. There might be two to four weeks between my first draft and my final script with thumbnails. There might be another two weeks between finished thumbnails/pencils and starting inks, and so on. I get stuck in my own head a lot, so those bits of time let me step away and come back to the project with fresh eyes and a fresh mind. It's especially important for me to take mental breaks from my work during the writing stage—that's the foundation of the entire project, so it needs to be well executed, thoughtful, and worth drawing.

Personally, I tend not to get huge initial bursts of excitement over ideas. My excitement is quieter, but it's long term, especially for bigger projects like *Galanthus*. I've certainly worked on projects that I've subsequently abandoned, but they weren't projects I was terribly excited about anyway. Sometimes I've realized that those ideas weren't very good, or they just weren't stories I was interested in telling anymore. Those realizations often come after the stretches of time between project stages, in many cases between first draft and final script. The bottom line is: If I feel that a story is worth telling, I'll finish it. If I genuinely feel, at some point, that it isn't worth telling, I'll scrap it. The decision to scrap a story (at least temporarily) can be difficult, but that sort of self-editing is important. If you don't care about an idea past its original novelty, if you don't feel it's worth all of those hours of work, then it'll show, and you'll hate making it.

Jenny Lin: I worked on a project that was a digital version of my accident story, and it took me several years to finish it because it involved using a software I had never used before and working with 3-D drawing for the first time. It was hard to keep going as it was such a slow and unsatisfying process for me, and I doubted it the whole time I was making it. I ended up working on other things on the side because I had to try to find ways to feel as though I was doing something, maybe getting more immediate gratification. I continued this project because I had received a grant to make it, so I felt obligated to complete it. In order to complete it and make something that I felt satisfied with, I had to really let go of my original idea and just respond to what I was able to do using this software and interactivity. I really had to acknowledge my limits and problem solve from there (at some point, it meant taking some of the 3-D content and working with a software I felt more at ease with, so kind of rescuing myself once in a while so that the entire process wasn't a struggle).

Another really long project I had was an animated video called *Covers* that is ten minutes long. It was a really lengthy process, and the main problem I encountered for this was just not having enough time in my week to focus on this in the way I wanted to (my paying jobs were taking too much time). I was able to find time for this because I had my accident and had a really long stretch of idle time during my recovery. The

> "Don't talk yourself out of making things! The world is always better with more comics in it than less comics." - Andi Santagata

motivating factor for this project was that it was really a project that helped me explore some really personal issues (even if it's not overtly visible in the animation).

For both of these long projects, I felt a little unsatisfied with the end result and felt like I could have continued to tweak both, but I also realize that they had to be finished at some point. It felt satisfying after the fact to have made projects that were tedious and difficult, that I could have easily given up on. I feel like long projects really can draw an audience into your experience and world, and that can really feel rewarding in a way that is really different in shorter projects. So, I guess, insisting on the project until it's done is really worthwhile.

Andi Santagata: Firstly, don't talk yourself out of making things! The world is always better with more comics in it than less comics. Once you're all excited and have hashed out the basics of what you want to do, write or thumbnail out the story, from beginning to end. Once you have *that,* you have a roadmap of where you're going! Using that initial pump of energy to write down some plans is critical since you'll inevitably lose steam as time goes on. As for continuing motivation, I find that the cool thing about comics in particular is watching your project grow—as you build, draw, and write, you can watch your comic visually complete itself. A lot of cartoonists I know post up their pages as they finish them on their wall or on a wire, so that they can read what they've done so far and have a visual way to track their work so far. There's nothing like looking up from your desk and seeing most of a graphic novel covering your room!

If you're having trouble finishing a comics project at all, I'd recommend starting with a shorter comic—tons of artists get tripped up by trying to write a big, long saga on their first go. Start with something shorter—way shorter, like four or eight pages—and work your way up from there. You'll also end up with a handy pile of comics you can submit to anthologies and zines!

If you can find it, get a copy of Alec Longstreth's zine *Draw Comics Forever!*. It lays down some solid advice on setting schedules, sustainability, and avoiding carpal tunnel. (Seriously, try to avoid carpal tunnel.)

Jade Lee: I'm a big believer in striking while the iron's hot, so to speak. When you get an idea for a project that pumps you up, take hold of that excitement and use it to hammer out a rough draft and/or thumbnails as soon as you can. It doesn't matter if that rough draft is filled with mistakes or plot holes because after you've got the first embryonic version of your project down on paper, you can then go through its nooks and crannies to revise. I also find that while you're going through revisions and creating subsequent drafts and thumbnails, it helps to have another creative colleague to show your drafts to and get editorial feedback. Sometimes having a fresh pair of eyes on something that you've been staring at for a dozen iterations will help you notice things you otherwise would have missed.

4.10 Exercise 5: Reverse Engineer a Movie Scene

In a classroom visit with essayist and cowriter of *World of Wakanda*, the spinoff to Marvel's *Black Panther*, Roxane Gay suggested the following exercise to practice panel transitions, detail and focus, and page layout. This exercise acts as a "translation" of a scene from a film or television episode into comics. As in most translations, certain aspects and nuances of the original will be lost, but our purpose for this exercise is to distill the essence of this scene into comics.

1. Find a scene from a film or television episode. In my classroom, we watched the "By Way of the Green Line Bus" scene from director Wes Anderson's film, *The Royal Tenenbaums*. Numerous film and TV scenes can be found on YouTube.
2. Mimic this scene on a one-to-two-page comic layout. Decide the sizes and shapes of the panels depending on the camera angles and sense of focus. Pay attention to these decisions as you watch (and rewatch) this scene:
    a. Are there wide shots that concentrate on landscapes to give the viewer a sense of setting? How can you translate a "wide shot" on your comics layout?
    b. What are the subjects or objects that the camera zooms in on? How can you translate these moments of zoom in your layout?
3. In the scene from *The Royal Tenenbaums*, the camera begins with a wide shot of Ritchie at the pier with a cruise ship in the background. The camera then adopts Ritchie's point of view, which focuses on a few Green Line buses arriving at the pier. We then see the camera tightening focus on Margot getting off the bus; the camera alternates zoom between Margot and Ritchie's faces.
4. Fill in the panels with key details from the scene you've selected. In *The Royal Tenenbaums* scene, as the camera alternates focus between Margot and Ritchie, we noticed Margot's kohl-lined eyes, Ritchie's sweatband and his thick beard; Margot's fur coat; and the symmetry of V-shapes between her coat and his jacket, implying their similarities and connection as siblings.

Reflection Questions

1. After completing this exercise, what did you choose to include in your "translation" of the scene into comics? Why?
2. What did you choose to leave out? Why?
3. Describe your choices of panel sizes and panel transitions.
4. Which details did you focus on and why?
5. How do Scott McCloud's ideas on iconography relate to your chosen details?

Variation

1. Choose a poem or song to translate into a two-page comic. As you make your comic, consider the following questions: Which details are the most significant to visually highlight? Which lines or lyrics should be used as word balloons or captions? Which panel sizes and panel transitions will you use? An important caveat: You aren't simply illustrating the song; you are looking for a way to create a comic that explores the image/text relationship and can stand on its own without the context of the poem or song.

4.11 Student Examples of Comics Final Projects

Below you will find a selection of excerpted final comics projects from various introductory comics students. These final projects were completed in the span of a ten-week quarter. The projects resulted in fifteen pages of comics and an artist statement where students reflected on their creative process, analysis of comics techniques used, and published comics they had read throughout the quarter that served as inspiration for their own work. It is amazing to see what is possible is such a short amount of time.

From Jacquelyn Nille's "In Which I Imagine I Swallow Thousands of Bees":

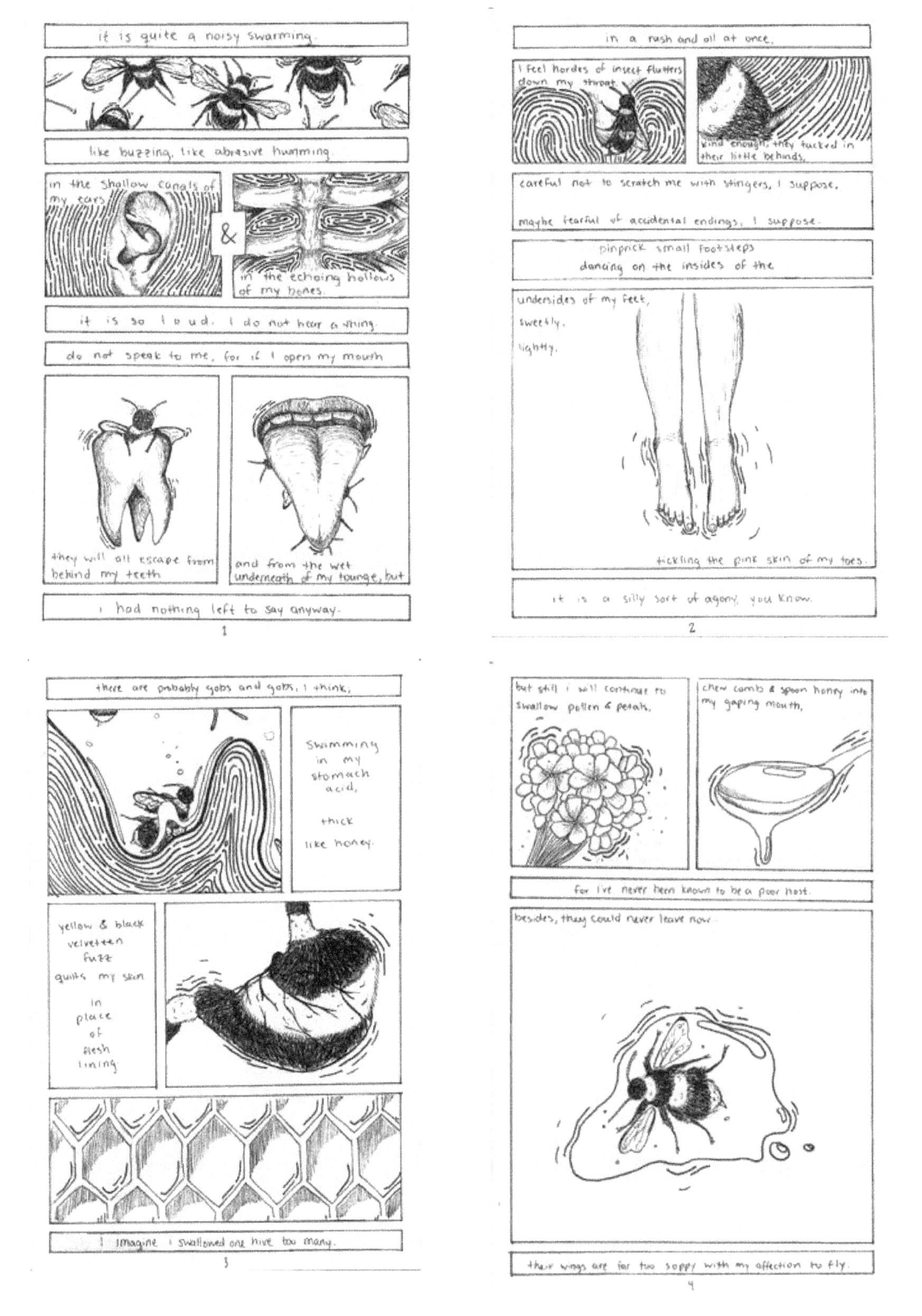

From Kini Sosa's "The Glades"

From Justin Jones's "Ginsburg"

From Lili Berni's "Mary, My Dear"

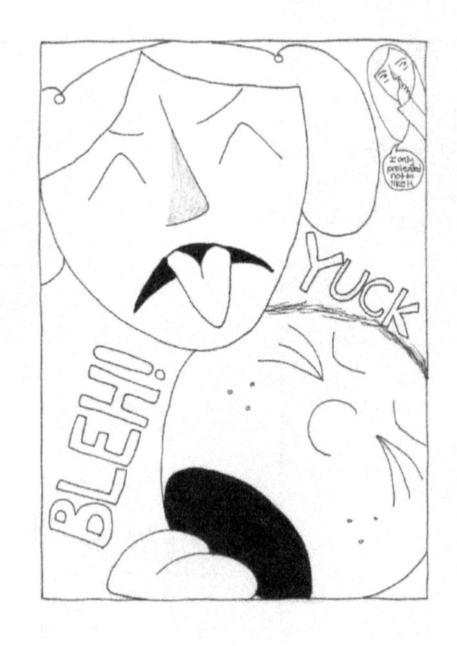

From Susana Martinez's "Crybaby"

4.12 Cartoonists on Advice for Students of Comics

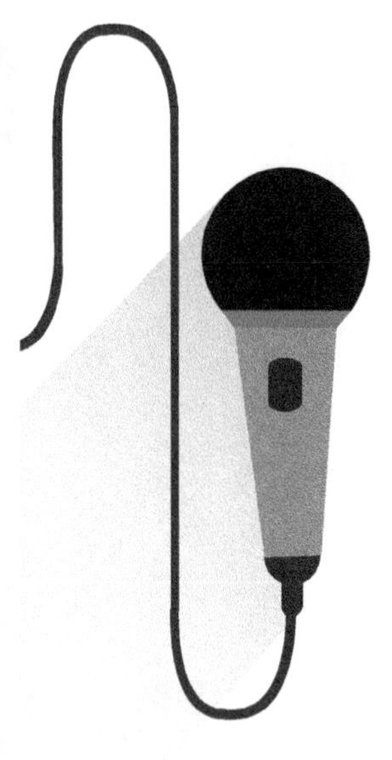

Question

What would you tell students who are just getting into creating comics? Any words of encouragement for beginning comics students who might be hesitant about their skills?

Gene Luen Yang: First, learn to finish. Learn to push past that feeling that everything you're doing is terrible. I mean, it might actually be terrible, but you'll get better by finishing. Finishing a terrible project will make you better faster than multiple false starts. Second, drawing and making comics are two different skills. Making good comics requires authenticity above all else, and a "rough" or "naïve" drawing style might communicate more authentically than a "polished" one.

Yumi Sakugawa: Make a lot of comics, try everything, and break all the rules! I used to get so stressed out about making comics because I thought I had to use the right paper size, pay attention to traditional comic page dimensions, the right kind of ink, make super-straight panels, etc. And then I realized that none of that really mattered. I made a lot of my best work on cheap computer paper, which is an archivist's worst nightmare but perfect for me because drawing on expensive paper really stresses me out.

Sign up for a table at your local indie comic fest or zine fest (to make it more fun, you can do it with a group of friends), and use that as an incentive to finish a short mini-comic. That was all I did for my first few years of self-publishing my own comics because, like most artists, I love/hate the pressure of a deadline to fully actualize a seed of an idea into a finished work of art.

Also, if you aren't confident in your own drawing and writing skills, I will say that authenticity and vulnerability go a very long way over technical skill. I will take a poorly drawn comic with a lot of heart over a very polished comic with no heart always. Make something that is honest and real to you, and release it into the world when you are ready. It will affect somebody out there who is meant to read your comic, and that is the whole magic of making comics for me: making a genuine emotional connection with your readers.

"Make a lot of comics, try everything, and break all the rules! I used to get so stressed out about making comics because I thought I had to use the right paper size, pay attention to traditional comic page dimensions, the right kind of ink, make super-straight panels, etc. And then I realized that none of that really mattered." - Yumi Sakugawa

Ryan North: Have fun (which is easy; comics is the most intrinsically fun written medium, both in reading and writing) and don't worry about sucking. As Jake the Dog said in *Adventure Time:* "Dude, sucking at something is the first step towards being kinda good at something." If you find something you like in comics, something that makes you happy—keep at it. Write every day (or draw every day) (you can take weekends off though; I'm not a MONSTER), and you'll get better despite yourself. And then one day you'll read a comic you wrote a few years ago and realize—"Wait a minute! This is actually good! I'VE BEEN GOOD FOR YEARS, AND NOBODY TOLD ME; WHERE'S MY MEDAL?"

Sonny Liew: Well, I'd say that although it's a visual medium, to some extent it's the storytelling that matters more than the drawings. You can have beautiful drawings and still make an unreadable comic—but if your story is good, the technical quality of the drawing doesn't usually matter as much. But whatever area you feel weaker at, the good thing is that we can all learn to be better at it—through practice and studying the craft.

Taneka Stotts: Please remember that self doubt is your worst enemy and should be ignored. Also, the myth that just an artist and writer makes a comic is false; when creating comics it is a full team. From your editor, inker, flatter, colorist, production tech, designer, letterer, pre-press, and more, comics are produced by a team of people with different skills that allow them to exceed expectations in great ways. Don't cut yourself short. There are many ways to influence what we love; continue doing you; never put your passions away and leave them neglected; continue to work and hone your craft; and let it make you smile.

Lucy Knisley: It's okay to copy at first, but don't try to claim it. Claim it once you've made it truly yours. This can be tough, at first, when you're just looking for someone who seems to have "made it" the way you want to "make it." Don't forget that success is usually measured by different yardsticks all across the board, and even the most adept artists have days when everything they make looks like a pile of poo to them. It takes a long time and a lot of work to get to a point where you're making consistent work, and I know that's not what anyone likes to hear, but it's sadly true. There's no magic bullet or secret idea that we all stumble upon; it's just work and friendliness at conventions and looking at other work that inspires you and reading and drawing and writing until something emerges.

"Write every day (or draw every day) (you can take weekends off though; I'm not a MONSTER), and you'll get better despite yourself. And then one day you'll read a comic you wrote a few years ago and realize—"Wait a minute! This is actually good! I'VE BEEN GOOD FOR YEARS, AND NOBODY TOLD ME; WHERE'S MY MEDAL?""

- Ryan North

Leela Corman: None but: Work very hard on your life-drawing skills. Get educated about the history of painting, design, and illustration. Learn everything you can about all art history, not only comics. In fact make comics history the LAST thing you study. Learn the larger history of visual art and communication and learn it well. Get deep inside the human figure and learn to draw it. Learn how to handle paint, charcoal, graphite, ink, and more. Take some graphic design classes. Don't be afraid to suck and to be a spaz. Develop your eye. Learn about your own body and its particular movement patterns and proclivities. Stand up straight, talk at an audible volume, and learn good grooming. Learn how to be present and not timid. Timidity is unprofessional and a turnoff. No one wants to lean close to you when you whisper. Speak up.

> "There are many ways to influence what we love; continue doing you; never put your passions away and leave them neglected; continue to work and hone your craft; and let it make you smile."
> - Taneka Stotts

Fred Van Lente: The key thing is to just start making comics. People don't want to see pitches or samples or scripts—the best thing for you is to finish comics. And have them be, you know, good, if you can. But keep at it. Most people give up. If you don't, that instantly gives you a leg up on your competition.

Nilah Magruder: You get better the more you do it. Study comics, study writing and drawing, study the work of artists and writers who do the type of work you want to do. And then, make some comics. Start small; just work on your technique, on panel layout, composition, dialogue, flow, toning and color, all that good stuff. Figure out a process, and challenge yourself with every step. And focus on the things that are most difficult for you. Learn to draw animals, backgrounds, cars. You get better the more you do it.

Rafael Rosado: You have to put in your time, your 10,000 hours. There are no short cuts to getting good, in comics or any other skill. But if you love the medium, and you love drawing and creating, it's hard to ignore that fire inside of you. Also, do different kinds of drawing, not just comics. Take life drawing classes; do some sculpture, some animation. It will all make you a better, more rounded artist.

Sophie Goldstein: Keep making comics and keep giving them to people. Give them to publishers and authors you admire. Trade them for mini-comics from other people at shows.

Be nice, and be generous. Show up. Don't quit.

Belle Yang: The comics format allows an artist or writer to be quirky, so there is room for every personality. That's the beauty of comics. You can be a super draftsman, but childlike drawings like Marjane Satrapi's art can be even more vivacious, superior as a storytelling vehicle. And the story has to be genuine to your own nature—especially memoirs—so comparing yourself to another person's work is hopeless and entirely unnecessary pain in comics.

> "Don't forget that success is usually measured by different yardsticks all across the board, and even the most adept artists have days when everything they make looks like a pile of poo to them."
> - Lucy Knisley

Danica Novgorodoff: I love comics because there's such an infinite variety of forms and formats, narrative and visual styles that you can use. They can be hyperrealistic or stylized, funny or sad; you can use stick figures or collage or photography or Photoshop or watercolor or any number of visual techniques. The possibilities are really endless, no matter what your drawing style or subject matter. My advice would just be to make

> "Start small; just work on your technique, on panel layout, composition, dialogue, flow, toning and color, all that good stuff. Figure out a process, and challenge yourself with every step." - Nilah Magruder

something that's meaningful to you. What do you love; what would you want to read?

Ashanti Fortson: Your comics can be about anything. You can *make* them about anything. There's sometimes this pressure, when you're starting to make comics, that your comics should look like *this* or like *that* and they should be about *these things.* I felt that when I started *Galanthus*. I thought space as a setting had to look a certain way, the way it's always portrayed. It doesn't! It can look like whatever I want it to. You can make comics about opera-singer mermaids or your relationship with your grandmother or the non-linear passage of time or so many other things. Make comics that you want to make, and the fact that you care will come through to the people who view your comics.

Overall, the most important thing in the path to improving at comics is to just make comics. Expand your horizons and try your best, and the rest will follow. If you make a short comic, and the art and/or writing aren't great? That's completely okay. The only thing that matters is that you made that comic, challenged yourself, and learned from it. You have to let yourself make things that aren't great; you have to let yourself fail. Failure, when coupled with self-reflection, leads to a better understanding of what to do next time.

Also: Pitch short comics to anthologies, if you're interested in the content! Keep pitching to different anthologies, even when you get rejected. Do your best with each pitch, but don't beat yourself up when editors say "no." Each pitch you write will help you get better at writing, conceptualizing stories, presenting your stories professionally, and more. You'll learn a lot, and you never know when someone will say yes.

Jenny Lin: I would say that it's good to just get the ideas out and realize that they might be rough at first, but if you just keep going with the idea, you can usually discover something in that that feels important and that communicates to others. Frustration and failure is really part of the process; at least for me it is. It's helpful to look at a ton of comics and art or watch films and read, maybe even borrow compositions of things you watch on screen, if that helps. Take lots of photos and work from that if you want something more specifically from your point of view.

Also, if you feel really inspired by one particular comic artist, it's always good to try to carefully consider if your work feels too similar and too influenced by that artist. It's easy to follow a format that's already there that you already admire, and it's inevitable to be influenced. It's good to acknowledge the importance of looking at other people's work but also to try to see if there are ways to come at your work that might have shared sentiments or sensibilities with another artist but to find a way to approach this sentiment differently. Just keep working.

> "My advice would just be to make something that's meaningful to you. What do you love; what would you want to read?" - Danica Novgorodoff

Self-publishing is also a really great way to get something out there. If you participate in zine fairs, it's really interesting to see what others are making and to have direct interactions with people who pass by your table. Also, putting stuff online is useful. I think all of this gives the work a bit of a feeling of being "done" or "somewhat done" with a potential audience and can feel motivating.

> "Self-publishing is also a really great way to get something out there. If you participate in zine fairs, it's really interesting to see what others are making and to have direct interactions with people who pass by your table." - Jenny Lin

Andi Santagata: The best advice I ever got was, "You need to get the bad comics out before you can make the good comics," which was a bastardization of the old "practice makes perfect" chestnut. Don't get discouraged and keep drawing. Everyone gets to a point where they tip into their own definition of "good"—you just have to keep working to get there. Practice drawing, writing, and finishing comics; then—and this is key!—show them to other people! Post them online, or show your friends, and get feedback. Use that feedback as a baseball bat to beat your next comic into shape, and then impress those same friends with your new, better, comic. Repeat!

Don't get too discouraged if you feel like you're not on a "professional" level yet. Everyone starts from somewhere, and you'd be very surprised if you saw some pro-level artists' and writers' early work. There's an old saying in comics—"Perseverance trumps talent"—so just imagine what you could do with both!

Rina Ayuyang: Draw every day even if it's just a couple of minutes on the bus or between classes. You won't realize it but you'll soon build a huge body of work as you do it. I've also found out when I wasn't making comics for about a year that you actually forget how to draw. Drawing every day prevents you from wasting good, precious time trying to figure out how to draw again. Also, don't stay too much in your head; otherwise, you'll just quit before you even start. Don't get bogged down wondering if you'll ever get published or not; just start drawing. Make mini-comics and share them with other cartoonists and readers at comics show. Drawing comics is such a solitary activity, so go out and meet other cartoonists at conventions, local drawing meetups, or at comics readings. They give you a different perspective on being a cartoonist and making comics and offer excellent constructive feedback on your work. Also, go look at art no matter what medium (museums, concerts, etc.) and read old comics to appreciate the history of the art form. As long as you are honest and true to yourself through your comics, you'll never have a reason to lack confidence as an artist.

Jade Lee: My advice is to keep in mind that EVERYONE sucks in the beginning. Drawing and writing is a skill that's learned and honed through practice, just like playing an instrument. The more you draw, the more you get your ideas out of your head and onto paper; even if it's something that you'll look back on in embarrassment, the better you will get. It's also important to remember that trying to create a perfect magnum opus in one go is the easiest way to paralyze yourself. Instead, look back on your previous works, figure out what you want to communicate, what you want

> "My advice is to keep in mind that EVERYONE sucks in the beginning." - Jade Lee

to improve upon, and give yourself room to mess up while setting small, chewable-sized goals to direct yourself through a piece.

4.13 Cartoonists on Pitching

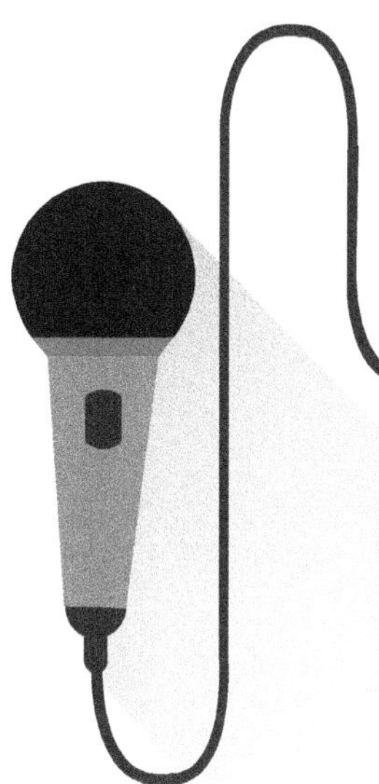

Question

Can you describe your process and trajectory as you decide and/or pitch certain projects? What excites you about the work you commit to writing or drawing?

Yumi Sakugawa: My first three published books have been a bit of an anomaly in the sense that they were both self-published works I either published online or printed myself, and then, very serendipitously, I found a publisher who was interested in turning those self-published works into printed books. So, I would describe that process as creating what excites you on your own timeline by your own terms and then trusting the universe that if it is meant to turn into a book, someone will want to make it into a book! Now that I have established a reputation as a published author, I will be pitching my next comic book in perhaps a more conventional way, where I will be pitching the idea and outline of a book to a publisher before it even exists. I do have an idea for a next full-length graphic book, and when it all comes down to it, it's an intuitive gut feeling. When you hit upon the book or project you are going to commit to, you just know, and it lights all your nerve endings on fire.

Ideally, every new project I commit to writing and drawing is a new internal frontier, a new depth for me to excavate and explore. I never want to repeat what I did before or rely on old tricks—the excitement is in the risk of trying something completely new, in revealing a new rawness or vulnerability I have never exposed before and not knowing at all how people are going to respond to my completely new work. Otherwise, I am not growing as an artist and not pushing myself, and that is boring.

Sonny Liew: We get ideas all the time—the ones we end up pursuing are a mixture of our own interests and what the marketplace finds compelling. I remember my first published comic at the age of nineteen—the whole idea that you could think up stories and characters and then get to share them with the rest of the world—that whole process felt so engaging I realised quite quickly it was something I'd want to try to spend the rest of my life doing, if I could.

Lucy Knisley: It depends on the book, of course. With travelogues, I never know quite what's going to come of it until I'm in the thick of it. Often travel and new experiences help to give form to the formless thoughts and changes we're experiencing, so I find these transitional periods of travel and growth interesting to write about and have developed a good sense of how to gather observations that adhere to a theme in those experiences. For more memoir-style books, like *Relish* and *Something New,* it's a process of talking things through with my editor, who really gets me and my work, and then piecing together my thoughts on things before writing an outline and doing some sketches to propose it as a book. My agent also helps, reigning me in if I'm going off the rails or making suggestions about what she'd like to read about. Then it's a matter of scripting the book, imagining the structure of it and how I want to share these experiences, and then moving on to the art.

“For more memoir-style books, like *Relish* and *Something New,* it's a process of talking things through with my editor, who really gets me and my work, and then piecing together my thoughts on things before writing an outline and doing some sketches to propose it as a book.”
- Lucy Knisley

Leela Corman: Pitching is a professional process that just involves my being able to clearly present and advocate for my ideas with editors. This is not hard once you get the hang of it. The trick is trusting your ideas and learning how to communicate and present yourself professionally. Because even in a business with very low barriers to entry and a lot of unprofessional behavior, you need to act like a pro in every aspect of your public presentation.

Rina Ayuyang: Usually the process of deciding what to make a comic about comes from a basic need to get a specific story or feeling out. Then I write notes like a stream of consciousness to at least document it all quickly on paper. I go through an outline to organize thoughts and plot out the entire book. I am excited when I find that readers have some sort of connection with the stories I share through my comics. A lot of my stories are personal and introspective, and so it's nice to see that readers have a similar feeling or emotion from something. At the same time, I get really excited to start writing a comic when it's just completely honest and it's emotionally freeing.

4.14 A List of Further Reading

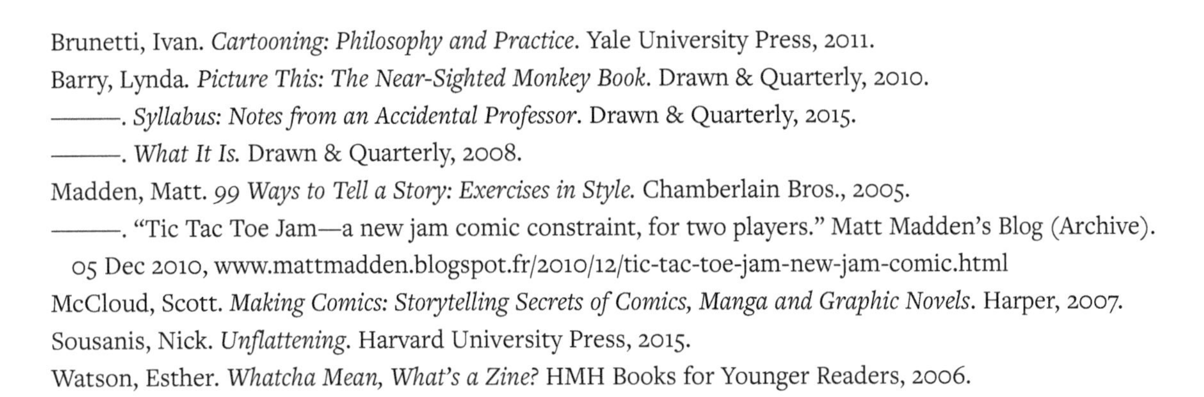

Brunetti, Ivan. *Cartooning: Philosophy and Practice*. Yale University Press, 2011.

Barry, Lynda. *Picture This: The Near-Sighted Monkey Book*. Drawn & Quarterly, 2010.

———. *Syllabus: Notes from an Accidental Professor*. Drawn & Quarterly, 2015.

———. *What It Is*. Drawn & Quarterly, 2008.

Madden, Matt. *99 Ways to Tell a Story: Exercises in Style*. Chamberlain Bros., 2005.

———. "Tic Tac Toe Jam—a new jam comic constraint, for two players." Matt Madden's Blog (Archive). 05 Dec 2010, www.mattmadden.blogspot.fr/2010/12/tic-tac-toe-jam-new-jam-comic.html

McCloud, Scott. *Making Comics: Storytelling Secrets of Comics, Manga and Graphic Novels*. Harper, 2007.

Sousanis, Nick. *Unflattening*. Harvard University Press, 2015.

Watson, Esther. *Whatcha Mean, What's a Zine?* HMH Books for Younger Readers, 2006.

Works Cited

Abel, Jessica, and Matt Madden. *Drawing Words, Writing Pictures: Making Comics from Manga to Graphic Novels*. First Second Books, 2008.

Aldama, Frederick Luis. *Graphic Borders: Latino Comics Past, Present and Future*. University of Texas Press, 2016.

———. *Multicultural Comics: from* Zap *to* Blue Beetle. University of Texas Press, 2010.

———. *Your Brain on Latino Comics: From Gus Arriola to Los Bros Hernandez*. University of Texas Press, 2009.

Barry, Lynda. *Picture This: The Near-Sighted Monkey Book*. Drawn & Quarterly, 2010.

———. *Syllabus: Notes from an Accidental Professor*. Drawn & Quarterly, 2015.

———. *What It Is*. Drawn & Quarterly, 2008.

Bennett, Tamryn. "Comics Poetry: Beyond 'Sequential Art.'" *Image and Narrative*, vol. 15, no. 2, 2014. www.imageandnarrative.be/index.php/imagenarrative/article/viewFile/544/397.

Betts, Tara. "When Comics and Poetry Intersect." The Ploughshares Blog, 16 July 2016, http://blog.pshares .org/index.php/when-poetry-and-comics-intersect/.

Brown, Jeffrey A. "Panthers and Vixens: Black Superheroines, Sexuality, and Stereotypes in Contemporary Comic Books." *Black Comics: Politics of Race and Representation*, doi:10.5040/9781472543424.ch-008.

Brunetti, Ivan. *Cartooning: Philosophy and Practice*. Yale University Press, 2011.

Carrier, David. *The Aesthetics of Comics*. Pennsylvania State University Press, 2000.

Chute, Hillary. *Why Comics? From Underground to Everywhere*. Harper, 2017.

Cohn, Neil. *The Visual Language of Comics: Introduction to the Structure and Cognition of Sequential Images*. Bloomsbury Academic, 2013.

"Comic Book Primer". ReadWriteThink, www.readwritethink.org/files/resources/lesson_images/lesson921/ ComicBookPrimer.pdf.

Duncan, Randy, Matthew J. Smith, and Paul Levitz. *The Power of Comics: History, Form and Culture*. 2nd ed., Bloomsbury Academic, 2015.

Eisner, Will. *Comics and Sequential Art: Principles and Practices from the Legendary Cartoonist*. W. W. Norton, 2008.

Fawaz, Ramzi. *The New Mutants: Superheroes and the Radical Imagination of American Comics*. New York University Press, 2016.

Fawaz, Ramzi. "The Difference A Mutant Makes." *Avidly*, Los Angeles Review of Books, 28 Jan. 2016. lareviewofbooks.org/2016/01/28/the-difference-a-mutant-makes/.

Gateward, Frances K., and John Jennings. *The Blacker the Ink: Constructions of Black Identity in Comics and Sequential Art*. Rutgers University Press, 2015.

Gay, Roxane, Yona Harvey, and Ta-Nehisi Coates. *Black Panther: World of Wakanda*. Marvel Worldwide. 2017.

Goldstein, Nancy. *Jackie Ormes: The First African American Woman Cartoonist*. University of Michigan Press, 2008.

Gordon, Ian. "Making Comics Respectable: How *Maus* Helped Redefine a Medium." *The Rise of the American Comics Artist*, 2010, pp. 179–193., doi:10.14325/mississippi/9781604737929.003.0013.

Hatfield, Charles. *Alternative Comics: An Emerging Literature*. University Press of Mississippi, 2005.

Howard, Sheena C., and Ronald L. Jackson. *Black Comics: Politics of Race and Representation*. Bloomsbury Academic, 2014.

Howard, Sheena. *Encyclopedia of Black Comics*. Fulcrum Publishing, 2017.

INK BRICK: The Press for Comics Poetry. *INK BRICK*—A Journal for Comics Poetry, 2014–2018, www.inkbrick.com.

Jennings, John, and Damian Duffy. *Kindred: A Graphic Novel Adaptation*. Abrams ComicArts, 2017.

Karasik, Paul, and Mark Newgarden. *How to Read* Nancy: *The Elements of Comics in Three Easy Panels.* Fantagraphics, 1994.

Knisley, Lucy. *Something New: Tales from a Makeshift Bride*. First Second, 2016.

Koyama-Richard, Brigitte. *One Thousand Years of Manga*. Flammarion, 2014.

Lai, Paul. *Comics Syllabus*. Podcast. Multiversity Comics, 2017–2018, http://www.multiversitycomics.com/tag/comics-syllabus/.

Lente, Fred Van, et al. *Comic Book History of Comics,* The IDW Publishing, 2017.

Lyn, Francesca. "Review of *Black Comics: Politics of Race and Representation*." *Image TexT* vol. 8, no. 1, 2015, n. pag. 18 December 2017.

Madden, Matt. *99 Ways to Tell a Story: Exercises in Style*. Chamberlain Bros., 2005.

———. "A History of American Comic Books in Six Panels." Matt Madden's Blog (Archive), 08 Aug 2012, www.mattmadden.blogspot.co.uk/2012/08/a-history-of-american-comic-books-in.html.

———. "Tic Tac Toe Jam—a new jam comic constraint, for two players." Matt Madden's Blog (Archive), 05 Dec 2010, www.mattmadden.blogspot.fr/2010/12/tic-tac-toe-jam-new-jam-comic.html.

Mateu-Mestre, Marcos. *Framed Ink: Drawing and Composition for Visual Storytellers*. Design Studio Press, 2015.

Mautner, Chris. "If You're Going to Fail, Just Make Sure You Fail Big: An Interview with Gene Luen Yang." *The Comics Journal,* 27 Nov 2013, http://www.tcj.com/if-youre-going-to-fail-just-make-sure-you-fail-big-an-interview-with-gene-luen-yang/.

Mazur, Dan, and Alexander Danner. *Comics: a Global History, 1968 to the Present*. Thames & Hudson, 2014.

McCloud, Scott. *Making Comics: Storytelling Secrets of Comics, Manga and Graphic Novels*. Harper, 2007.

McCloud, Scott. *Understanding Comics:* [*the Invisible Art*]. New York: HarperPerennial, 1994.

Molotiu, Andrei. "List of Terms for Comics Studies by Andrei Molotiu." *Comics Forum*, Comics Forum, 26 Sept. 2016, comicsforum.org/2013/07/26/list-of-terms-for-comics-studies-by-andrei-molotiu/.

North, Ryan. *Dinosaur Comics*. Dinosaur Comics, 2003–2018, www.qwantz.com.

Powers, Thom. "The Lynda Barry Interview." *The Comics Journal*, 2 Jan 1989, www.tcj.com/the-lynda-barry-interview/.

Sabin, Roger. *Comics, Comix & Graphic Novels*. Phaidon Press, 2010.

Sakugawa, Yumi. *There is No Right Way to Meditate*. Adams Media, 2015.

———. *Your Illustrated Guide to Becoming One with the Universe*. Adams Media, 2014.

Sicate, Keith, director. *Komikero Chronicles*. Cine Totoo, 2014.

Smith, Matthew J., and Randy Duncan, eds. *Critical Approaches to Comics: Theories and Methods*. Routledge, 2012.

Sousanis, Nick. *Unflattening*. Harvard University Press, 2015.

Stotts, Taneka. *Elements: Fire—An Anthology by Creators of Color*. Beyond Press, 2017.

"Strip Panel Naked". YouTube, uploaded by HassanOE, https://www.youtube.com/channel/UCYJAToPH5GSGShP7Yoc3jsA.

Tabachnick, Stephen, ed. *Teaching the Graphic Novel*. The Modern Language Association of America, 2009.

Van Lente, Fred, and Ryan Dunlavey. *Comic Book History of Comics*. IDW Publishing, 2017.

Watson, Esther. *Whatcha Mean, What's a Zine?* HMH Books for Younger Readers, 2006.

Whaley, Deborah Elizabeth. *Black Women in Sequence: Re-Inking Comics, Graphic Novels, and Anime*. University of Washington Press, 2016.

Wolk, Douglas. *Reading Comics: How Graphic Novels Work and What They Mean*. Da Capo Press, 2007.

Wright, Bradford. *Comic Book Nation: The Transformation of Youth Culture in America*. John Hopkins University Press, 2003.

Yang, Belle. *Forget Sorrow*. W. W. Norton, 2011.

Yang, Gene Luen, and Lark Pien. *American Born Chinese*. Square Fish, 2008.

Yang, Jeff, and Keith Chow. *Secret Identities: the Asian American Superhero Anthology*. New Press, 2009.

About the Author and Editor

Rachelle Cruz is from Hayward, California. She is the author and editor of a comics textbook, *Experiencing Comics: An Introduction to Reading, Discussing and Creating Comics* (Cognella, 2018); a poetry collection, *God's Will for Monsters*, which won an American Book Award in 2018 and the 2016 Hillary Gravendyk Regional Poetry Prize (Inlandia, 2017); and an anthology, *Kuwento: Lost Things, an anthology of Philippine Myths* (Carayan Press, 2015), which she co-edited with Melissa Sipin. She hosts The Blood-Jet Writing Hour. She is a Lecturer in the Creative Writing Department at the University of California, Riverside where she teaches comics and poetry. An Emerging Voices Fellow, a Kundiman Fellow and a VONA writer, she lives and writes in Southern California.

CPSIA information can be obtained
at www.ICGtesting.com
Printed in the USA
LVHW062321180119
604498LV00003B/21/P